*Flavorful*

# Flavorful

150 *Irresistible* Desserts
in *All-Time Favorite* Flavors

TISH BOYLE

*Photography by* **ANDREW MEADE**

Houghton Mifflin Harcourt
Boston   New York
2015

www.hmhco.com

Library of Congress Cataloging-in-
Publication Data
Boyle, Tish.
Flavorful : 150 irresistible desserts in
all-time favorite flavors / Tish Boyle;
photography by Andrew Meade.
pages  cm
Includes bibliographical references.
ISBN 978-1-118-52355-1 (hardcover)
ISBN 978-0-544-18640-8 (ebook)
1.  Desserts.  I. Title.
TX773.B6928 2015
641.86 — DC23      2015004678

Printed in China
C&C 10 9 8 7 6 5 4 3 2 1

*To Mickey.*

# Contents

# INTRODUCTION

*There's no accounting for taste,* as the saying goes, and this is certainly true when it comes to desserts. Consider three people dining together at a restaurant. What makes one person order the lemon soufflé, another the flourless chocolate cake, and the third the espresso-soaked tiramisu? Why do some people love the puckery tartness of a lemon meringue pie, while others swoon over a rich chocolate layer cake or a caramel mousse? If there's a chocolate item on a dessert menu, for example, that's the one I'll order every time. Everyone's palate is a little different.

I've always been curious about flavor. In my years as editor of *Chocolatier* and *Pastry Art & Design* magazines, I frequently asked pastry chefs how they planned their dessert menus. Many cited seasonality as an important factor in selecting items for their menus—desserts with apples or pears for the fall; citrus for winter; strawberry and rhubarb for the spring; and stone fruits and berries in the summer. Working with the seasons makes perfect sense, because a big part of a pastry chef's job is getting ahold of the very best raw ingredients throughout the year. After all, if you start with oversized, flavorless strawberries, your strawberry shortcake will never be any good, regardless of how pretty it looks on the plate.

But even more critical than working with the seasons is the pastry chef's underlying goal of selling as many desserts as possible. As one chef put it, "You can make the best prune tart in the world, but if people don't like prunes, it's just not going to sell." A good pastry chef knows what flavors sell, and his or her menu will focus on these flavors. These are the desserts that people will order time after time, regardless of the season or, for that matter, anything else.

Many factors come into play when we taste a dessert. Our tongues can identify four tastes: sweet, salty, sour, and bitter. Simply put, it is how we react to the combination of these four tastes that dictates our flavor preferences. My personal research, based on interviewing countless pastry chefs, led me to a list of the nine hottest flavors in the dessert world: vanilla, chocolate, caramel, coffee, nuts, apple, berries and cherries, sweet cheese (as in cheesecake), and citrus fruit. My objective in this book is to present a collection of exceptional desserts in these—America's favorite—flavors. No matter which is *your* favorite, there is something for everyone here, from caramel devotees to chocolate fanatics to cheesecake aficionados to coffee junkies to lemon lovers. Capturing flavor is the first, and probably most important, step in creating a great dessert. Adding textural contrasts and presenting that dessert in a visually appealing way also contribute to its success. Each recipe in this book has been developed with the goal of maximizing flavor and visual appeal—an excellent foundation for developing a repertoire of memorable desserts that you can depend on and return to time after time.

## Recipe Notes

With just a few exceptions, the recipes in this book don't require special pans or molds, unusual equipment, or extravagant ingredients. They were all tested in my home oven, which is electric. Recipes indicate a range of time for baking—always check *5 minutes before* the earliest time given in the baking range, just to be on the safe side. Ovens do vary considerably, so always use an oven thermometer to make sure you are baking at the correct temperature. Unless specified in the recipe, your oven rack should be positioned in the center of the oven. If you are baking two sheets at one time, arrange the oven racks close to the center of the oven, rather than at the top and bottom, and switch positions of the baking sheets halfway through baking.

### ESSENTIAL BAKING EQUIPMENT

Following is a list for the well-equipped pastry kitchen. The tools that I deem essential have an asterisk next to them.

Apple corer

Bench scraper

Cake turntable

Cardboard cake rounds

Cherry pitter

*Citrus juicer

*Citrus zester

*Digital scale

Electric juicer

*Electric mixer

Food processor

*Knives

*Measuring equipment (1-cup and 1-quart glass liquid measuring cups, nested metal dry measuring cups, and metal measuring spoons)

Microplane zester/grater

*Mixing bowls

Parchment paper

*Pastry bags

Pastry brushes

*Pastry cutters

*Pastry tips

Pastry wheel

Propane or butane torch

*Rolling pin

Saucepans

*Sieve

Sifter

Silicone baking mats

*Spatulas

*Thermometers (candy, instant-read, and oven)

*Vegetable peeler

*Whisks

*Wire racks

*Wooden spoons

# INGREDIENT NOTES

*Using the best quality* ingredients possible is an important first step in making a great cake, pie, pudding, or other dessert. Following are notes on some of the basic ingredients used in the book, with some suggestions on brands.

## Flours

ALL-PURPOSE, CAKE, AND WHOLE WHEAT FLOUR. When baking, it's important to use the type of flour called for in each recipe, whether it's all-purpose, cake, or whole wheat flour. Using the wrong flour can have a dramatic impact on your dessert or baked good, and not in a good way. Use a high-quality brand and measure accurately, preferably by weight. Invest in a good digital scale and get into the habit of using it to weigh your ingredients, especially flour. If you must use volume measurements, measure carefully. Stir the flour with a whisk to aerate it first, then spoon it into the dry measuring cup, overfilling it. Use the back of a butter knife to sweep away the excess flour and level the top.

For *all-purpose flour*, I use King Arthur unbleached flour. For *cake flour*, I use Swans Down or Pillsbury Softasilk enriched bleached cake flour (unless specified, never use self-rising cake flour, which has baking powder and salt in it). For *whole wheat flour*, I recommend King Arthur unbleached. Always store whole wheat flour in an airtight container in the refrigerator as it turns rancid more quickly than white flour.

## Sugars and Sweeteners

GRANULATED, TURBINADO, AND DEMERARA SUGAR. In recipes that call for *granulated sugar*, you can use any sugar labeled "granulated cane sugar." You can use organic cane sugar, if you like, but it is more expensive. Some recipes call for *turbinado* sugar or *demerara* sugar. Both are coarse-textured, pale blond raw sugars with a delicate caramel flavor, although demerara is a little moister than turbinado and has slightly larger crystals. I like to use them when I want to add a little texture to a cake, cookie, or muffin, or for caramelizing the top of a tart or crème brûlée.

CONFECTIONERS' SUGAR is granulated sugar that has been processed commercially to a fine powder. Although a small amount of cornstarch is added to prevent clumping, it should always be sifted before use.

BROWN SUGAR is granulated sugar with molasses added. There are two basic types: light and dark. Light brown sugar has a more delicate flavor and lighter color than its darker counterpart, which contains more molasses. Because it has a tendency to dry out and become rock-hard, brown sugar should be stored tightly wrapped in a plastic bag inside an airtight container. To rehabilitate hardened brown sugar, place the amount you need in a microwave-safe bowl and cover with a wet paper towel. Tightly cover the bowl with plastic wrap and microwave on high for 1½ to 2 minutes. Break up the sugar with a fork and then stir; use the sugar immediately, as it will harden as it cools.

HONEY is an amber-colored syrup with a distinct flavor and a slightly higher sweetening power than sugar. Its flavor varies depending on the flowers the bees fed on, and can range from pale and mild to dark amber and robust. Orange blossom, acacia, and clover honeys are relatively mild, while wildflower, buckwheat, and fireweed honeys are robust and will significantly affect the flavor of a recipe.

MAPLE SYRUP is made from the concentrated sap of the sugar maple tree. It is available in different grades, ranging from Grade AA, which is thin in texture and mild in flavor, to Grade C, which is thick and robust. The recipes in this book either call for Grade A or Grade B syrup, both of which are available in supermarkets.

GOLDEN SYRUP. Also known as refiner's syrup, golden syrup is a by-product of the sugar-refining process. It can be used interchangeably with light corn syrup, but I really prefer its more complex flavor profile. Look for Lyle's Golden Syrup in the same aisle as honey in the supermarket.

CORN SYRUP is 100 percent glucose, and shouldn't be confused with the high-fructose corn syrup that is used commercially. There are two types of corn syrup, light and dark, which can generally be used interchangeably. The dark has a richer flavor reminiscent of brown sugar. Some manufacturers add high-fructose corn syrup to their syrup; look for a brand that does not contain high-fructose corn syrup, such as Karo, which is what I use.

## Gelling Agents and Thickeners

GELATIN is available in granulated or sheet form. The recipes in this book call for powdered gelatin exclusively. I use Knox brand unflavored gelatin, which comes in ¼-ounce (7-gram) packets (just over 2¼ teaspoons). To use, open the packet(s) and measure the required amount of gelatin granules with a measuring spoon.

PECTIN is a gelling agent extracted from citrus fruits or apple skins. It is commonly used as a thickener for jams and jellies, but is also used for confections, such as Raspberry-Mint Pâtes de Fruits (page 67). Pectin is available in powdered or liquid form, but the recipes in this book call exclusively for liquid pectin.

CORNSTARCH. Made from ground corn, cornstarch is primarily used as a thickening agent in sauces, fruit pies, puddings, and custards, though it is also used with flour to produce a tender crumb in cakes, shortbread, and other baked goods. Cornstarch is also used as an anti-caking agent in confectioners' sugar.

TAPIOCA. This starch is derived from the root of the cassava (or manioc) plant and is used as a thickening agent in fruit pies and crisps.

## Dairy Products

MILK is labeled according to its fat content. Whole milk is at least 3 percent milk fat; reduced-fat milk is 2 percent milk fat; low-fat milk is 1 percent milk fat; and fat-free milk is less than 0.1 percent milk fat. For most recipes in this book, I recommend using whole milk, which has better body and a richer flavor than lower-fat milk. If you must, you can use 2 percent milk, but I don't recommend using 1 percent or fat-free milk in these recipes.

CREAM. In recipes where *heavy cream* is called for, use cream that is labeled either "heavy cream" or "heavy whipping cream," which contains 36 to 40 percent butter-fat. "Whipping cream" often contains stabilizers and emulsifiers to ensure it keeps its shape when whipped. Do not use light cream. Pastry chefs prefer to use cream with 40 percent butterfat, which is even better; you can find 40 percent cream in gourmet stores.

SOUR CREAM is cultured cream that contains 16 to 22 percent fat. For recipes that call for sour cream, use the full-fat version, never reduced-fat or fat-free.

CRÈME FRAÎCHE is made by adding a bacterial culture to cream that has about 28 percent butterfat. It has a higher fat content and is thicker than sour cream. It is available in gourmet food stores and better supermarkets, but you can also easily make it at home (see page 20).

SWEETENED CONDENSED MILK is evaporated milk with added sugar, which yields a very thick, sweet product. Sold in cans, my preference is Eagle Brand.

BUTTERMILK. Originally the by-product of churning milk into butter, buttermilk is now usually made by adding a bacterial strain to fat-free milk. It has a thick texture and slightly sour flavor. You can make your own buttermilk in a pinch: Spoon 1 tablespoon freshly squeezed lemon juice into a liquid measuring cup and add milk (2 percent, 1 percent, or fat-free) to fill to the 1-cup mark. Allow to stand at room temperature for 5 minutes before using.

CREAM CHEESE. American-style cream cheese is a soft, fresh cheese that contains stabilizers such as carob bean gum and carrageenan. For the recipes in this book, I recommend Philadelphia brand cream cheese.

MASCARPONE is a soft, slightly sweet Italian cheese. It's a key component of tiramisu and makes a great addition to other desserts, too. Happily, it's available in the dairy section of most supermarkets now.

YOGURT is a cultured milk product that is made from whole, low-fat, or fat-free milk and is available plain or flavored. *Greek yogurt* is yogurt that has been strained to remove the whey, giving it a very thick consistency. For recipes that call for yogurt, use whichever fat content you prefer.

## *Eggs*

EGGS are graded for quality and freshness as AA, A, or B. Grade AA eggs are best for baking; they have thick whites and strong yolks. Eggs should be stored in the coldest part of the refrigerator, in their original carton, with the pointed end down. Because of the potential threat of salmonella poisoning, keep eggs refrigerated until shortly before using them. Bring the eggs to room temperature by setting them in a bowl of very warm water for 10 to 15 minutes (dry the shells before cracking the eggs). Do not use eggs with cracked shells. If you're left with extra whites or yolks, they can both be frozen for use in the future.

Recipes in this book call for large eggs, and that is what you should use. Do not use small, extra-large, or jumbo eggs—it will greatly affect the texture and consistency of whatever you're making. Because I am fond of hens and believe in good karma, I also look for eggs that are labeled organic and "free-range" or "cruelty-free." Organic eggs are produced by hens whose feed is composed of ingredients that were grown with minimal use of pesticides, fungicides, herbicides, and commercial fertilizers. Free-range hens have daily access to the outdoors. The production cost of these eggs is higher, and the hens produce fewer eggs, so they're more expensive, but organic, free-range eggs generally have brighter yolks and better flavor.

*Pasteurized eggs* are available as whole eggs, yolks, or whites, and in refrigerated or frozen liquid form. Use them in desserts that are uncooked or lightly cooked to reduce the instance of food-borne illness.

## Fats

Fats make baked goods rich and tender and provide aeration to help leaven batter or dough. They also add flavor and moisture, act as emulsifiers, and lubricate the gluten in flour. There are several types of fat, each with its own properties that result in particular flavors and textures.

BUTTER. Always use unsalted butter in baking, as it permits you to control the salt content in a recipe. Butter can be stored in the freezer, wrapped in plastic, for up to six months. If a recipe calls for softened butter, you can either allow it to soften at room temperature or in the microwave. Just microwave the unwrapped cold butter on 50 percent power for 20 to 30 seconds. Softened butter should still be cool to the touch. In contrast, room temperature butter should look and feel slightly greasy.

SOLID VEGETABLE SHORTENING is 100 percent fat and contains no water or minerals. It is soft and has the ability to surround air bubbles well, providing good aeration in batters. I also like to use shortening to grease my pans because cakes will unmold easily, without sticking. Look for a brand of shortening that is free of trans fats, such as Crisco.

VEGETABLE OIL. When a recipe calls for vegetable oil as an ingredient, it's best to use a neutral-flavored oil. My top choice is safflower oil because of its clean flavor, but it is more expensive than soy-based oils. Whatever oil you choose, always give it a good sniff before using it to make sure it is not rancid.

## Leaveners

BAKING SODA produces carbon dioxide bubbles when combined with an acid such as buttermilk or yogurt. It has an almost indefinite shelf life if stored in a dry place.

BAKING POWDER is composed of baking soda, cream of tartar, and cornstarch. When combined with a liquid, it releases carbon dioxide. Always use double-acting baking powder, the most common type, which releases some carbon dioxide when it is combined with a liquid and the rest when exposed to oven heat. Baking powder has a shelf life of about a year, after which it loses its strength. To test it, sprinkle some over hot water. If it fizzes, it is still active.

## Nuts, Raisins, and Coconut

**NUTS.** When using nuts, always taste a few to make sure they are fresh and not rancid. Even slightly rancid nuts will ruin the flavor of your dessert or baked good. See instructions for toasting various types of nuts on page 13.

**RAISINS.** These are grapes of a certain type, usually Thompson, that have been dried either in the sun or in a special dehydrating process. Sun-Maid makes a "baking raisin" that is exceptionally moist and plump and is wonderful in cakes and other baked items. Golden raisins have been treated with sulfites to keep them from darkening, so if you're sensitive to sulfites, use black raisins instead. To rehydrate hard, dry raisins, cover them with the liquid of your choice (orange or apple juice or dark rum, for example) in a small saucepan and heat gently over medium heat until the liquid begins to bubble and the raisins become plump. Drain before using.

**COCONUT** is available as sweetened flakes or unsweetened desiccated (dried) flakes, and I use both types. The unsweetened variety can usually be found in the organic or health food aisle of the supermarket. To toast coconut, place it in a large skillet and cook over medium heat, stirring frequently, until the flakes are mostly golden brown.

## Flavor Accents

**CITRUS ZEST AND JUICE.** For *citrus zest,* it's best to use organic citrus fruit, which is free of toxic chemicals and pesticides. If you are not using organic fruit, scrub the fruit well with a vegetable brush under running water and dry before zesting. For *citrus juice,* use freshly squeezed and strained juice.

**DARK RUM.** Several recipes in this book call for dark rum. I recommend the Myers's and Mount Gay brands, both of which are excellent.

**ORANGE BLOSSOM WATER** (also known as *orange flower water*) is distilled from the petals of bitter orange blossoms and has a sweet, perfumed fragrance. It is used frequently in Middle Eastern cuisine in both sweet and savory dishes. Use a product that is all natural, such as Cortas brand (available from amazon.com). Cheaper brands use a combination of chemicals and orange oil instead of real orange blossoms and water.

**SALT.** I use *fine sea salt* for the recipes in this book. *Kosher salt* has slightly larger crystals, so if you use it, increase the amount of salt by 25 percent (for example, for 1 teaspoon of fine salt, you would use 1¼ teaspoons of kosher salt).

VANILLA BEANS, VANILLA EXTRACT, AND VANILLA BEAN PASTE. *Vanilla beans* add a wonderful, full-bodied flavor to desserts. My favorite types are Bourbon, Madagascar, Ugandan, and Tahitian beans. Whatever type you use, always make sure the beans are moist and plump and have a slightly oily skin. Store beans wrapped in plastic in an airtight container at cool room temperature. Do not store them in the refrigerator —this moist environment can promote the growth of a particular mold specific to vanilla. Another trick (which I learned from Sarabeth Levine of Sarabeth's Bakery) is to cut off ⅛ inch from the bottom of your vanilla beans and place them, cut side down, in a tall jar. Pour about 2 inches of dark rum in the jar and place the lid on the jar. Allow the beans to stand for at least two weeks before using. To extract the seeds, simply squeeze the beans like a tube of toothpaste. The rum keeps the beans plump and very moist; you can store them like this for up to six months.

For *vanilla extract,* use a high-quality pure vanilla extract, such as the Nielsen-Massey brand, or make your own (see page 27). *Vanilla bean paste* is made by infusing vanilla bean pods and seeds into a thick, sweet syrup base. Since vanilla paste contains the tiny seeds of the pod, it will add a lovely speckled look to your dessert without the hassle of dealing with a vanilla bean. Vanilla paste is usually substituted in equal proportions for vanilla extract, but check the label, as concentrations can vary. If you want to substitute a vanilla bean for vanilla extract or paste, use one-third of a bean for every 1 teaspoon of extract or paste.

## Chocolate

There are many excellent chocolates available today. My general advice for desserts is to use the best chocolate you can find, as it will make all the difference. To store chocolate, wrap it first in plastic wrap, then in heavy-duty aluminum foil, and place it in an airtight container. Ideally, chocolate should be stored in a cool, dry place with a consistent temperature of around 65°F. White chocolate must be stored away from light because of the milk solids it contains. Light will accelerate its oxidation, so that the chocolate may turn rancid overnight. Store it, well wrapped, in a dark place. Properly stored, unsweetened and dark chocolate may keep for as long as two years. Milk chocolate will keep for one year and white chocolate for seven or eight months. See page 17 for instructions on tempering chocolate.

UNSWEETENED CHOCOLATE. Also known as baking chocolate, this consists of pure chocolate liquor (ground cacao nibs, also called cocoa solids) and lecithin (a stabilizer). It does not contain sugar, and it cannot be used as a substitute for semisweet or bittersweet chocolate. Scharffen Berger is my favorite brand of unsweetened chocolate — it's a little pricey, but really worth it

**BITTERSWEET AND SEMISWEET CHOCOLATES.** These are the chocolates used most often in baking. Sugar, lecithin, vanilla, and more cocoa butter are added to unsweetened chocolate to create these chocolates, which are interchangeable (the FDA does not distinguish between the two categories). Both varieties must contain at least 35 percent chocolate liquor. *Semisweet chocolate* is generally sweeter than *bittersweet chocolate*, though this varies according to brand, and one company's semisweet chocolate may be comparable in sweetness to another's bittersweet chocolate. It is best to use your own taste as a guide in choosing between the two. Because there are so many different chocolates with varying cocoa solid percentages available today, I specify a range of percentages for both semisweet and bittersweet chocolates in this book. My favorite brands of bittersweet and semisweet chocolates are Guittard and Valrhona.

**MILK CHOCOLATE.** Milk chocolate contains much less chocolate liquor (a minimum of 10 percent) than bittersweet. It also contains a minimum of 3.7 percent milk fat and 12 percent milk solids. Because of the milk component, it is sensitive to heat, and therefore requires more attention when you melt it. For baking, I love Guittard Orinoco and Valrhona Jivara Lactee.

**WHITE CHOCOLATE.** White chocolate contains no chocolate liquor at all, just chocolate's natural fat, cocoa butter. Different products contain various proportions of cocoa butter, butterfat, sugar, milk solids, lecithin, and flavorings. Avoid at all costs the so-called "coating" products, which are made with vegetable fat instead of cocoa butter. My favorite brands of true white chocolate include El Rey, Valrhona, Green & Black's, and Guittard.

**CHOCOLATE MORSELS.** Chocolate morsels, or chips, are formulated especially to retain their shape when used in cookies, cakes, and other desserts. The manufacturers achieve this by substituting vegetable fat for some portion of the cocoa butter. Because of this, chocolate morsels should not be substituted for semisweet or bittersweet chocolate, especially for melting.

**COCOA POWDER.** There are two types of unsweetened cocoa powder: alkalized, or *Dutch-processed,* and non-alkalized, or *natural.* Dutch-processed cocoa powder has been treated with an alkali to neutralize its acidity, a process that creates a darker cocoa with a smoother flavor. Natural cocoa powder tends to have a more chocolaty flavor. Recipes in this book will specify which type of cocoa powder to use. My two favorite brands of cocoa powder are Valrhona (which is alkalized) and Scharffen Berger (natural).

**CACAO NIBS** are the seeds of the cacao pod and can be used to add a light chocolate flavor and crunch to recipes. I also use them to garnish puddings, mousses, and cakes.

# Basics

✤ ✤

# Vanilla Sugar

*This fragrant sugar* adds vanilla flavor to cookies, cakes, pie and tart dough, and almost any baked item you can think of. Substitute it in equal amounts for the sugar in a recipe; if there is already vanilla in the recipe, omit it, or leave it in for an extra flavor boost. It's also great in coffee, tea, and hot chocolate.

**MAKES 2 CUPS**

2 cups (400 g/14 oz) granulated sugar

1 vanilla bean

1. Place the sugar in a jar with a lid or another airtight container.

2. Using a small paring knife, slit the vanilla bean lengthwise to expose the seeds. Using the knife, scrape the seeds into the sugar. Add the vanilla pod to the sugar and spoon sugar over it so that it's covered. Cover the jar or container and let stand for 1 week before using.

# Sugared Vanilla Beans

*These sugared beans* make a pretty garnish for all sorts of desserts, but particularly vanilla flavored ones.

**MAKES 8 GARNISHES**

2 vanilla beans

¼ cup (50 g/1.76 oz) granulated sugar

Preheat the oven to 350°F. Line a baking sheet with parchment paper. Using a paring knife, cut each of the vanilla beans lengthwise in half and then in half again, to make 4 strips each. Place the sugar in a small bowl and toss the vanilla bean strips in it. Place the vanilla bean strips on the prepared baking sheet and bake for about 5 minutes, or until the sugar sticks to the beans. Set aside to cool.

# Toasted Nuts

*Toasting brings out* the full flavor of nuts. Watch the nuts carefully as they toast — they can over-brown or burn easily.

NOTE: To remove the skin from toasted hazelnuts, wrap the hot nuts in a clean dishtowel and let them stand for 5 to 10 minutes. Then, vigorously rub the nuts against themselves in the towel to remove most of the skins.

Preheat the oven to 350°F. Spread nuts in a single layer on a baking sheet and toast for 5 to 12 minutes (the time will vary depending on the nut variety; see Toasting Times, below), shaking the pan once or twice during baking, until they are golden (if the nuts have skins, look beneath the skin) and fragrant. Transfer to a plate to cool. The nuts can be stored in an airtight container for up to 1 day.

## Toasting Times

SLIVERED OR SLICED ALMONDS: 5 to 10 minutes

WHOLE ALMONDS: 10 to 15 minutes

WALNUTS AND PECANS: 5 to 10 minutes

HAZELNUTS: 8 to 12 minutes

PISTACHIOS: 5 to 7 minutes

# Candied Pecans or Walnuts

*This method of candying* nuts is super-quick and fuss-free. Candied nuts make a beautiful garnish and add texture to smooth desserts, such as ice cream, puddings, and mousses.

MAKES ½ CUP

½ cup (50 g/1.76 oz) pecans or walnuts, whole or coarsely chopped

1 teaspoon (4 g/0.14 oz) vanilla extract

2 teaspoons (8 g/0.3 oz) granulated sugar

Pinch of fine sea salt

Preheat the oven to 350°F. Place the pecans or walnuts in a small bowl and toss well with the vanilla, sugar, and salt. Scatter the nuts on a baking sheet and bake for 9 to 12 minutes, tossing them once during baking, until they are lightly browned and fragrant. Set aside to cool. Store in an airtight container at room temperature for up to 2 weeks.

*Basics*

# Apple Butter

*Slow-simmered apple butter* is far better than the jarred variety found in stores. It does take a while to cook — four to five hours — but it doesn't require much attention, only some occasional stirring with a wooden spoon. Use this as you would use jam or preserves. It is especially good spread on a warm croissant or added to hot oatmeal.

MAKES ABOUT 1 QUART

6 medium (1.36 kg/3 lb) Granny Smith apples

2 cups (480 g/17 oz) apple cider or juice

⅔ cup firmly packed (144 g/ 5 oz) light brown sugar

½ teaspoon (1 g/0.03 oz) ground cinnamon

⅛ teaspoon (0.25 g/0.009 oz) ground cloves

⅛ teaspoon (0.8 g/0.03 oz) salt

1. Peel and core the apples, then cut each one into 8 wedges. Place the apples and the remaining ingredients in a 4-quart saucepan and bring to a boil, stirring occasionally. Reduce the heat so that the mixture is at a low simmer and cook, stirring every 30 minutes, until almost all the liquid has evaporated and the mixture is dark brown, 4 to 5 hours.

2. Remove the pan from the heat and stir or whisk vigorously to break up any remaining apple pieces. Cool the apple butter completely, then transfer to a container, cover, and refrigerate for up to 1 week.

# Almond Cream

*Also known as frangipane,* baked almond cream makes a delicious filling for fruit tarts. It's used in my Apple and Almond Tart (page 124) and Raspberry Almond Tartlets (page 89). To create your own fruit tart, fill a fully baked tart shell with Almond Cream and bake at 350°F for 40 to 45 minutes, or until a toothpick inserted into the filling comes out clean (bake tartlets 25 to 30 minutes). Allow the filling to cool and top it with slices of fresh fruit or berries.

MAKES ABOUT 2 CUPS

1 cup (85 g/3 oz) unblanched sliced almonds

½ cup (100 g/3.5 oz) granulated sugar, divided

7 tablespoons (100 g/3.5 oz) unsalted butter, softened

2 large eggs

2 tablespoons (16 g/0.58 oz) all-purpose flour

1 teaspoon (5 g/0.17 oz) vanilla extract

Pinch of salt

1 tablespoon (15 g/0.5 oz) dark rum

1. In the bowl of a food processor, process the almonds and 2 tablespoons (25 g/0.88 oz) of the sugar until the nuts are finely ground.

2. In the bowl of an electric mixer fitted with the paddle attachment, mix the butter and the remaining 6 tablespoons (75 g/2.6 oz) sugar together at medium speed until well combined and smooth, about 2 minutes. Add the ground almonds and mix until combined. Add the eggs one at a time, mixing well after each addition. Add the flour, vanilla, salt, and rum and mix until combined. Store the unbaked almond cream in an airtight container in the refrigerator for up to 1 week, or in the freezer for up to 1 month.

# Quick Puff Pastry

*Puff pastry can be* a little tricky to make, but this recipe is fairly foolproof, and really quick. The dough is made like a pie crust, and then folded several times like classic puff pastry dough. If you've never made puff pastry before, give this recipe a try — you may never buy frozen packaged sheets again!

**MAKES 2 POUNDS 2 OUNCES (964 GRAMS)**

3 cups plus 2 tablespoons (414 g/14.6 oz) all-purpose flour

1 teaspoon (6.7 g/0.23 oz) salt

32 tablespoons (454 g/1 lb) cold unsalted butter, cut into ½-inch pieces

½ cup plus 1 tablespoon (133 g/4.7 oz) ice cold water

1. In the bowl of an electric mixer fitted with the paddle attachment, combine the flour and salt at low speed. If your mixer has a splatter shield attachment, attach it now. Add the butter, one-third at a time, and mix for just a few seconds. The mixture will be very crumbly, with large pieces of butter in it. While continuing to mix at low speed, add the water and mix just until the dough starts to come together. (Large pieces of butter should remain.)

2. Scrape the dough onto a floured work surface and pound and pat it into a rough rectangle with a rolling pin. Roll the dough into an 8-by-16-inch rectangle, dusting the dough with flour as needed. Arrange the dough with a short side closest to you. Brush off any excess flour on the dough with a pastry brush. Fold the bottom third up over the center, and then the top third over the bottom, as if you were folding a business letter. The dough now has three layers. Rotate the dough 90 degrees, so that the short sides are at the top and bottom. Roll the dough out again to an 8-by-16-inch rectangle. Fold it in thirds again. The dough has now been "turned" twice. Wrap the dough well in plastic wrap and refrigerate for 30 minutes.

3. Remove the dough from the refrigerator and place it back on the floured work surface so that the short ends are on the top and bottom. Roll and fold the dough as before, to make two more turns. Use the dough immediately, or wrap it well in plastic wrap and store it for future use, refrigerated for up to 3 days or frozen for up to 1 month.

# Tempered Chocolate

*Tempering gives chocolate* its glossy sheen and snap. Use it when you are making chocolate confections such as White Chocolate Holiday Bark and Mendiants (page 219) or to coat cookies or confections such as Peanut Honeycomb (page 223) with chocolate. Since it's difficult to temper small quantities of chocolate, it's best to work with a minimum of 1 pound. Any leftover chocolate can be allowed to set and retempered at a later date. Though there are a few ways to temper chocolate, this is the easiest, and my favorite.

**SPECIAL EQUIPMENT:**
Instant-read thermometer

1 pound (450 g) high-quality chocolate of any type, finely chopped

1. Put one-third of the chocolate in a bowl and set aside.

2. Have an instant-read thermometer at hand. Fill a medium pot one-third full with water and bring it to a gentle simmer over medium heat. Place the remaining two-thirds chocolate in a bowl that will fit snugly on top of the pot but not touch the water. Reduce the heat to low and place the bowl over the pot. Heat until the chocolate is completely melted, stirring occasionally with a silicone spatula. Check its temperature frequently to make sure it's not warmer than the desired melting temperature (see Temperature Guide, below). Once the chocolate reaches the proper temperature, remove the bowl from the heat, stir in the reserved chocolate to lower the temperature, and let the chocolate set until it reaches the proper cooling temperature for its type (see Temperature Guide). Once that temperature is reached, return the bowl of chocolate to the pot and briefly heat it so the chocolate reaches its proper working temperature.

3. Use the tempered chocolate as directed in the recipe.

### Temperature Guide

| TYPE OF CHOCOLATE | MELTING TEMP | COOLING TEMP | WORKING TEMP |
|---|---|---|---|
| Dark | 122–131°F | 82–84°F | 87°F |
| Milk | 113–118°F | 80–82°F | 86°F |
| White | 113–118°F | 78–80°F | 84°F |

# Caramel Cream

*Silky smooth, with* a deep caramel flavor and a subtle tang, this whipped cream is wonderful as an accompaniment to or topping for a cake or dessert. Note that the caramel must chill for two hours before the whipped cream can be completed, so plan ahead.

MAKES ABOUT 3 CUPS

¾ cup (150 g/5.3 oz) granulated sugar

3 tablespoons (44 g/1.5 oz) water

Pinch of cream of tartar

2 cups (464 g/16.3 oz) heavy cream, divided

1 teaspoon (4 g/0.14 oz) vanilla extract

1. Fill a cup with water and place a pastry brush in it (this will be used for washing down the sides of the pan to prevent crystallization). In a small, heavy saucepan, combine the sugar, water, and cream of tartar and place over medium heat. Cook, stirring constantly, until the sugar dissolves. Increase the heat to high and cook without stirring, occasionally brushing down the sides of the pan with the wet pastry brush, until the syrup caramelizes and turns a golden amber color, about 4 minutes. Remove the pan from the heat and slowly stir in ½ cup (116 g/4 oz) of the cream (the mixture will bubble up), stirring until smooth. Carefully pour the caramel into a heatproof glass measuring cup and loosely cover the top with plastic wrap. Refrigerate the caramel until chilled, about 2 hours.

2. In the bowl of an electric mixer fitted with the whisk attachment, beat the remaining 1½ cups (348 g/12.2 oz) cream with the vanilla at medium speed just until blended. Add the chilled caramel and beat at high speed until the mixture forms soft peaks. Refrigerate, covered, until ready to serve, up to 8 hours.

# Clarified and Browned Butter

*Clarifying is a process* that removes the milk solids from butter. Clarified butter has a much higher smoking point—the temperature at which smoke becomes visible—than regular butter. To make browned butter (*beurre noisette*), which adds a delicious, nutty flavor to cakes and cookies, continue cooking the clarified butter until the milk solids turn dark brown and the butter has a nutty fragrance.

**Unsalted butter, as needed (use 33 percent, or one-third, more solid butter than you need of clarified butter; for example, if you need 16 tablespoons/ 8 oz/225 g clarified butter, start with 21 tablespoons/ 10.5 oz/300 g solid butter)**

1. Cut the butter into tablespoons and place in a heavy saucepan over medium heat, partially covered to prevent spattering. Once the butter is melted, reduce the heat to low and cook, uncovered, until the solids drop to the bottom of the pan and begin to turn brown, about 20 minutes for 454 g/ 1 lb of butter.

2. For *beurre noisette,* continue to cook the clarified butter until the solids turn dark brown, 2 to 3 minutes more.

3. Strain the butter through a fine-mesh sieve or a cheesecloth-lined strainer and discard the solids. Let cool, then store in an airtight container in the refrigerator for up to 3 months.

# Homemade Crème Fraîche

*These days, rich and tangy* crème fraîche can be found in the dairy section of many supermarkets, but, if you prefer, it can also be made at home.

**MAKES ABOUT 2¼ CUPS**

**SPECIAL EQUIPMENT:**
Instant-read thermometer

2 cups (464 g/16.3 oz) heavy cream (preferably not ultra-pasteurized)

¼ cup (60 g/2.1 oz) buttermilk

1. Combine the cream and buttermilk in a small saucepan and place over medium-low heat. Heat just until the mixture registers 110°F on an instant-read thermometer. Remove the pan from the heat and pour the mixture into a glass container.

2. Cover the container loosely with plastic wrap and place it in a warm place, such as on top of the refrigerator or the stove. Let stand, without stirring, for 8 to 14 hours (ultra-pasteurized cream may take up to 36 hours), until slightly thickened but still pourable. Transfer the crème fraîche to an airtight container and refrigerate for 3 hours before using (it will continue to thicken as it chills). Store in an airtight container in the refrigerator for up to 2 weeks.

# Red Berry Sauce

*This simple berry sauce* comes together quickly and really dresses up a plain slice of cheesecake or a bowl of ice cream. Start by adding the lesser amount of sugar and check the sauce for balance. If needed, add more sugar until it's just right.

**MAKES ABOUT 1⅓ CUPS**

2 cups (226 g/8 oz) fresh raspberries

1 cup (113 g/4 oz) hulled and sliced strawberries

⅓ to ½ cup (42 g/1.5 oz to 64 g/2.2 oz) confectioners' sugar, depending on the sweetness of the berries

2 teaspoons freshly squeezed lemon juice

Put all the ingredients in the bowl of a food processor and process until smooth. Strain the sauce through a fine-mesh sieve into a bowl or storage container. Cover the sauce and refrigerate until ready to serve, up to 2 weeks.

# Brown Sugar–Rum Sauce

*This dark caramel sauce* goes so well with a variety of desserts, from vanilla ice cream to chocolate cake to espresso semifreddo. The rum gives it a musky sweetness, without the taste of alcohol.

MAKES 1 CUP

¾ cup (174 g/6.13 oz) heavy cream

1 cup firmly packed (216 g/7.6 oz) light brown sugar

¼ cup (60 g/2.1 oz) dark rum

Pinch of salt

3 tablespoons (42 g/1.5 oz) unsalted butter

1 teaspoon (5 g/0.17 oz) vanilla extract

1. In a 1½-quart saucepan, bring the cream, brown sugar, rum, and salt to a boil over high heat, stirring just until the sugar is dissolved. As soon as it reaches a boil, reduce the heat to low or medium-low, so that the mixture is at a simmer. Continue to simmer, stirring occasionally, until the mixture thickens slightly, 8 to 10 minutes.

2. Remove the pan from the heat and add the butter and vanilla, stirring until the butter is melted. The sauce should be served warm. It can be prepared ahead and refrigerated, covered, for up to 1 week. To reheat the sauce, microwave on high power until it is warmed through, about 30 seconds.

# Vanilla

✤ ✤

Ah, you flavor everything; you
are the vanilla of society.

— SYDNEY SMITH
English essayist (1771–1845)

*Flowery and aromatic,* there's nothing plain about vanilla. Known as the queen of spices, it is the second most expensive spice in the world (saffron has the distinction of being the priciest), a fact borne out by the high price of a small container of vanilla extract. Vanilla also happens to be the most popular flavor in the world — quite an honor, when you consider how much competition there is.

Vanilla's nuanced flavor comes from the vanilla bean, a pod fruit from a vine in the orchid family. The pod contains many tiny seeds, the source of vanilla's fragrant flavor and aroma. To make vanilla extract, vanilla beans are infused in a combination of alcohol and water (for instructions on making your own, see page 27).

The best vanilla beans come from Tahiti (flowery notes of cherry and anise), Madagascar (sweet and creamy), and Mexico (bold and smoky). Ugandan beans are also excellent, similar in flavor to creamy Madagascar beans, but with additional notes of milk chocolate. To use vanilla beans, slit them lengthwise with a paring knife and either infuse them into a liquid (such as melted butter, caramel, or heavy cream), or scrape out the seeds and add them directly to batter, dough, or whatever element you want to flavor. There are now several excellent online sources for buying vanilla beans from all over the world (see Sources, page 361). Many of these sources allow you to purchase small amounts — a single bean, if you like — so you can mix and match and order a variety of beans to decide which ones you like the best.

Another wonderful product is vanilla bean paste, which is made by infusing pods and seeds into a sweet syrup base. The advantage of using this product instead of extract is that you get the speckled look of the tiny seeds along with vanilla flavor, without the hassle of storing perishable vanilla beans. For example, I always use vanilla bean paste in my whipped cream because I love the way the seeds look in contrast to the snowy white cream.

Vanilla is frequently relegated to the role of flavor enhancer, used to round out the other flavors in a dessert or baked good. But in this chapter, it's the star ingredient: bold, flowery, and voluptuous. From simple butter cookies to a silky pudding to a show-stopping white chocolate vanilla mousse cake, there is something for everyone (even hard-core chocoholics) to love.

# Silky Vanilla Pudding

*Vanilla pudding is* one of life's great pleasures. When executed perfectly, this classic custard is rich, satisfying, and full of vanilla essence. This version is all that and more; it uses less cornstarch than most recipes, relying more on egg yolks for thickening. This gives it a beautiful, ultra-smooth texture and soft richness that will impress even the most discriminating pudding connoisseur.

MAKES 6 SERVINGS

6 large egg yolks

½ cup (100 g/3.5 oz) granulated sugar, divided

3 tablespoons (22 g/0.8 oz) cornstarch

¼ teaspoon (1.6 g/0.06 oz) salt

2½ cups (605 g/21.3 oz) whole milk

½ cup (116 g/4 oz) heavy cream

3 tablespoons (42 g/1.5 oz) unsalted butter, cut into tablespoons

1 vanilla bean (Tahitian, Ugandan, or Madagascar), split lengthwise and seeds scraped out, or 2 teaspoons (8 g/ 0.28 oz) vanilla bean paste or extract

1. Place the egg yolks in a medium bowl and set aside.

2. Prepare an ice bath by filling a large bowl one-third full with ice water.

3. In a 2-quart saucepan, whisk together ¼ cup (50 g/1.76 oz) of the sugar with the cornstarch and salt. Gradually whisk in the milk and cream. Place the pan over medium heat and cook, whisking occasionally, until the mixture comes to a simmer.

4. Meanwhile, whisk the egg yolks with the remaining ¼ cup (50 g/1.76 oz) sugar until well blended. When the milk mixture has reached a simmer, whisk about ½ cup (118 ml/4 fl oz) of the hot milk mixture into the yolks to temper them, then whisk the yolk mixture into the remaining milk mixture in the pan. Cook over medium heat, whisking constantly, until the pudding thickens slightly and just begins to bubble, 2 to 3 minutes. Whisk in the butter until it is completely melted. Pour the pudding through a fine-mesh sieve into a medium bowl. Stir in the vanilla seeds (or paste or extract), then place the bowl into the ice bath. Let the pudding stand in the ice bath, stirring frequently, until it is completely cool.

5. Divide the pudding among 6 serving glasses (about ½ cup per serving). Cover each pudding with a piece of plastic wrap. Refrigerate for at least 3 hours (or up to 24 hours) before serving.

# Homemade Vanilla Extract

*Making vanilla extract* is surprisingly easy, and a lot less expensive than buying those little bottles from the supermarket. It does take three months for the vanilla bean flavor to infuse the vodka, but the result is a fragrant vanilla essence full of tiny vanilla seeds. My favorite source for vanilla beans is Amadeus Vanilla Beans (amadeusvanillabeans.com). Try various beans to see which you like best; my current favorite is the Ugandan bean.

MAKES 1½ CUPS

6 plump vanilla beans (see Sources, page 361)

1½ cups (320 g/11.3 oz) vodka

Split the vanilla beans lengthwise and scrape the seeds into a jar with a screw-on lid (I use a Mason jar). Cut the vanilla pods into 1-inch pieces and add them to the jar along with the vodka. Put the lid on and shake the jar really well. Store in a dark cupboard for 3 months, giving it a good shake every day. Strain, discarding the pod pieces, and store in the covered jar in a dark place, like the back of a cabinet, for up to 3 years.

# Vanilla-Scented Jasmine Rice Pudding

*Rice pudding falls squarely* into the category of comfort food, though there's nothing old-fashioned about this version, which is made with jasmine rice. From Thailand, jasmine rice has a floral aroma that makes it ideal for desserts. The rice is cooked in the oven, which allows you to control the cooking temperature more accurately than on the stovetop. The texture of the cooked pudding should be loose, as it will firm up during chilling (and there's nothing worse than gloppy rice pudding). Once chilled, I fold whipped cream into it, which gives it a light, ultra-creamy texture. The dark rum is optional, but it really brings out the vanilla flavor in the pudding without making it boozy; it just adds a subtle sweetness. If you prefer your rice pudding hot, leave out the whipped cream and cut the sugar down to ¼ cup.

**MAKES 6 SERVINGS**

2⅓ cups (564 g/19.9 oz) whole milk

⅓ cup (66 g/2.3 oz) granulated sugar

½ teaspoon (1 g/0.03 oz) finely grated orange zest

½ vanilla bean, or 1½ teaspoons (6 g/0.21 oz) vanilla bean paste or extract

½ cup (85 g/3 oz) uncooked jasmine rice

2 large egg yolks

2 tablespoons (30 g/1 oz) dark rum (optional)

½ cup (116 g/4 oz) heavy cream

1. Preheat the oven to 350°F. In a medium ovenproof saucepan with a lid, combine the milk, sugar, and orange zest. If using a vanilla bean, use a paring knife to split it in half lengthwise and scrape the seeds into the pan. Add the vanilla bean pod and bring the mixture to a boil over medium-high heat. Stir in the rice.

2. Cover the pot with the lid, place it in the oven, and bake, whisking the rice vigorously every 10 minutes during baking, for about 30 minutes, until the rice is tender (not all the milk will have been absorbed). Remove the pan from the oven and whisk the egg yolks into the hot rice. Place the pan over medium heat and cook, whisking constantly, until the mixture thickens slightly, about 2 minutes. Stir in the rum, if using, and the vanilla bean paste or extract, if using. Set the mixture aside to cool completely.

3. Transfer the rice mixture to a medium bowl, cover, and refrigerate until chilled, at least 2 hours.

4. Remove the vanilla bean pod from the chilled rice mixture. In the bowl of an electric mixer fitted with the whisk attachment, whip the cream at high speed until it forms medium peaks. Gently fold the whipped cream into the chilled rice pudding. Divide the pudding among 6 serving glasses (about ½ cup each), cover with plastic wrap, and refrigerate until ready to serve, up to 2 days.

# Honey-Vanilla-Chamomile Ice Cream

*Made with chamomile tea,* which is reputed to aid digestion and induce sleep, this subtly flavored ice cream makes an ideal ending to a heavy dinner. You can alter the character of the ice cream by using different varieties of honey, but stick to a mild one so the soft flavors of chamomile and vanilla are not overwhelmed. Good choices are orange blossom, clover, acacia, or tupelo. I like to serve the ice cream topped with sliced strawberries that have been tossed with a little sugar and allowed to macerate for 30 minutes, making them sweet and juicy.

**MAKES ABOUT 1 QUART**

**SPECIAL EQUIPMENT:**
Ice cream maker

1 vanilla bean, or 1 teaspoon (4 g/0.14 oz) vanilla bean paste or extract

2 cups (464 g/16.3 oz) heavy cream

1¼ cups (302 g/10.7 oz) whole milk

5 tablespoons (62 g/2.2 oz) granulated sugar, divided

5 (6.5 g/0.22 oz) chamomile tea bags

6 large egg yolks

¼ teaspoon (1.7 g/0.06 oz) salt

3 tablespoons (60 g/2.1 oz) mild honey

1. If using a vanilla bean, use a paring knife to split it lengthwise down the center. Scrape the vanilla seeds into a medium heavy-bottomed saucepan and add the pod. Add the cream, milk, 3 tablespoons of the sugar, and the tea bags and heat over medium-high heat, stirring to dissolve the sugar, until the mixture begins to bubble around the edge of the pan and steam rises from the surface. Remove the pan from the heat, cover, and allow to steep for 30 minutes.

2. In a heatproof bowl, whisk the remaining 2 tablespoons sugar, the egg yolks, and salt until thickened and lightened in color. Remove the tea bags from the cream, squeezing them to remove excess liquid. Return the infused cream to medium heat and heat until it starts to bubble around the edges again. Gradually whisk about 1 cup of the warm cream mixture into the yolks to temper them. Return the yolk mixture to the saucepan and stir over medium heat until the custard has thickened and coats the back of a wooden spoon. Strain the custard through a fine-mesh strainer into a medium bowl and whisk in the honey (and vanilla paste or extract, if using). Prepare an ice bath by filling a large bowl one-third full with ice and water and set the bowl of custard in it. Let the custard cool to room temperature, stirring occasionally. Press a piece of plastic wrap directly on the surface of the custard and refrigerate for at least 6 hours or, preferably, overnight.

3. Freeze the cold custard in an ice cream maker according to the manufacturer's instructions. Pack into an airtight container and freeze for at least 3 hours (or up 1 week) before serving.

# Vanilla Gelato

*Gelato has a lower fat content* than ice cream and, consequently, is less rich. Because it is made with more milk than cream, it also has a more pronounced flavor — there are fewer fat molecules to coat the tongue and mask the flavor — which is what I love most about it.

**MAKES 1¼ QUARTS**

**SPECIAL EQUIPMENT:**
Ice cream maker, instant-read thermometer

1 plump vanilla bean, preferably Tahitian, or 2 teaspoons (8 g/ 0.28 oz) vanilla bean paste or extract

3½ cups (847 g/30 oz) whole milk

1 cup (232 g/8.18 oz) heavy cream

1½ cups (300 g/10.5 oz) granulated sugar, divided

8 large egg yolks

¾ teaspoon (5 g/0.17 oz) salt

1. If using a vanilla bean, use a paring knife to split it lengthwise down the center. Scrape the vanilla seeds into a large heavy-bottomed saucepan and add the pod. Add the milk, cream, and 1¼ cups (250 g/8.8 oz) of the sugar and heat over medium-high heat, stirring to dissolve the sugar, until the mixture begins to bubble around the edge of the pan and steam rises from the surface.

2. Meanwhile, in a medium heatproof bowl, vigorously whisk together the remaining ¼ cup (50 g/1.76 oz) sugar, the egg yolks, and salt until well blended. Slowly pour about 1 cup of the hot milk into the yolk mixture to temper it, whisking constantly. Return the mixture to the saucepan with the remaining milk mixture and cook over medium heat, stirring constantly with a heatproof spatula, until the custard registers 185°F on an instant-read thermometer. Immediately strain the custard through a fine-mesh strainer into a large heatproof bowl. Return the strained vanilla bean pod to the custard. Prepare an ice bath by filling a large bowl one-third full with ice and water, and place the bowl of custard in it. Allow the custard to chill in the ice bath, stirring occasionally, until cold, about 20 minutes. Remove the bowl of custard from the ice bath. Stir in the vanilla paste or extract, if using. Press a piece of plastic wrap directly on the surface of the custard to prevent a skin from forming. Refrigerate the custard for at least 6 hours, or, preferably, overnight.

3. Remove the vanilla bean pod from the custard. Freeze the custard in an ice cream maker according to the manufacturer's instructions. Pack into a freezer container, cover, and freeze for at least 3 hours before serving. (Unlike ice cream, gelato is best served the day it is made.)

# Frozen Vanilla Yogurt Parfaits with Granola Streusel

*The parfait in this layered* dessert is made from a *pâte à bombe* (egg yolks whipped with a sugar syrup), so it has a soft texture, similar to that of a semifreddo. The mild vanilla-honey flavor of the parfait is a perfect match for the cinnamon-scented granola streusel and tart raspberries. This is a refreshing summer dessert and can be made up to three days ahead, making it ideal for entertaining.

**MAKES 6 PARFAITS**

**SPECIAL EQUIPMENT:**
Candy thermometer

**GRANOLA STREUSEL**

1 cup (122 g/4.3 oz) granola

¼ cup (33 g/1.16 oz) all-purpose flour

¼ cup firmly packed (54 g/ 1.9 oz) light brown sugar

½ teaspoon (1 g/0.03 oz) ground cinnamon

3 tablespoons (42 g/ 1.5 oz) unsalted butter, slightly softened and cut into ½-inch pieces

**VANILLA YOGURT CREAM**

6 large egg yolks

½ cup (100 g/3.5 oz) granulated sugar, divided

¼ cup (84 g/2.96 oz) honey

¼ cup (59 g/2 oz) water

Pinch of salt

1½ cups (348 g/12.27 oz) heavy cream

¾ cup (181 g/6.4 oz) Greek yogurt

1½ teaspoons (6 g/0.21 oz) vanilla bean paste or extract

(CONTINUED)

## Make the streusel

1. Preheat the oven to 350°F. In a small bowl, stir together the granola, flour, brown sugar, and cinnamon. Add the butter pieces, and stir and mash with a fork until the mixture is crumbly. Spread the mixture out on a baking sheet and bake for 10 to 12 minutes, tossing it once during baking, until golden brown. Cool on the baking sheet set on a wire rack.

## Make the yogurt cream

2. Place the egg yolks and 2 tablespoons of the sugar in the bowl of an electric mixer fitted with the whisk attachment and begin whipping them at medium speed. Meanwhile, in a small saucepan, combine the remaining 6 tablespoons sugar, the honey, and water and place over medium-high heat. Cook, without stirring, occasionally brushing down the sides of the pan with a wet pastry brush to prevent crystallization, until the syrup reaches 248°F on a candy thermometer.

3. With the mixer on medium speed, quickly pour the hot syrup into the egg yolks in a continuous stream near the side of the bowl, trying to avoid getting it on the whisk attachment (to prevent spattering). Add the salt. Raise the mixer speed to high and whip the egg yolks until they become pale, have tripled in volume, and are cool, about 7 minutes.

**GARNISH**

½ cup (56 g/2 oz) fresh raspberries

4. Whip the cream until soft peaks just begin to form. Add the yogurt and vanilla and whip just until blended. Scrape the whipped cream into the whipped yolk mixture and fold until well combined.

### Assemble the parfaits

5. Divide half the mixture among 6 serving glasses. Sprinkle the top of each with about 2½ tablespoons of the granola streusel and then top with the remaining parfait. Set the remaining streusel aside, covered, until ready to serve the parfaits. Cover the parfaits with plastic wrap and freeze for at least 4 hours (or up to 3 days).

6. Remove the parfaits from the freezer about 5 minutes before serving. Sprinkle the tops with the remaining streusel and the raspberries and serve.

# Perfect Vanilla Soufflés

*If you haven't made* a soufflé since you saw Julia Child demonstrate one on *The French Chef* back in the 1960s, it's been too long. There's a reason this retro dessert is a classic—it is as beautiful as it is delicious, with a puffy, golden brown exterior and soft vanilla fragrance. To ensure a perfect rise, follow the instructions to run your thumb around the edge of each ramekin right before they go into the oven and don't open the oven door during baking. To enjoy the frisson of hot and cold, serve with a scoop of ice cream on top. I like pistachio, rum-raisin, or, if you're a purist, vanilla!

MAKE 6 SOUFFLÉS

3 tablespoons (42 g/1.5 oz) unsalted butter, cut into tablespoons

2 tablespoons plus 1½ teaspoons (20 g/0.7 oz) all-purpose flour

1¼ cups (290 g/10.2 oz) heavy cream

½ cup (100 g/3.5 oz) granulated sugar, divided

1 vanilla bean, split lengthwise and seeds scraped out, or 2 teaspoons (8 g/0.28 oz) vanilla bean paste

5 large eggs, separated, plus 1 large egg white, at room temperature

1 tablespoon (15 g/0.5 oz) dark rum, brandy, or Grand Marnier (optional)

¼ teaspoon (0.75 g/0.03 oz) cream of tartar

⅛ teaspoon (0.83 g/0.03 oz) salt

Confectioners' sugar, for dusting

Ice cream of your choice, for serving

1. Position a rack in the lower third of the oven and preheat the oven to 375°F. Brush the interior of six 12-ounce ramekins generously with softened butter (try not to miss any spots). Coat with sugar, tilting the ramekins to cover the entire surface of the interior. Arrange the ramekins on a rimmed baking sheet and set aside.

2. Place the 3 tablespoons butter in a small saucepan and melt over medium heat. Whisk in the flour and cook, whisking constantly, for 30 seconds. Gradually whisk in the cream, ¼ cup (50 g/1.76 oz) of the sugar, and the vanilla bean pod and seeds (or paste). Raise the heat to medium-high and cook, whisking constantly, until the mixture comes to a boil, about 2 minutes. Remove the pan from the heat and let cool slightly, about 5 minutes, whisking once or twice.

3. Place the egg yolks in a large bowl and whisk to blend. Gradually whisk the hot cream mixture into the yolks until blended. Remove the vanilla bean pod and whisk in the rum, if using. Set aside while you whip the egg whites.

4. In the bowl of an electric mixer fitted with the whisk attachment, whip all the egg whites at medium speed until foamy, about 1 minute. Add the cream of tartar and salt and whip at medium-high speed until the whites just begin to hold soft peaks. Gradually add the remaining ¼ cup (50 g/1.76 oz) sugar, then raise the mixer speed to high and whip until the whites are stiff, but not dry (if you overwhip the whites, you will have small clumps of unblended egg white in your soufflé batter, which is not a good thing). Gently fold

one-third of the whipped whites into the yolk mixture to lighten it. Gently fold in the remaining whites in two additions, until just blended.

**5.** Spoon the batter into the prepared ramekins, dividing it evenly. Using a small offset metal spatula or spoon, smooth the tops of the soufflés so that they are level. Run your thumb around the inside edge of each soufflé (this will ensure that the soufflés rise evenly). Bake for 20 to 25 minutes, or until the soufflés have puffed up nicely and are golden brown on top. To check for doneness, you can insert a bamboo skewer horizontally into the side of a soufflé, just to the center — it should come out just slightly moistened.

**6.** Dust the soufflés lightly with confectioners' sugar and serve immediately, with a scoop of ice cream popped into the center at the final moment.

# Vanilla Bean Panna Cotta with Strawberries and Lavender

*This could be the easiest* dessert you'll ever make. I find that most panna cotta recipes overdo the gelatin, which makes the finished dessert rubbery and unappealing. I like to use just enough gelatin to set the dessert and not a pinch more, and this yields a silky texture that melts on the tongue. There are two key steps in this recipe: First, make sure the gelatin is completely dissolved, otherwise some of it will end up in the strainer and there won't be enough to bind the dessert properly. Second, chill the hot base slightly in an ice bath as directed—this will ensure the vanilla bean seeds are evenly distributed throughout the dessert instead of sinking to the bottom. I think the earthy, floral scent of lavender is an ideal match for vanilla, but if lavender reminds you too much of your grandmother's soap, you could substitute 1 teaspoon fresh lemon verbena, or simply omit it. Because this recipe does not have a lot of gelatin in it, don't try to unmold the desserts—it's more fragile than standard panna cotta. Dried lavender buds are available from myspicesage.com.

**MAKES 6 SERVINGS**

### VANILLA BEAN PANNA COTTA

¼ cup (60 g/2.1 oz) cold water

2½ teaspoons (7.8 g/0.27 oz) powdered gelatin

2¾ cups (638 g/22.5 oz) heavy cream

½ cup (100 g/3.5 oz) granulated sugar

Pinch of salt

1 vanilla bean, or 1 teaspoon (4 g/0.24 oz) vanilla bean paste or extract

### LAVENDER SYRUP

¾ cup (150 g/5.3 oz) granulated sugar

1 cup (236 g/8.3 oz) water

1 teaspoon (0.25 g/0.009 oz) dried lavender buds (see note, above)

(CONTINUED)

## Make the panna cotta

1. Place the water in a heatproof glass measuring cup and sprinkle the gelatin on top. Let stand to soften for 5 minutes.

2. Meanwhile, place the cream, sugar, and salt in a small saucepan and place over medium-high heat. Cook, stirring to dissolve the sugar, just until the cream starts to bubble around the edges.

3. If using a vanilla bean, slit it lengthwise with a paring knife and scrape the seeds into a saucepan; add the pod. Once the cream begins to bubble, remove the pan from the heat, cover, and let stand for 30 minutes. (If you are using paste or extract, you will add it later; you can skip this steeping step.)

4. Reheat the cream over medium heat. Turn off the heat and add the softened gelatin mixture to the hot cream, stirring until it is thoroughly dissolved. Be patient with this step—it's ready when you don't you see any small lumps of gelatin. Strain the mixture through a fine-mesh sieve into a medium bowl. Stir in the vanilla paste or extract, if using. Prepare an ice bath by filling a larger bowl

**2 cups (312 g/11 oz) strawberries, washed, hulled, and sliced**

**2 teaspoons (30 g/1 oz) freshly squeezed lemon juice**

one-third full with ice and water, and place the bowl of panna cotta in it. Let the mixture stand, stirring occasionally, until it is slightly chilled to the touch, about 10 minutes.

**5.** Transfer the panna cotta to a small pitcher or glass measure with a pouring spout and divide it among six 6- to 8-ounce serving glasses (I like to use wine glasses, but you can use also ramekins or martini glasses). Refrigerate, uncovered, until firm, about 3 hours (after this the panna cottas can be covered with plastic wrap and refrigerated for up to 3 days).

### *Make the lavender syrup*

**6.** Combine all the ingredients in a small saucepan and bring to a boil over medium heat, stirring to dissolve the sugar. Remove from the heat, cover, and allow to infuse for 20 minutes.

**7.** Strain the syrup through a sieve into a small bowl and refrigerate, covered, until chilled, about 2 hours.

### *Make the topping and assemble the dessert*

**8.** In a medium bowl, toss the strawberries with the lemon juice and ½ cup (128 g/4.5 oz) of the lavender syrup. Spoon the strawberries with some of the syrup on top of the panna cottas (about ⅓ cup on each), dividing them evenly. Serve the remaining lavender syrup alongside.

# Vanilla-Flecked Marshmallows

*Homemade marshmallows are miles* above the commercial varieties, which usually have the texture of pencil erasers. These are pillow-soft because there's not too much gelatin in them, and they are infused with wonderful vanilla flavor. Serve them on top of a cup of homemade hot chocolate or coffee that has been enriched with a little melted dark chocolate — wow! This recipe yields cube-shaped marshmallows, but you could also pipe the mixture into rosette or kiss shapes on a baking sheet that has been dusted with confectioners' sugar. Or spread it onto a sugar-dusted 10-by-15-inch jelly-roll pan and use cookie cutters to cut out shapes.

MAKES ABOUT FIFTY 1-INCH MARSHMALLOWS

SPECIAL EQUIPMENT:
Candy thermometer

½ cup (118 g/4.16 oz) plus
⅓ cup (78 g/2.75 oz) cold
water, divided

1 tablespoon plus 2 teaspoons
(14.5 g/0.51 oz) powdered
gelatin

¼ cup (32 g/1.1 oz)
confectioners' sugar

¼ cup (28 g/1 oz) cornstarch

1½ cups (300 g/10.6 oz)
granulated sugar

3 tablespoons plus
1½ teaspoons (71 g/2.5 oz)
light corn syrup

4 large (120 g/4.2 oz) egg
whites

Seeds from 1 vanilla bean, or
1½ teaspoons (6 g/0.21 oz)
vanilla bean paste

1. Place the ⅓ cup (78 g/2.75 oz) water in a small bowl and sprinkle the gelatin evenly over it. Set aside to soften.

2. Spray the bottom and sides of a 9-inch square baking pan with nonstick cooking spray and line it with plastic wrap. Combine the confectioners' sugar and cornstarch in a bowl and then sift some of it over the plastic wrap so that it covers the bottom of the pan.

3. In a small heavy-bottomed saucepan, combine the remaining ½ cup (118 g/4.16 oz) water, the granulated sugar, and corn syrup and place over medium-high heat. Bring to a boil, occasionally brushing down the sides of the pan with a wet pastry brush to prevent crystals from forming, and continue to boil until the syrup registers 248°F on a candy thermometer. Remove from the heat and add the softened gelatin mixture to the hot syrup, stirring to dissolve.

4. Place the egg whites in the bowl of an electric mixer fitted with the whisk attachment and beat on high speed until they are opaque and doubled in volume. Reduce the speed to medium and gradually add the hot syrup in a slow stream. Add the vanilla bean seeds or paste to the beating egg whites. Raise the mixer speed to high and beat until cool, about 8 minutes. Using a rubber spatula, scrape the meringue into the prepared pan and spread it into an even layer. Sift a layer of the confectioners' sugar mixture on top (reserve the remaining mixture for later use). Let stand at room temperature, uncovered, for at least 6 hours or up to 1 day.

**5.** Dust a cutting board well with the confectioners' sugar mixture. Invert the marshmallows onto the cutting board and gently peel off the plastic wrap. Cut into 1-inch cubes with a sharp knife (dust it with more of the confectioners' sugar mixture after each cut). After the marshmallows are cut, dust with more of the confectioners' sugar mixture to keep the pieces apart. Store the marshmallows in an airtight container at room temperature for up to 1 week.

# Vanilla Palmiers

*These palm leaf–shaped* cookies will fill your house with the heavenly scent of vanilla as they bake. They are crunchy, buttery, and absolutely delicious. If you don't have vanilla sugar on hand and don't want to make it, combine ½ cup sugar with ½ teaspoon ground vanilla powder. Nielsen-Massey makes an excellent version; it's available at King Arthur Flour (kingarthurflour.com) and amazon.com.

MAKES ABOUT 44 PALMIERS

1½ cups (200 g/7 oz) all-purpose flour

½ teaspoon (3.3 g/0.12 oz) salt

16 tablespoons (226 g/8 oz) cold unsalted butter, cut into ½-inch cubes

⅓ cup (77 g/2.7 oz) cold heavy cream

½ cup (100 g/3.5 oz) Vanilla Sugar (page 12)

1. In the bowl of an electric mixer fitted with the paddle attachment, combine the flour and salt at low speed. Add the butter, one-third at a time, and mix for just a few seconds. The mixture will be very crumbly, with large pieces of butter in it. While continuing to mix at low speed, add the cream and mix just until the dough starts to come together (large pieces of butter should still be visible).

2. Scrape the dough onto a lightly floured work surface and pound and pat it into a rough rectangle with a rolling pin. Roll the dough into an 8-by-16-inch rectangle, dusting the dough with flour as needed. Arrange the dough with a short side closest to you. Brush off any excess flour on the dough with a pastry brush. Fold the bottom third up over the center, and then fold the top third over the bottom, as if you were folding a business letter. The dough now has three layers. Rotate the dough 90 degrees, so that the short sides are at the top and bottom. Roll the dough out again to an 8-by-16-inch rectangle. Fold it again to make three layers. The dough has now been "turned" twice. Wrap the dough in plastic wrap and refrigerate for 30 minutes.

3. Remove the dough from the refrigerator and place it so that the short ends are on the top and bottom. Roll and fold the dough as before to make two more turns. Wrap the dough in plastic wrap and chill for at least 1 hour before forming the cookies.

4. Cut the dough into two rectangles. Wrap one piece in plastic wrap and refrigerate while you roll the other piece. Sprinkle a work surface liberally with some of the Vanilla Sugar and roll out the dough to a 9-by-15-inch rectangle, sprinkling it with more of

the sugar as you go along to prevent sticking. Using a chef's knife, cut off the ragged edges from the long sides of the dough rectangle. With one of the long sides facing you, fold the dough in half lengthwise, then unfold it (this will give you a reference line for folding the dough). Fold the long sides halfway to the center line, then fold both sides so that they meet in the center. Fold one long side over the other, as if you were closing a book. Place the log of dough on a baking sheet, cover with plastic wrap, and refrigerate. Repeat with the remaining piece of dough, and refrigerate the logs for 1 hour. (Set aside the remaining Vanilla Sugar, which you will use later.)

5. Preheat the oven to 375°F. Line a baking sheet with a silicone baking mat or piece of parchment paper.

6. Using a chef's knife, cut the rough end off one of the dough logs. Cut the log into ½-inch slices and dredge the slices lightly with more Vanilla Sugar on both sides. Arrange the cookies, flat side down, on the prepared baking sheet, spacing them 2 inches apart.

7. Bake for 12 to 15 minutes, until the undersides of the cookies are golden brown and caramelized (the tops will still be light colored). Using a metal spatula, flip each cookie over and bake for another 8 to 10 minutes, until the bottoms are caramelized. Transfer the cookies to a cooling rack and cool completely. Store in an airtight container in a cool, dry place for up to 5 days.

# Vanilla Shortbread

*I love the sandy,* slightly chewy texture of these buttery vanilla cookies. The endnote is pure, perfumy vanilla. If you can, use the seeds from a real vanilla bean — my favorites are Ugandan (notes of honey and jasmine) and Tahitian (fruity and floral) beans. Second choice would be Nielsen-Massey vanilla paste, and a distant third is pure vanilla extract (imitation vanilla should be banished forever from your home). I order my beans online from Amadeus Vanilla Beans (amadeusvanillabeans.com), which has an excellent selection and great prices.

**MAKES 24 WEDGES OR 20 BARS**

1 vanilla bean, split lengthwise, or 2 teaspoons (8 g/0.28 oz) vanilla bean paste or extract

1½ cups (200 g/7 oz) all-purpose flour

½ cup (60 g/2.1 oz) cornstarch

¼ teaspoon (1.7 g/0.06 oz) salt

⅔ cup (133 g/4.7 oz) granulated sugar

16 tablespoons (226 g/8 oz) cold unsalted butter, cut into ½-inch cubes

1 tablespoon plus 1½ teaspoons (19 g/0.66 oz) demerara or turbinado sugar, for sprinkling

1. Position a rack in the lower third of the oven and preheat to 300°F. Have two 9-inch fluted tart pans with removable bottoms or one 9-inch square baking pan at hand.

2. If using a vanilla bean, use a paring knife to scrape the seeds into a small bowl and set aside.

3. Place the flour, cornstarch, and salt in the bowl of a food processor and pulse on and off until blended. Add the granulated sugar and vanilla seeds (or paste or extract) and process for a few seconds until blended. Scatter the butter cubes over the flour mixture and process in on/off pulses 6 or 7 times. Then process for another 6 seconds. The crumbs should be fine and powdery. Process for another 5 to 9 seconds, until the crumbs are clumpier and the dough holds together easily when pressed. If you are using the tart pans, divide the crumbs evenly between the pans and press them firmly onto the bottoms, forming a smooth layer. If you are using the square baking pan, press all the crumbs onto the bottom of the pan. Sprinkle the shortbread with the demerara or turbinado sugar. For the shortbread in the tart pans, use a paring knife to score each round into 12 wedges. Using the tines of a fork, lightly prick each wedge 3 times, spacing the holes evenly apart. For the shortbread in the baking pan, use a paring knife to score the shortbread into 20 bars. Lightly prick each bar twice with the fork on the diagonal, spacing the holes evenly apart.

4. Bake the shortbread for 45 to 50 minutes, until it is just barely colored a creamy beige (don't let it brown), switching the position of the tart pans halfway through baking. Place the pan(s) on a wire rack and let cool for 15 minutes.

5. Recut the shortbread along the scoring lines while it is still very warm (remove the rims of the pans if using the tart pans). Transfer the shortbread to the wire rack and cool completely. Store in an airtight container at room temperature for up to 1 week.

# Vanilla Swirl Cookies

*I love the versatility* of these pretty piped cookies—you can dip them in chocolate, sandwich them with jam, sprinkle them with nuts, or drizzle them with icing. They are tender, hold their shape nicely, and have a velvety vanilla flavor. The first few cookies are a little hard to pipe, but then the batter softens up and it gets easier. This recipe can easily be doubled or tripled.

**MAKES 20 COOKIES**

**SPECIAL EQUIPMENT:**
Pastry bag and medium closed star tip

12 tablespoons (170 g/6 oz) unsalted butter, softened

⅓ cup (42 g/1.5 oz) confectioners' sugar

1 teaspoon (4 g/0.14 oz) vanilla bean paste or extract

Pinch of salt

1⅓ cups (177 g/6.2 oz) all-purpose flour

1½ teaspoons demerara sugar, for sprinkling (optional)

1. Line two baking sheets with silicone baking mats or parchment paper. In the bowl of an electric mixer fitted with the paddle attachment, beat the butter with the confectioners' sugar at high speed until creamy and light, about 2 minutes. Reduce the speed to medium and add the vanilla and salt, mixing until blended. Reduce the speed to low, add the flour, and mix just until blended. Transfer the dough to a pastry bag fitted with a medium closed star tip, such as Ateco #6.

2. Pipe the dough into 1½-inch rosettes on the baking sheets, spacing them about 2 inches apart. Sprinkle the cookies with demerara sugar, if desired. Let the piped cookies stand at room temperature for 30 minutes. Meanwhile, preheat the oven to 350°F.

3. Bake the cookies, one sheet at a time, for 14 to 16 minutes, until they are lightly browned around the edges. Cool completely on the baking sheet set on a wire rack. Store the cookies in an airtight container at room temperature for up to 5 days.

# Vanilla Pecan Blondies

*Brown sugar, toasted pecans,* and vanilla are the flavors that take center stage in these chewy, slightly salty blondies. I like to use Green & Black's organic white chocolate, because it has a prominent vanilla flavor and a smooth, creamy texture. The white chocolate pieces on top of the blondies turn light tan as they toast, imparting a delicious dulce de leche flavor to the bars.

MAKES 20 BLONDIES

2 cups (265 g/9.3 oz) all-purpose flour

1¼ teaspoons (6.25 g/0.22 oz) baking powder

½ teaspoon (3.3 g/0.12 oz) salt

16 tablespoons (226 g/8 oz) unsalted butter, cut into tablespoons

1 cup firmly packed (216 g/ 7.6 oz) light brown sugar

1 cup (200 g/7 oz) granulated sugar

2 large eggs

2 teaspoons (8 g/0.28 oz) vanilla extract

2 cups (200 g/7 oz) toasted pecan halves (see page 13)

3.5 oz (99 g) good-quality white chocolate (preferably Green & Black's), cut into ½-inch pieces (½ cup)

1. Preheat the oven to 350°F. Line a 13-by-9-inch baking pan with aluminum foil and spray the foil with nonstick cooking spray.

2. In a medium bowl, whisk together the flour, baking powder, and salt.

3. Melt the butter in a small saucepan over medium heat. Transfer it to a medium bowl and stir in the brown sugar, making sure that all lumps are dissolved. Stir in the granulated sugar, eggs, and vanilla until well blended. Stir in the flour mixture one-third at a time, then stir in half the pecans and half the white chocolate pieces. Scrape the batter into the prepared pan, smoothing it into an even layer. Sprinkle with the remaining pecans and white chocolate pieces.

4. Bake for 25 to 28 minutes, until the blondies are golden brown on top, puffed, and set in the middle; a toothpick inserted into the center should come out with a few moist crumbs clinging to it. Cool in the pan on a wire rack.

5. Cut the blondies into 20 rectangles. Store in an airtight container at room temperature for up to 3 days.

# Vanilla Whoopie Pies with Malted Vanilla Buttercream Filling

*Whoopie pies are almost* always chocolate, but here's my all-vanilla version, which makes a nice change from the standard. Most whoopie pie fillings are either made with commercially prepared marshmallow or with American-style buttercream, but I prefer the luxurious texture of a Swiss meringue buttercream, which elevates these down-home cakes to a memorable treat.

MAKES ABOUT 17 WHOOPIE PIES

**SPECIAL EQUIPMENT:**
Instant-read thermometer

**WHOOPIE PIES**

2 cups (265 g/9.3 oz) all-purpose flour

½ teaspoon (2.5 g/0.09 oz) baking powder

½ teaspoon (2.5 g/0.09 oz) baking soda

¼ teaspoon (1.7 g/0.06 oz) salt

8 tablespoons (113 g/4 oz) unsalted butter, melted and still warm

¾ cup firmly packed (162 g/ 5.7 oz) light brown sugar

½ cup (121 g/4.2 oz) sour cream

½ cup (121 g/4.2 oz) whole milk

1 large egg

1 large egg yolk

2 teaspoons (8 g/0.28 oz) vanilla bean paste or extract

(CONTINUED)

## Make the whoopie pies

1. Position two racks near the center of the oven and preheat the oven to 375°F. Line two baking sheets with silicone baking mats or parchment paper.

2. Sift the flour, baking powder, baking soda, and salt into a medium bowl and gently whisk to combine.

3. In another bowl, whisk together the warm melted butter and brown sugar until smooth, breaking up any lumps of brown sugar. Add the sour cream, milk, egg, egg yolk, and vanilla and whisk until well blended. Stir in the dry ingredients one-third at a time just until combined. Transfer the batter to a pastry bag fitted with a medium plain tip, such as Ateco #6, and pipe 2-inch mounds onto the baking sheets, spacing them about 2 inches apart—I pipe 12 mounds on each sheet. Or, if you're not so good in the piping department, you can scoop the batter onto the sheet using a 1-ounce scoop or even spoon it into 2-inch rounds. Dip your index finger in water and smooth over any peaks on the mounds.

4. Bake the cakes, both sheets at a time, for 14 to 16 minutes, switching the position of the baking sheets after 7 minutes, until the whoopie pies are light brown on the bottom (lift one up with a metal spatula to check). Cool the cakes on the sheets for 5 minutes, then transfer to wire racks to cool completely. Repeat with any remaining batter.

⅔ cup (133 g/4.7 oz) granulated
sugar

3 large egg whites (90 g/
3.17 oz), at room temperature

2 tablespoons (30 g/1 oz) cold
water

20 tablespoons (282 g/
9.9 oz) unsalted butter, slightly
softened

¼ cup (34 g/1.2 oz) malted
milk powder, dissolved in
2 tablespoons (30 g/1 oz) hot
water

1 teaspoon (4 g/0.14 oz) vanilla
bean paste or extract

## Make the buttercream filling

**5.** Pour enough water into a skillet so that it comes ½ inch up its sides. Bring the water to a simmer; reduce the heat to medium-low to maintain a simmer.

**6.** In the bowl of an electric mixer, combine the sugar, egg whites, and water. Place the bowl in the skillet of water and whisk gently until the mixture registers 150°F on an instant-read thermometer.

**7.** Transfer the bowl to the mixer stand and, using the whisk attachment, beat at high speed until the meringue is cool and forms stiff, shiny peaks, about 5 minutes.

**8.** Reduce the speed to medium and beat in the butter, 1 tablespoon at a time. Beat in the dissolved malted milk powder and the vanilla. Beat at high speed until the buttercream is smooth and silky, about 1 minute.

## Assemble the whoopie pies

**9.** Scrape the buttercream into a pastry bag fitted with a closed star tip, such as Ateco #5. Pipe 3 swirls of buttercream onto the bottom of a whoopie pie to cover, and top it with another whoopie pie half. Repeat with the remaining buttercream and whoopie pie halves to make 17 sandwiches. Serve the whoopie pies right away, or store them in a covered container in the refrigerator for up to 3 days; bring them to room temperature before serving.

# Crème Brûlée Cupcakes

*For professional pastry chefs,* crème brûlée is much more than a dessert — the rich custard is frequently used as a filling for cakes and other desserts. Here I use it as a filling and topping for a simple vanilla cupcake. For "brûléeing" the tops, you can use a propane or butane torch, both of which are available at hardware stores. I use a small butane torch, which is very user-friendly — not scary at all.

**MAKES 12 CUPCAKES**

**SPECIAL EQUIPMENT:**
Propane or butane torch

**CRÈME BRÛLÉE FILLING AND TOPPING**

1 vanilla bean

2 cups (472 g/16.6 oz) heavy cream

8 large egg yolks

½ cup (100 g/3.5 oz) granulated sugar

**VANILLA CUPCAKES**

1½ cups (192 g/6.7 oz) cake flour

1¼ teaspoons (6.25 g/0.22 oz) baking powder

¼ teaspoon (1.7 g/0.06 oz) salt

8 tablespoons (113 g/4 oz) unsalted butter, softened

1 cup (200 g/7 oz) granulated sugar

2 large eggs

1½ teaspoons (6 g/0.21 oz) vanilla bean paste or extract

½ cup (121 g/4.2 oz) whole milk

**BRÛLÉE TOPPING**

2 tablespoons (25 g/0.88 oz) demerara sugar or granulated sugar

## Make the crème brûlée filling and topping

1. Preheat the oven to 275°F. Arrange six 5- or 6-ounce ramekins in a baking pan.

2. Using a paring knife, split the vanilla bean in half lengthwise and scrape the seeds into a small saucepan. Add the pod and the cream to the saucepan and cook over medium-high heat until the cream just begins to simmer. Remove the pan from the heat.

3. In a medium bowl, whisk the egg yolks with the sugar until well blended. Remove the vanilla bean pod from the cream and whisk the cream into the yolk mixture. Strain the mixture through a fine-mesh sieve into a heatproof glass measuring cup with a pouring spout. Divide the custard mixture among the ramekins. Pour enough hot tap water into the baking pan so that it comes about one-third of the way up the sides of the ramekins. Bake the custards until they are just set but still slightly jiggly, 60 to 75 minutes. Remove the ramekins from the water, place them on a wire rack, and cool completely.

4. Cover the ramekins with plastic wrap and refrigerate for at least 6 hours. The custard can be prepared up to 3 days in advance.

## Make the cupcakes

**5.** Preheat the oven to 350°F. Line a standard 12-cup muffin pan with cupcake liners.

**6.** In a medium bowl, sift together the flour, baking powder, and salt and whisk to combine.

**7.** In the bowl of an electric mixer fitted with the paddle attachment, beat the butter at medium speed until creamy, about 30 seconds. Gradually add the sugar and beat at high speed for 3 minutes, until well blended and light. Scrape down the sides of the bowl with a rubber spatula, reduce the speed to medium, and add the eggs one at a time, beating well after each addition and mixing until blended. Beat in the vanilla. Reduce the speed to low and add the flour mixture in three additions, alternating it with the milk in two additions. Mix just until blended. Scrape the batter into the prepared muffin cups, dividing it evenly.

**8.** Bake the cupcakes for 20 to 24 minutes, until they are a light golden brown and a toothpick inserted into the center of a cupcake comes out clean. Cool the cupcakes in the pan set on a wire rack for 5 minutes. Transfer the cupcakes to the wire rack and cool completely.

## Fill and finish the cupcakes

**9.** Fill the cupcakes right before serving them. Using a paring knife, cut a cone-shaped piece about 1¼ inches in diameter from the center of each cupcake (its tip should be about ½ inch from the bottom of the cupcake) and remove it (you don't need the cone shapes for this recipe, but they're nice little treats for the cook or anyone within range). Stir the custard in one of the ramekins vigorously until smooth. Spoon or pipe (no need to use a pastry tip) 2½ to 3 tablespoon of the custard into the center of a cupcake, letting it fill the hole and spill over the top a bit so that the custard is about ½ inch from the edge of each cupcake. Repeat with the remaining custard and cupcakes. (You may have some custard left over after filling all the cupcakes, but you will probably be able to figure out what to do with it.)

**10.** Working with one cupcake at a time, sprinkle the custard evenly with ½ teaspoon of the demerara or granulated sugar and then, using a propane or butane torch and holding it about 4 inches above the surface, heat the sugar until it bubbles and browns, being careful to keep the torch moving so that the sugar doesn't burn. Let the cupcakes stand for a minute before serving.

# Big Vanilla Pavlova with Fresh Berries

*This classic Australian dessert*—a baked meringue shell topped with sweetened whipped cream and fresh fruit—was named for the Russian ballerina Anna Pavlova, who probably appeared as light as air as she fluttered across the stage. My version is super-sized, so it's perfect for a crowd. Because it's big, it does require some time to dry out in the oven; I make the meringue the night before I'm going to serve it so it can cool in the oven overnight and be ready for assembly the next day. I like it best with a simple vanilla-flavored whipped cream filling, but if you want to make the filling tangier, substitute ¼ cup crème fraîche or sour cream for an equal amount of the cream. You can also customize the fruit topping, but it's best to stick to slightly tart fruits like berries, because they go so well with the sweet meringue. Make this in the summer, when berries are in season, and get the fruit from a local farmers' market, if possible.

MAKES ONE 9-INCH PAVLOVA, SERVING 12

### MERINGUE

8 large egg whites

⅛ teaspoon (0.4 g/0.01 oz) cream of tartar

1¾ cups (350 g/12.3 oz) granulated sugar, divided

2 tablespoons (30 g/1 oz) cold water

2 tablespoons (15 g/0.5 oz) cornstarch

1 teaspoon (5 g/0.17 oz) white vinegar

2½ teaspoons (10 g/0.35 oz) vanilla extract

### WHIPPED CREAM FILLING

1¾ cups (406 g/14.3 oz) heavy cream

¼ cup (32 g/1.1 oz) confectioners' sugar, sifted

2 teaspoons (8 g/0.28 oz) vanilla bean paste or extract

(CONTINUED)

## Make the meringue

1. Preheat the oven to 250°F. Line a baking sheet with a piece of parchment paper. Using a 9-inch cake pan as a guide, trace a circle onto the parchment and then turn the paper over so that the pencil or pen marks are on the underside.

2. Place the egg whites in the bowl of an electric mixer fitted with the whisk attachment and whip at medium-low speed until just foamy. Add the cream of tartar and beat at medium speed until soft peaks form. Gradually add 1 cup (200 g/7 oz) of the sugar and beat at high speed until the whites are stiff and glossy. Remove the bowl from the mixer stand and, using a rubber spatula, gently fold in the remaining ¾ cup (150 g/5.3 oz) sugar. In a small bowl, combine the water, cornstarch, vinegar, and vanilla and then gently fold this mixture into the whites. Pile the meringue into the outlines of the 9-inch circle, spreading it with a rubber spatula and leaving a shallow well in the center (this will hold the whipped cream and berry filling).

3. Place the meringue in the oven and bake for about 2 hours, until the exterior of the meringue is crisp and a light creamy beige color. Turn the oven off and let the meringue cool in the oven for at least

## BERRY TOPPING

2 cups (226 g/8 oz) assorted fresh berries, such as sliced strawberries, red or yellow raspberries, blackberries, and blueberries

2 teaspoons (25 g/0.88 oz) granulated sugar

1 teaspoon (5 g/0.17 oz) freshly squeezed lemon juice

## GARNISH

Confectioners' sugar, for dusting

8 hours. (The meringue can be prepared and stored in a cool, dry place for up to 24 hours before serving.)

### Make the filling

4. In the bowl of an electric mixer fitted with the whisk attachment, whip the cream at high speed until it just begins to form soft peaks. Add the confectioners' sugar and vanilla and whip until stiff peaks just start to form. (The whipped cream can be prepared and refrigerated, covered, up to 3 hours before serving.)

### Make the topping

5. In a medium bowl, gently toss the berries with the granulated sugar and lemon juice. Allow to stand at room temperature for 30 minutes, until the sugar is dissolved. (The berries can be prepared up to an hour before serving.)

### Assemble the dessert

6. Place the meringue base on a cake stand or plate. When ready to serve, spoon the whipped cream into the center and top with the berries. Sprinkle with confectioners' sugar and serve immediately.

# Vanilla Buttermilk Pound Cake with Bourbon Soaking Glaze

*This tender pound cake* gets its vanilla flavor from a technique commonly used by pastry chefs: Sugar and vanilla bean seeds are blended together in a food processor before they are creamed with the butter. This releases the essential oils of the vanilla and infuses the sugar (and the cake) with a wonderful flavor. The bourbon soaking glaze is just right for this simple cake—the musky notes of bourbon and vanilla go so well together—but if you want to skip the bourbon, just substitute an equal amount of water.

MAKES ONE 10-INCH CAKE, SERVING 10 TO 12

## VANILLA BUTTERMILK POUND CAKE

2¼ cups (450 g/15.8 oz) granulated sugar

1 vanilla bean, or 2 tablespoons (24 g/0.8 oz) vanilla bean paste or extract

3 cups plus 2 tablespoons (400 g/14.1 oz) all-purpose flour

½ teaspoon (2.5 g/0.08 oz) baking soda

¾ teaspoon (5 g/0.17 oz) salt

22 tablespoons (310 g/11 oz) unsalted butter, softened

5 large eggs

1 cup (242 g/8.5 oz) buttermilk

## SOAKING GLAZE

1½ cups (192 g/6.7 oz) confectioners' sugar, sifted

¼ cup (60 g/2.1 oz) bourbon

3 tablespoons (45 g/1.6 oz) water

1 tablespoon (12 g/0.42 oz) vanilla bean paste or extract

(CONTINUED)

### Make the cake

1. Preheat the oven to 300°F. Butter and flour a 10-inch (12-cup) Bundt pan.

2. Place the sugar in the bowl of a food processor. If using a vanilla bean, use a paring knife to split the bean lengthwise to expose the seeds. Scrape out the seeds and pulp and add them to the sugar in the food processor. If using the vanilla paste or extract, simply add it to the sugar. Process the sugar mixture for about 1 minute, until the vanilla pulp and oils are incorporated into the sugar. Set aside.

3. In a medium bowl, sift together the flour, baking soda, and salt.

4. In the bowl of an electric mixer fitted with the paddle attachment, beat the butter at medium-high speed until creamy, about 1 minute. Gradually add the vanilla sugar and beat at high speed until light, about 3 minutes. Reduce the speed to medium-low and add the eggs one at a time, mixing well after each addition and scraping down the sides of the bowl as necessary. Reduce the speed to low and add the flour mixture in three additions, alternating with the buttermilk in two additions and mixing just until blended. Scrape the batter into the prepared pan and smooth the top.

5. Bake the cake for 55 to 60 minutes, until the cake is golden and a toothpick inserted into the center comes out clean. Cool the cake

Sweetened whipped cream
(optional)

Sugared Vanilla Beans
(page 12), for garnish
(optional)

in the pan for 15 minutes. Invert the cake onto a wire rack. Make
the soaking glaze right away.

## Make the soaking glaze and finish the cake

6. Whisk together all the glaze ingredients in a medium bowl until
smooth (the glaze will be very thin). Using a bamboo skewer, poke
holes all over top and sides of the cake, spacing them about 2 inches
apart. Brush the glaze all over the top and sides of the cake, letting
it soak in and using all the glaze.

7. Serve slices of the cake alone or with sweetened whipped cream
and garnished with Sugared Vanilla Beans, if desired.

# Vanilla Tres Leches Cake

*The base of this Latin-American* classic is a light sponge cake that doesn't contain fat (other than what is in the eggs), so it's fairly dry—better to soak up all the deliciousness of the triple milk mixture for which the cake is named. I like to add a little dark rum to the milk mixture; it adds some depth to the vanilla-milk flavor without overwhelming it, but feel free to leave it out if you prefer. I realize that candied violets are not a typical garnish for this cake, but I love the way the sugary purple flowers look against all that snow-white cream. Candied violets from France are best; they are available online from L'epicerie (lepicerie.com).

MAKES ONE 9-INCH CAKE, SERVING 10

### VANILLA SPONGE CAKE

4 large eggs, separated

⅔ cup (133 g/4.7 oz) granulated sugar, divided

⅓ cup (80 g/2.8 oz) whole milk

1½ teaspoons (6 g/0.21 oz) vanilla bean paste or extract

¼ teaspoon (1.6 g/0.05 oz) salt

1 cup (114 g/4 oz) cake flour, sifted

### THREE-MILK SOAK

1 cup (317 g/11.2 oz) sweetened condensed milk

1 cup (242 g/8.5 oz) evaporated milk

⅓ cup (77 g/2.7 oz) heavy cream

1 teaspoon (4 g/0.14 oz) vanilla bean paste or extract

1 tablespoon (15 g/0.5 oz) dark rum (optional)

(CONTINUED)

## *Make the sponge cake*

1. Preheat the oven to 350°F. Coat the bottom and sides of a 9-inch springform pan with nonstick cooking spray. Line the bottom of the pan with a round of parchment paper and spray the paper. Bring a pot of water to a gentle simmer.

2. In the bowl of an electric mixer, whisk together the egg yolks and ⅓ cup (66 g/2.3 oz) of the sugar by hand. Place the bowl over the pot of simmering water and whisk the yolks (so that they don't cook) until the mixture is warm to the touch and slightly thickened. Remove the bowl from over the water and place it in the mixer stand. Using the whisk attachment, whip the yolk mixture at high speed until thickened and very pale, about 5 minutes. Transfer the whipped yolks to a large bowl and gently whisk in the milk and vanilla. Clean the dirty mixer bowl and whisk attachment and dry them well.

3. Place the egg whites and salt in the clean, dry mixer bowl and using the clean whisk attachment, whip them at medium-high speed until they are foamy. Slowly add the remaining ⅓ cup (66 g/2.3 oz) sugar and whip at high speed until the whites form soft (not stiff) peaks. Gently fold the whipped whites into the yolk mixture one-third at a time. Sift one-third of the flour over the mixture and gently fold it in. Add the remaining flour in two additions. Scrape the batter into the prepared pan.

*Vanilla*

1¾ cups (406 g/14.32 oz) heavy cream

1½ teaspoons (6 g/0.21 oz) vanilla bean paste or extract

3 tablespoons (24 g/0.8 oz) confectioners' sugar, sifted

GARNISH

Candied violets (optional)

4. Bake the cake for 20 to 25 minutes, until the top is lightly browned and a toothpick inserted into the center of the cake comes out clean. Cool the cake in the pan on a wire rack for 15 minutes (the cake will fall slightly, which is okay). Remove the side of the springform pan, invert the cake onto the rack, peel off the parchment paper, and let the cake cool completely.

## Make the soaking mixture and soak the cake

5. In a 1-quart measure or small pitcher, combine the condensed milk, evaporated milk, cream, vanilla, and rum (if using).

6. Using a bamboo skewer, poke holes all over the top and sides of the cake at 1-inch intervals. Return the cake (still inverted) to the springform pan and wrap the bottom of the pan with a large piece of aluminum foil to prevent the soaking mixture from leaking out. Place the pan on a serving plate that has a lip. Very slowly, drizzle the soaking mixture over the top of the cake, allowing it to soak in as you pour. This takes some patience—if you pour too quickly, the soaking mixture will simply run off the top. If some of the mixture pools at the bottom of the cake, carefully remove the foil and pour the liquid over the top of the cake again. When you've used all the mixture, carefully remove the foil and the side of the pan and slide the cake off its base onto the serving plate.

## Make the whipped cream and top the cake

7. In the bowl of an electric mixer fitted with the whisk attachment, whip the cream and vanilla at high speed until soft peaks just begin to form. Add the confectioners' sugar and whip until stiff peaks begin to form.

8. Transfer the whipped cream to a pastry bag fitted with either a star tip, such as Ateco #6, or a St. Honore tip, such as Ateco #880, and pipe the cream over the top of the cake, covering it completely. If you are using the star tip, pipe large rosettes. If you are using the St. Honore tip, pipe straight lines across the top. Garnish the cake with candied violets, if you like.

# Twenty-Layer Vanilla Cream Crêpe Cake

*"Ethereal" is the word* that comes to mind when I eat a piece of this amazing cake. Originally made famous by the Lady M Confections boutique in New York, it's composed of twenty paper-thin crêpes that are layered with a light vanilla-and-orange-scented cream filling. The crêpes meld with the cream, so each forkful melts in your mouth, with the subtle flavors of sweet orange and vanilla lingering behind. The top of the cake is sprinkled with sugar and caramelized with a blow torch just before serving, adding a crackly sweetness to the dessert. Like anything really wonderful, this cake takes some time to make, but once the crêpes and pastry cream are made, assembly is relatively fast. Note that a 10-inch skillet will make an 8-inch crêpe.

MAKE ONE 8-INCH CRÊPE CAKE, SERVING 8

SPECIAL EQUIPMENT:
Propane or butane torch

CRÊPES

7 tablespoons (98 g/3.5 oz) unsalted butter, cut into tablespoons

1½ cups (192 g/6.7 oz) all-purpose flour

½ cup (100 g/3.5 oz) granulated sugar

Pinch of salt

6 large eggs

2 cups (484 g/17 oz) whole milk

1½ teaspoons (6 g/0.21 oz) vanilla extract

½ teaspoon (1 g/0.03 oz) finely grated orange zest

¾ cup (174 g/6.13 oz) heavy cream

Vegetable oil or melted butter, for coating the pan

VANILLA PASTRY CREAM FILLING

2 cups (484 g/17 oz) whole milk

(CONTINUED)

## Make the crêpes

**1.** Place the butter in a small saucepan and cook over medium heat until it melts and then turns brown and has a nutty fragrance, 4 to 6 minutes. Remove the pan from the heat.

**2.** Place the flour, sugar, and salt in the bowl of a food processor and pulse until blended. In a medium bowl, whisk together the eggs, milk, and vanilla until blended, then gradually add to the flour mixture while running the processor. Mix just until blended. Scrape down the sides of the bowl with a rubber spatula, then turn the processor on and add the orange zest and browned butter until combined. Add the cream and process until just blended. Transfer the batter to a pitcher or container with a pouring lip. Cover the container and refrigerate the batter for at least 2 hours (or up to 3 days). Don't skip this step—chilling the batter will allow the flour to absorb the liquid and the gluten to relax.

**3.** To make the crêpes, take the batter out of the refrigerator and bring it to room temperature (otherwise the crêpes will be too thick). Stir the crêpe batter well to re-blend.

**4.** Place a 10-inch nonstick skillet over medium heat and allow it to get hot. Brush the pan with a little vegetable oil or melted butter, then pour in a scant ¼ cup crêpe batter, rolling the pan from side to side to coat it evenly. When the bottom of the crêpe has begun to

6 large egg yolks

½ cup (3.5 oz/100 g) granulated sugar

¼ cup (0.1 oz/30 g) cornstarch

2 tablespoons (28 g/1 oz) unsalted butter, divided

1 vanilla bean, or 1 tablespoon (12 g/0.42 oz) vanilla bean paste or extract

ASSEMBLY

2 cups (464 g/16.3 oz) heavy cream

5 tablespoons (62 g/2.2 oz) granulated sugar

1 tablespoon (15 g/0.5 oz) Cointreau or Grand Marnier (optional)

brown, after 30 seconds to 1 minute, turn the crêpe (I use a long, nonstick offset spatula to flip it, but you can use a silicone spatula to lift up an end, then turn the crêpe over with your fingers or, if you're really competent, you can flip it over in the air) and cook on the other side for another 10 to 15 seconds. Place the cooked crêpe on a piece of parchment paper on a plate. Continue cooking the crêpes until all the batter has been used, stacking the crêpes one on top of another as they are finished. You will need 20 perfect crêpes for this cake. Cover and store in the refrigerator until needed. The crêpes can be made 1 day ahead of time; just bring them to room temperature before using.

## Make the pastry cream filling

5. In a medium saucepan, bring the milk to a boil over medium heat. Remove from the heat.

6. In a medium bowl, whisk together the egg yolks and sugar until pale. Sift the cornstarch into the mixture and whisk to combine. Whisk about one-quarter of the milk into the yolk mixture to temper it, then whisk the yolk mixture into the pan with the remaining milk. Cook over medium-high heat, whisking constantly, until the pastry cream thickens and boils. Remove the pan from the heat and whisk in the butter until it is completely melted. Strain the pastry cream through a fine-mesh sieve into a medium stainless steel bowl to remove any lumps. If you are using a vanilla bean, split it lengthwise with a paring knife, scrape out the seeds, and whisk them into the pastry cream (or whisk in the vanilla paste or extract). Prepare an ice bath by filling a larger bowl one-third full with ice and water, then set the bowl of pastry cream in the ice bath and stir frequently until cold. Press a piece of plastic wrap directly onto the surface of the pastry cream to prevent a skin from forming and refrigerate until ready to use.

## Assemble the cake

7. In the bowl of an electric mixer fitted with the whisk attachment, whip the cream with 3 tablespoons (37 g/1.3 oz) of the sugar at high speed until it forms soft peaks. Remove the pastry cream from the refrigerator. Whisk it until it is smooth and stir in the Cointreau.

## WHITE CHOCOLATE–VANILLA MOUSSE

3.5 ounces (100 g) high-quality white chocolate, chopped

¼ cup plus 1 tablespoon plus 1½ teaspoons (81 g/2.8 oz) water, divided

1½ teaspoons (4.7 g/0.16 oz) powdered gelatin

6 large egg yolks

⅔ cup (132 g/4.6 oz) granulated sugar

1 teaspoon (4 g/0.14 oz) vanilla bean paste or extract

1½ cups (348 g/12.3 oz) heavy cream

## ASSEMBLY

½ cup (154 g/5.4 oz) raspberry jam, divided

## WHIPPED CREAM TOPPING

1 cup (232 g/8.18 oz) heavy cream

3 tablespoons (24 g/0.8 oz) confectioners' sugar, sifted

½ teaspoon (2 g/0.07 oz) vanilla bean paste or extract

## *Make the syrup*

**5.** In a small saucepan, combine the sugar and water and bring to a boil over medium-high heat, stirring occasionally, just to dissolve the sugar. Remove the pan from the heat and let stand at room temperature until cool.

**6.** Stir in the liqueur and set aside until ready to use.

## *Make the mousse*

**7.** Place the white chocolate and 1 tablespoon plus 1½ teaspoons (22 g/0.7 oz) of the water in a medium bowl and place the bowl over a pan filled one-third full with barely simmering water. Heat, stirring frequently, until the white chocolate is melted. Remove the pan from the heat and remove the bowl from the pan. Set the white chocolate aside and cool until barely warm.

**8.** Pour the remaining ¼ cup (60 g/2.1 oz) water into a small, heatproof cup and sprinkle the gelatin on top. Set aside to soften for 5 minutes.

**9.** In a medium bowl, whisk together the egg yolks and sugar. Set the bowl over a pan filled one-third full with simmering water. Heat the yolks, whisking constantly, until they are hot and register 160°F on an instant-read thermometer. Remove the bowl from the pan of water. Whisk the vanilla into the yolk mixture.

**10.** Set the cup of softened gelatin into the pan of simmering water and turn the heat off. Stir the mixture until the gelatin dissolves completely. Whisk the gelatin mixture into the yolk mixture, then whisk the yolk mixture into the melted white chocolate. Set aside to cool until tepid.

**11.** In the bowl of an electric mixer fitted with the whisk attachment, beat the cream at high speed until firm peaks just begin to form. Gently fold about one-third of the whipped cream into the cooled yolk mixture. Fold in the remaining whipped cream.

*Vanilla*

## Assemble the cake

**12.** Using a long, serrated knife, slice the chiffon cake in half horizontally to form two layers. Place one of the layers, cut side up, in the bottom of a 9-inch springform pan. Brush the cake with half the soaking syrup, letting it soak into the cake. Top the cake with ¼ cup (77 g / 2.7 oz) of the raspberry jam and spread the jam evenly over the cake. Spoon about 2 cups of the mousse over the cake and spread it into an even layer—it's okay if some of the mousse drips over the edge of the cake. Place the other cake layer, cut side up, on top of the mousse. Brush the cake with the remaining syrup and spread it with the remaining ¼ cup (77 g / 2.7 oz) jam. Scrape the remaining mousse on top of the cake and spread it into an even layer, letting it fill the gap between the cake and the edge of the pan. Refrigerate the cake for at least 4 hours (the cake can be prepared to this point up to 24 hours before serving).

## Top and serve the cake

**13.** Up to 3 hours before serving, dip a paring knife in hot water and wipe it dry. Run the knife around the edge of the pan to loosen the cake. Remove the side of the pan. Run a small metal spatula around the side of the cake to smooth out any bare or rough spots.

**14.** In the bowl of an electric mixer fitted with the whisk attachment, beat the cream at high speed until soft peaks begin to form. Add the confectioners' sugar and vanilla and whip until firm peaks begin to form. You can either spread or pipe the cream on top of the cake. To spread it, scrape the whipped cream on top of the cake and, using a small metal spatula, spread the cream into decorative swirls. To pipe it, place it in a pastry bag fitted with a medium star tip, such as Ateco #6, and pipe rosettes of cream to cover the top of the cake. Serve the cake immediately, or refrigerate for up to 3 hours before serving.

# Berries
# and
# Cherries

✧ ✧

Berries, eh?
There's good cheer
when there's berries.

**— CHARLES DICKENS,**
*The Haunted Man*

**5.** Using the ends of the plastic wrap as handles, carefully lift the confection out of the pan. Cut the *pâte de fruit* block into 1-inch squares (or any size or shape you like) and roll them in the remaining sugar until they are well coated on all sides. Store the *pâtes de fruits* in an airtight container between layers of parchment or waxed paper, at room temperature, for up to 1 month.

## Strawberry-Basil Pâtes de Fruits

Substitute basil leaves for the mint leaves and fresh strawberries, washed and hulled, for the raspberries.

# Berry-Topped Phyllo Cups with Mascarpone Cream

*This is a quick* summer dessert that makes a memorable impression. A medley of saucy berries tops a sweet mascarpone filling in crispy phyllo dough cups. Make this in midsummer, when berries are at their peak.

MAKES 6 SERVINGS

## PHYLLO CUPS

Six 9-by-14-inch sheets (68 g/2.4 oz) phyllo dough

4 tablespoons (57 g/2 oz) unsalted butter, melted

6 tablespoons (48 g/1.7 oz) confectioners' sugar

## SAUCY MIXED BERRY TOPPING

2 cups (227 g/8 oz) fresh strawberries, hulled and sliced, divided

2 tablespoons (16 g/0.5 oz) confectioners' sugar

½ teaspoon (2.5 g/0.09 oz) freshly squeezed lemon juice

1 cup (113 g/4 oz) fresh raspberries

1 cup (140 g/5 oz) fresh blueberries

## MASCARPONE CREAM

½ cup (116 g/4 oz) heavy cream

½ cup (123 g/4.3 oz) mascarpone cheese

½ teaspoon (2 g/0.07 oz) vanilla extract

3 tablespoons (24 g/0.8 oz) confectioners' sugar

## *Make the phyllo cups*

1. Preheat the oven to 350°F. Have a standard 6-cup muffin pan at hand.

2. Unroll the phyllo sheets and place them on a work surface. Cover the sheets with a piece of plastic wrap and then a damp kitchen towel to prevent them from drying out as you work. Place one of the sheets on a cutting board and brush it all over with some of the melted butter. Sift 1 tablespoon (8 g/0.3 oz) of the confectioners' sugar evenly over the buttered sheet. Top with another phyllo sheet and repeat layering with more butter and sugar, then top with another phyllo sheet so that you have a stack of 3 phyllo sheets. Brush the top sheet with butter and dust with another tablespoon of sugar. Cut the phyllo stack into six 4½-inch squares. Press each stack of squares into a separate muffin cup to form 6 cup shapes.

3. Repeat with the remaining 3 sheets of phyllo dough, using the remaining melted butter and confectioners' sugar. Cut the phyllo stack into six 4½-inch squares, as before. Press the squares into the phyllo cups you've already made, pressing them into the bottom of the molds. Using your fingers, try to separate the phyllo sheets a little around the edges to give the cups a more delicate look. Bake the cups for 10 to 12 minutes, until lightly browned. Let the cups cool completely in the pan set on a wire rack.

## Make the topping

**4.** Place 1 cup (113 g/4 oz) of the sliced strawberries, the confectioners' sugar, and lemon juice in the bowl of a food processor. Process until the berries are pureed and the mixture is smooth. Place the remaining sliced strawberries in a medium bowl with the raspberries and blueberries and toss with the strawberry puree. Set the mixture aside while you make the mascarpone cream.

## Make the mascarpone cream

**5.** In the bowl of an electric mixer fitted with the whisk attachment, beat the cream, mascarpone, and vanilla at high speed until the mixture just begins to form soft mounds. Add the confectioners' sugar and continue to beat at high speed until the cream forms medium-firm peaks.

## Assemble the cups

**6.** Divide the mascarpone cream among the phyllo cups (they will almost be filled). Place each cup into a shallow bowl or on a dessert plate and top with a generous amount of the berry topping, letting it spill over into the bowl or onto the plate. Serve immediately.

# Red Berry Whipped Yogurt Parfaits

*This summery parfait* is a quick, easy dessert that combines the flavor of fresh red berries with a tangy yogurt cream. Roasting strawberries for a short time really concentrates their flavor, which is good, but it also makes them soggy, which is not so good. I solved this texture problem by pureeing the roasted berries and tossing them with fresh sliced strawberries and raspberries to make a really flavorful berry layer. The yogurt cream is made with Greek yogurt that is lightened with whipped cream, sweetened with honey, and flavored with fragrant orange blossom water (see page 8).

MAKES 6 PARFAITS

### RED BERRY LAYER

3¼ cups (364 g/12.8 oz) fresh strawberries, hulled, divided

3 tablespoons (37 g/1.3 oz) granulated sugar

1 teaspoon (5 g/0.17 oz) freshly squeezed lemon juice

1⅓ cups (170 g/6 oz) fresh raspberries

### WHIPPED YOGURT LAYER

1¾ cups (14 oz/400 g) Greek yogurt (any fat content)

1 cup (232 g/8.18 oz) heavy cream

¼ cup (84 g/3 oz) honey

1 teaspoon (2 g/0.07 oz) finely grated orange zest

½ teaspoon (1 g/0.03 oz) orange blossom water

## Make the berry layer

1. Preheat the oven to 375°F. Slice 1½ cups (213 g/7.5 oz) of the strawberries ½ inch thick and place them in a ceramic or glass pie dish. Sprinkle them with the sugar and toss to coat. Roast the berries for about 8 minutes, just until softened. Set aside to cool.

2. In the bowl of a food processor, puree the cooled roasted strawberries with the lemon juice. Transfer the puree to a medium bowl.

3. Slice the remaining 1¾ cups (248 g/8.7 oz) strawberries ¼ inch thick and add them to the puree along with the raspberries. Stir to coat the berries with the puree. Cover the bowl and refrigerate until ready to use.

## Make the yogurt layer

4. In the bowl of an electric mixer fitted with the whisk attachment, combine the yogurt, cream, honey, orange zest, and orange blossom water. Whip on medium-high speed until medium peaks form.

## Assemble the parfaits

5. Spoon ¼ cup of the berries into each of 6 parfait or wine glasses. Top with ½ cup of the yogurt layer, then top with the remaining berries, dividing them evenly among the glasses. Refrigerate the parfaits for at least 30 minutes before serving.

# Cherry-Vanilla Frozen Pops

*These frozen treats* pay homage to cherry-vanilla ice cream, with layers of cherry- and vanilla-flavored ice and nuggets of fresh cherry. Tart cherry juice (such as from Lakewood Organic or R.W. Knudsen) is available in the health food section of the supermarket or at natural food stores. If you can't find it, you can substitute pomegranate juice, or, if you have a juicer, you can make your own.

**MAKES 8 FROZEN POPS**

**SPECIAL EQUIPMENT:**
Cherry pitter; eight 3-ounce frozen pop molds and wooden popsicle sticks

½ cup (100 g/3.5 oz) granulated sugar

½ cup (118 g/4.16 oz) water

1¾ cups (255 g/9 oz) sweet cherries, pitted

⅓ cup (80 g/2.8 oz) tart cherry juice

1 teaspoon (5 g/0.18 oz) freshly squeezed lemon juice

½ cup (121 g/4.3 oz) full-fat or low-fat Greek yogurt

¾ cup (174 g/6.13 oz) heavy cream

½ teaspoon (2 g/0.07 oz) vanilla extract

1. Combine the sugar and water in a small saucepan and bring to a boil over high heat, stirring until the sugar is dissolved. Remove from the heat and let cool for 10 minutes, or until just warm.

2. Cut 4 of the cherries into 8 pieces each and reserve, covered, in the refrigerator. Place the remaining cherries in a blender with ⅓ cup (106 g/3.7 oz) of the sugar syrup and the cherry juice and process until smooth, about 1 minute. Strain through a fine-mesh sieve into a bowl and stir in the lemon juice. Divide half the cherry mixture among eight 3-ounce frozen pop molds (about 1¼ tablespoons per mold). Freeze the pops for 30 minutes. Cover the remaining cherry mixture and refrigerate until ready to use.

3. After 30 minutes, place the wooden sticks in the molds and freeze for another 30 minutes.

4. While the cherry mixture is freezing, make the vanilla layer. In a bowl, whisk together the yogurt, cream, vanilla, and the remaining sugar syrup until smooth. Divide the mixture among the pop molds, pouring it over the cherry layer (about 2½ tablespoons per mold). Add 4 of the reserved cherry pieces to each mold, pushing them down into the vanilla layer with a spoon. Freeze for 30 minutes.

5. Stir the remaining cherry mixture well and pour it over the vanilla layer in each mold, dividing it evenly (you may have a little of the mixture left over). Freeze the pops for at least 4 hours.

6. To unmold the pops, run the molds under hot water and pull on the stick until the pops release. Serve immediately, or place the unmolded pops in an airtight container and freeze until ready to serve.

# Strawberry-Fennel Sorbet

*The earthy licorice flavor* of fennel is a natural match for sweet, ripe strawberries in this simple sorbet. You'll be amazed how the addition of a few fennel seeds infused in water can turn strawberry sorbet into a completely different — and delightful — flavor. I like to serve this topped with strawberry slices that have been tossed with a little honey and lemon juice.

**MAKES 1½ QUARTS**

**SPECIAL EQUIPMENT:**
Ice cream maker

½ cup (118 g/4.16 oz) water

2 teaspoons (3 g/0.1 oz) fennel seeds, coarsely ground with a mortar and pestle

4 pints (908 g/2 lb) fresh strawberries, hulled and halved

1½ cups (300 g/10.5 oz) granulated sugar

2 teaspoons (10 g/0.34 oz) freshly squeezed lemon juice

Pinch of salt

1. Place the water and fennel seeds in a small microwave-safe cup and microwave on high until the water just begins to boil, about 1 minute. Cover the cup and set aside for 15 minutes to infuse.

2. Place the strawberries and sugar in the bowl of a food processor and process until smooth. Transfer to a medium bowl and strain the fennel water into it (discard the fennel seeds). Stir until blended. Add the lemon juice and salt and stir to combine. Cover the bowl and refrigerate the sorbet base for at least 4 hours (or up to 2 days).

3. Process the sorbet base in an ice cream maker according to the manufacturer's instructions. Transfer the sorbet to a covered container and freeze for at least 2 hours before serving.

# Strawberry—Pink Peppercorn Ice Cream

*The first time* I made this ice cream I ate half of it straight from the ice cream maker — it's that good. It's got just enough buttermilk in it to balance the sweetness of the berries, and the pink peppercorns give it a mild, peppery kick at the end.

**MAKES 1½ QUARTS**

**SPECIAL EQUIPMENT:**
Instant-read thermometer; ice cream maker

1¼ cups (302 g/10.6 oz) whole milk

1½ cups (348 g/12.3 oz) heavy cream

1 cup (200 g/7 oz) granulated sugar, divided

2 tablespoons (41 g/1.4 oz) light corn syrup

4 large egg yolks

⅛ teaspoon (0.8 g/0.03 oz) salt

¼ cup (60 g/2.1 oz) buttermilk

1 teaspoon (4 g/0.14 oz) vanilla extract

1 pint (227 g/8 oz) strawberries, hulled and chopped

1 tablespoon (3 g/0.1 oz) pink peppercorns, ground with a mortar and pestle or spice grinder

1. In a medium saucepan, combine the milk, cream, ½ cup (100 g/3.5 oz) of the sugar, and the corn syrup. Bring to a simmer over medium heat, stirring just to dissolve the sugar. Remove from the heat. In a bowl, whisk the yolks with ¼ cup (50 g/1.76 oz) of the sugar and the salt. Whisk in about 1 cup of the hot milk mixture. Return this mixture to the remaining milk mixture in the saucepan and cook over medium heat, stirring constantly, until the mixture thickens and reaches 180°F. Strain through a fine-mesh sieve and stir in the buttermilk and vanilla. Prepare an ice bath by filling a large bowl one-third full with ice and water, and place the bowl of custard in it. Refrigerate the ice cream base for 6 hours or overnight.

2. Place the strawberries in a bowl and sprinkle with the remaining ¼ cup (50 g/1.76 oz) sugar. Stir to coat, then cover and refrigerate for 45 minutes.

3. Place the strawberries and their juices in the bowl of a food processor or blender and process until smooth. Add about 1 cup of the chilled ice cream base and the pink peppercorns to the strawberries and process until smooth. Add this mixture to the remaining ice cream base and stir well to combine. Transfer to an ice cream maker and process according to the manufacturer's instructions. This ice cream is best served the day it's made; it gets a little icy the next day.

# Sweet Cherry and Peach Crisp

*A crisp is a great way* to showcase summer fruit, and it doesn't require the fuss of rolling out pastry for a pie. Sweet cherries and juicy peaches are a good match here, and both fruits complement the crunchy almond topping.

MAKES 8 SERVINGS

SPECIAL EQUIPMENT:
Cherry pitter

### CRUMBLY ALMOND TOPPING

1 cup (84 g/3 oz) unblanched sliced almonds, divided

7 tablespoons (98 g/3.5 oz) unsalted butter, softened

½ cup firmly packed (108 g/ 3.8 oz) light brown sugar

¾ cup (99 g/3.5 oz) all-purpose flour

⅛ teaspoon (0.83 g/0.03 oz) salt

½ cup (50 g/1.76 oz) old-fashioned rolled oats

### CHERRY AND PEACH FILLING

About 2½ (454 g/1 lb) ripe peaches

3¼ cups (454 g/1 lb) fresh sweet cherries

3 tablespoons (22 g/0.8 oz) cornstarch

⅓ cup firmly packed (71 g/ 2.5 oz) light brown sugar

½ cup (120 g/4.2 oz) fresh or bottled cherry or peach juice

1 teaspoon (2 g/0.07 oz) finely grated lemon zest

2 teaspoons (30 g/1 oz) freshly squeezed lemon juice

¼ teaspoon (0.5 g/0.02 oz) ground cinnamon

Pinch of salt

2 tablespoons (28 g/1 oz) unsalted butter, cut into cubes

## Make the topping

1. Preheat the oven to 375°F. Butter the bottom and sides of a 9-by-13-inch baking pan (preferably glass). Place ½ cup (42 g/1.5 oz) of the sliced almonds in the bowl of a food processor and pulse until finely ground.

2. In the bowl of an electric mixer fitted with the paddle attachment, beat together the ground almonds, butter, and brown sugar on medium speed until smooth, about 2 minutes. With the mixer on low speed, gradually add the flour and salt and mix just until crumbly. Stir in the oats and the remaining ½ cup (42 g/1.5 oz) almonds. Set the topping aside while you prepare the fruit filling.

## Make the fruit filling

3. Halve and pit the peaches and cut them into ½-inch slices. Pit the cherries. In a medium bowl, combine the peaches and cherries with the cornstarch, brown sugar, cherry or peach juice, lemon zest, lemon juice, cinnamon, and salt. Transfer the filling to the prepared baking dish. Scatter the butter pieces over the filling. Sprinkle the topping evenly over the fruit.

4. Bake the crisp for 25 to 30 minutes, or until the top is golden brown and the fruit filling is bubbling around the edges. Serve warm.

# Blueberry Cornmeal Scones

*It's difficult to find* a good scone these days, even at respectable bakeries. Most are dry, tough, and flavorless. The solution is to make your own, using a good recipe and a light touch. These scones are tender and bursting with juicy blueberries, just right for a weekend breakfast, brunch, or afternoon snack. The yellow cornmeal gives them a slightly nutty flavor and hearty texture that stands up to the berries, while a little lemon zest offers a bright note. This recipe makes eight triangular scones, but you can cut out rounds from the dough if you prefer—just pat the scraps back together and cut out more scones until you've used up all the dough. I like to eat these with nothing more than a smear of soft Irish butter, but add your favorite jam and clotted cream, if you like.

MAKES 8 SCONES

1⅔ cups (221 g/7.8 oz) all-purpose flour, plus more for dusting

⅓ cup (58 g/2 oz) yellow cornmeal

⅓ cup (66 g/2.3 oz) granulated sugar

2¼ teaspoons (11 g/0.4 oz) baking powder

¼ teaspoon (1.6 g/0.06 oz) salt

1½ teaspoons (3 g/0.1 oz) finely grated lemon zest

5⅓ tablespoons (75 g/2.6 oz) cold unsalted butter, cut into ½-inch cubes and frozen for 15 minutes

¾ cup plus 2 tablespoons (203 g/7.16 oz) heavy cream

1¼ cups (160 g/5.6 oz) fresh blueberries

1 egg, lightly beaten with 1 teaspoon water, for egg wash

Demerara or turbinado sugar, for sprinkling

1. Preheat the oven to 400°F. Line a baking sheet with parchment paper or a silicone baking mat.

2. In the bowl of a food processor, combine the flour, cornmeal, sugar, baking powder, salt, and lemon zest and pulse until blended. Add the butter and process until the mixture forms coarse crumbs. Turn the mixture into a medium bowl and form a well in the center. Add the cream to the center of the well and, using a wooden spoon or rubber spatula, gradually stir the flour mixture into the liquid. Add the blueberries and knead the dough *very lightly* just a few times, just until it comes together. Transfer the dough to a lightly floured work surface and gently pat it into an 8-inch round. Using a chef's knife, cut the round into 8 wedges and arrange them on the prepared baking sheet, spacing them at least 1 inch apart. Brush the scones with egg wash, then sprinkle them with demerara sugar.

3. Bake the scones for 16 to 20 minutes, until light golden brown. Serve the scones warm. Store in an airtight container at room temperature for up to 3 days.

# Strawberry Shortcakes with Fresh Mint Cream

*I love the combination* of tender, sweet biscuits, juicy berries, and pillowy whipped cream in this classic dessert. My only twist is that I infuse the cream with mint leaves, which gives it a fresh flavor and very pale green hue. Every component for this dessert can be made ahead—the shortcakes the day before, the berries and cream up to eight hours ahead—and assembled just before serving.

**MAKES 6 SERVINGS**

### FRESH MINT CREAM

2 cups (464 g/16.3 oz) heavy cream

1 cup packed (20 g/0.7 oz) mint leaves

¼ cup (32 g/1 oz) confectioners' sugar

### SHORTCAKES

1¾ cups (232 g/8.17 oz) all-purpose flour

¼ cup (50 g/1.76 oz) granulated sugar

1 tablespoon plus 1½ teaspoons (22.5 g/0.8 oz) baking powder

¼ teaspoon (1.6 g/0.05 oz) salt

6 tablespoons (85 g/3 oz) unsalted butter, cut into ½-inch cubes and frozen for 15 minutes

½ cup plus 1 tablespoon (130 g/4.6 oz) heavy cream or half-and-half, divided

Demerara sugar, for sprinkling (about 1½ teaspoons)

### STRAWBERRIES

2 pints (454 g/1 lb) fresh strawberries, hulled

¼ cup (1.76 oz/50 g) granulated sugar

1 teaspoon (2 g/0.07 oz) lemon zest

## Make the mint cream

1. Heat the cream in a small saucepan over medium-high heat until it just begins to bubble around the edges. Stir in the mint leaves, cover the pan, and let stand for 30 minutes until the mint flavor is infused into the cream.

2. Strain the cream through a sieve into a bowl and discard the mint leaves. Cover the bowl and refrigerate the cream for at least 4 hours or overnight. Set aside the confectioners' sugar until ready to whip the cream.

## Make the shortcakes

3. In the bowl of a food processor, combine the flour, sugar, baking powder, and salt by pulsing the machine a few times. Add the butter cubes and, using a fork, toss them in the flour mixture. Pulse until the mixture resembles coarse meal. Add ½ cup (113 g/4 oz) of the cream and pulse just until the mixture comes together (don't over-process the dough—it will make the shortcakes tough, and that's a guarantee). Turn the dough out onto a work surface and gently pat it into a round that is about ¾ inch thick (it's okay if it's a little cracked on top). Transfer the dough to a plate, cover with plastic wrap, and refrigerate for at least 1 hour (this will relax the gluten in the dough).

4. Preheat the oven to 375°F. Line a baking sheet with parchment paper or a silicone baking mat. Remove the dough from the

refrigerator and, using a 2½-inch biscuit or cookie cutter, cut out as many shortcakes as possible from the dough (3 or 4). Arrange them on the baking sheet. As gently as possible, pat together the remaining dough and cut out more shortcakes (you should be able to make 6 or 7 in total). Brush the tops with the remaining 1 tablespoon (14 g/0.5 oz) cream and sprinkle with demerara sugar.

5. Bake the cakes for 15 to 17 minutes, until the tops are light golden brown. Let the shortcakes cool on the baking sheet set on a wire rack for 2 minutes. Transfer the cakes to the rack and let cool completely.

## Prepare the strawberries

6. Cut the strawberries in half lengthwise (or quarters, if large) and place in a medium bowl. Toss them with the sugar and lemon zest, cover the bowl loosely with plastic wrap, and let stand at room temperature for 30 minutes.

## Whip the cream and assemble the shortcakes

7. In the bowl of an electric mixer fitted with the whisk attachment, whip the mint cream on high speed until soft peaks just begin to form. Add the confectioners' sugar and whip until stiff peaks just begin to form.

8. Using a serrated knife or a fork, split the shortcakes in half horizontally and place each bottom half, cut side up, on a plate. Spoon some of the strawberry juice over each bottom half. Divide the strawberries among the shortcakes. Top the strawberries on each cake with a large dollop of the whipped mint cream and more strawberry juice. Set each shortcake top on the cream, placing it slightly off-center. Serve the shortcakes immediately, with any remaining cream in a bowl alongside.

# Blueberry Hand Pies with Lemon Glaze

*I love the rustic appearance* of these individual pies, with the purplish-blue filling spilling out of the vents on top. Traditionally, hand pies are deep-fried, but they are just as delicious, and a bit more wholesome, when baked. A hint of cinnamon and lemon enhances the jammy blueberry filling, while a drizzle of lemon glaze adds a pretty finish. If you prefer a more down-home look, skip the glaze and sprinkle the pies with a little turbinado or demerara sugar before baking.

MAKES 6 INDIVIDUAL PIES

## PIE DOUGH

1⅔ cups (220 g/7.8 oz) all-purpose flour

1 teaspoon (4 g/0.15 oz) granulated sugar

1 teaspoon (2 g/0.07 oz) finely grated lemon zest

½ teaspoon (3.3 g/0.12 oz) salt

9 tablespoons (127 g/4.5 oz) unsalted butter, cut into ½-inch cubes and frozen for 30 minutes

1 teaspoon (5 g/0.17 oz) white vinegar

¼ cup (59 g/2 oz) ice-cold water

## BLUEBERRY FILLING

1⅔ cups (234 g/8 oz) fresh blueberries

⅓ cup (66 g/2.3 oz) granulated sugar

2½ teaspoons (6.25 g/0.22 oz) cornstarch

½ teaspoon (1 g/0.03 oz) finely grated lemon zest

1 teaspoon (5 g/0.17 oz) freshly squeezed lemon juice

⅛ teaspoon ground cinnamon

Pinch of salt

(CONTINUED)

## Make the dough

1. Place the flour, sugar, lemon zest, and salt in the bowl of a food processor and pulse a few times to combine. Add the butter pieces and toss lightly with a spoon to coat them with flour. Blend the butter and flour with about five 1-second pulses or until the mixture is the texture of coarse meal with some butter pieces the size of peas. Put the vinegar in a small bowl and stir in the cold water. Sprinkle the water mixture over the flour mixture and process continuously until the dough begins to clump together. Do not overprocess; the dough should not form a ball on the blade. Turn the dough out onto a work surface and shape it into a thick, 4-inch-wide disc. Wrap the dough in plastic wrap and refrigerate until firm enough to roll, about 1 hour.

2. Place the unwrapped dough on a cutting surface and cut it into 6 equal-size pieces. Working with one piece of dough at a time, shape the dough into a small disc and place it on a lightly floured work surface. Roll the disc out to a 6-inch circle. Using a 5½-inch plate or can as a guide, cut out a 5½-inch circle from the dough. Place the circle on a dinner plate and refrigerate while you roll out the next circle. Repeat with the remaining dough, placing each dough circle on the plate (it's okay to overlap them) and refrigerating them as you roll out the next. Keep the dough circles in the refrigerator while you make the filling.

ASSEMBLY

1 egg, whisked with 1 teaspoon
water, for egg wash

LEMON GLAZE

1 cup (128 g/4.5 ounces)
confectioners' sugar

2 tablespoons (30 g/1 oz)
freshly squeezed lemon juice

## Make the filling

**3.** In a medium bowl, stir together the blueberries, sugar, cornstarch, lemon zest, lemon juice, cinnamon, and salt. Let stand at room temperature for 10 minutes. Stir the mixture well again to combine.

## Assemble and bake the pies

**4.** Place one of the pie dough circles on a work surface and brush ½ inch of the outer edge of the circle with egg wash. Spoon a generous ¼ cup of the blueberry filling into the center of the dough circle. Bring two opposite sides of the round together and pinch them together in the center. Gradually work your way down each side, pinching the edges of the dough together firmly to contain the filling in a crescent-shaped pie. Crimp the edges of the dough by pinching them together along the sealed edge. Place each pie in the freezer after it has been formed. When all the pies have been made, cover the bowl containing the egg wash and refrigerate it. Freeze the pies for 30 minutes. Meanwhile, preheat the oven to 400°F. Line a baking sheet with a silicone baking mat or piece of parchment paper.

**5.** Remove the pies from the freezer and arrange them on the prepared baking sheet. Brush the tops of the pies with the egg wash. Using a sharp paring knife, cut three ¾-inch slits, 1 inch apart, in the top of each pie. Bake the pies for 25 to 30 minutes, until they are evenly browned and the filling is bubbling. Let the pies cool completely on the baking sheet set on a wire rack.

## Make the glaze

**6.** Place the confectioners' sugar in a medium bowl and whisk in the lemon juice to make a smooth glaze. Pour the glaze into a small sealable plastic bag and seal the bag. Snip off a tiny piece of one corner and drizzle the glaze diagonally over the top of each pie. Allow the glaze to set for 10 minutes before serving the pies. Store the pies in an airtight container at room temperature for up to 2 days.

# Lattice-Topped Sour Cherry Pie

*Sour cherries have* a very short season—just a few weeks—and they are highly perishable, which is why they are rarely sold fresh at supermarkets. They are not meant to be eaten raw; they are too tart to enjoy au naturel, but their complex flavor shines through when they're baked, which is why they are known as "pie cherries." They can be found at farmers' markets from late June to mid-July, and that's when I stock up, storing them in sealable plastic bags and tucking them in my freezer to enjoy throughout the year. The flavor of sour cherries needs little embellishment, just some sugar and a pinch of cinnamon. I also add a little almond extract, which brings out the cherry flavor; believe it or not, cherry pits actually taste like almonds (though I don't recommend eating them). I also add some whole wheat flour to the crust, which gives the pie a slightly nutty flavor and texture. If you just can't get hold of sour cherries, you can use sweet ones in a pinch; just reduce the sugar in the filling to ¾ cup.

MAKES ONE 9-INCH PIE, SERVING 8

**SPECIAL EQUIPMENT:**
Cherry pitter (if using fresh cherries)

**PIE DOUGH**

2½ cups (332 g/11.7 oz) all-purpose flour

⅓ cup (41 g/1.45 oz) whole wheat flour

3 tablespoons (37 g/1.3 oz) granulated sugar

1 teaspoon (6.7 g/0.23 oz) salt

16 tablespoons (227 g/8 oz) unsalted butter, cut into ½-inch cubes and frozen for 30 minutes

2 teaspoons (10 g/0.35 oz) cider vinegar or white vinegar

4 to 5 tablespoons (59 g to 74 g/2 oz to 2.6 oz) ice-cold water

(CONTINUED)

## Make the dough

1. Place the flours, sugar, and salt in the bowl of a food processor and pulse until blended. Add the butter cubes and, using a spoon, toss to coat them in flour. Pulse the machine on and off just until the mixture resembles coarse crumbs. Combine the vinegar with 3 tablespoons of the water. With the processor on, add the vinegar mixture through the feed tube and process until the mixture just starts to come together. If the dough seems dry, add as much of the remaining 2 tablespoons water as necessary and process, but not so much that the dough forms a ball on the blade, or the resulting crust will be tough.

2. Turn the dough out onto a work surface, divide it in half, and shape each half into a thick disc. Wrap the discs in plastic wrap and refrigerate for at least 2 hours.

## Make the filling

3. In a large bowl, toss the cherries with the sugar, cornstarch, lemon juice, almond extract, cinnamon, and salt. Let stand for 20 minutes, stirring occasionally, to release the cherries' juices.

## CHERRY FILLING

5 cups (810 g/1.75 lb) fresh or frozen sour cherries, pitted

1 cup (200 g/7 oz) granulated sugar

¼ cup (30 g/1 oz) cornstarch

2 teaspoons (10 g/0.35 oz) freshly squeezed lemon juice

¼ teaspoon (1 g/0.03 oz) almond extract

¼ teaspoon (0.5 g/0.02 oz) ground cinnamon

Big pinch of salt

## ASSEMBLY

2 tablespoons (28 g/1 oz) unsalted butter, cut into ¼-inch cubes

1 egg, whisked with 1 teaspoon water, for egg wash

1 tablespoon demerara or turbinado sugar, for sprinkling

Vanilla ice cream, for serving

## *Assemble and bake the pie*

**4.** Butter a 9-inch pie pan. Place one of the chilled dough discs on a lightly floured work surface and sprinkle some flour over it. Roll out the dough from the center in every direction, flouring the work surface as necessary to prevent sticking. You want a round about ⅛ inch thick or slightly thinner and about 12 inches in diameter.

**5.** Transfer the dough to the prepared pie pan by rolling it loosely around the rolling pin and unrolling it carefully over the pan. Press the dough into the bottom of the pan and then against the sides. Trim the edges with scissors, leaving about ¾ inch of overhang. (Patch any holes or cracks with dough scraps.) Tuck the overhang underneath itself. Prick the bottom of the crust with a fork at 1-inch intervals. Refrigerate the pie shell while you roll out the top.

**6.** Remove the second dough round from the refrigerator and, on a lightly floured surface, roll it into a 12-inch round. Using a pastry wheel or a chef's knife, cut the round into ½-inch-wide strips.

**7.** Remove the pie shell from the refrigerator and pile the cherry filling into it. Dot the top of the filling with the butter. Lay half of the pastry strips on top of the filling in one direction, spacing them 1 inch apart and leaving a small overhang at the edges. Lay the remaining strips on top, crossing the other strips diagonally and creating a lattice pattern (I don't bother to weave them), leaving an overhang. Tuck the edges of the dough strips under the outer edge of the pie crust and, using your thumb and index finger, crimp the edge. Refrigerate the pie for 30 minutes, until firm.

**8.** Position a rack in the lowest part of the oven and place a baking sheet on the rack. Preheat the oven to 425°F. Brush the top of the lattice crust with the egg wash, then sprinkle with demerara sugar. Place the pie on the baking sheet and bake for 20 minutes. Reduce the heat to 375°F and bake until the crust is golden and the filling is bubbling, 30 to 40 minutes more (cover the pie with a piece of vented foil during baking if it looks like the crust is browning too quickly). Let the pie cool completely, about 2 hours, before serving with vanilla ice cream.

# Frozen Raspberry-Blackberry Pie

*This is one* of my favorite summer desserts — in fact, I'm fairly certain I could eat a whole pie by myself if left to my own devices. It's similar to an ice cream pie, but the filling is softer and creamier than ice cream, more like a semifreddo. The crust is made from buttery cookie crumbs, a good textural foil to the creamy berry filling. This can be made up to two days in advance — just cover the frozen pie well with plastic wrap to preserve its fresh berry flavor.

MAKES ONE 9-INCH DEEP-DISH PIE, SERVING 8 TO 10

SPECIAL EQUIPMENT: 9-inch deep-dish pie pan, candy thermometer

### SHORTBREAD COOKIE CRUST

35 (283 g/10 oz) shortbread cookies, such as Lorna Doone

1 tablespoon (12 g/0.4 oz) granulated sugar

4 tablespoons (56 g/2 oz) unsalted butter, melted

### RASPBERRY-BLACKBERRY FILLING

3 cups (283 g/10 oz) frozen raspberries, thawed

2 teaspoons (10 g/0.35 oz) freshly squeezed lemon juice

2 tablespoons (38 g/1.3 oz) seedless blackberry preserves

2 cups (464 g/16.3 oz) heavy cream

6 large egg yolks

¾ cup (150 g/5.3 oz) granulated sugar, divided

3 tablespoons (44 g/1.5 oz) water

Pinch of salt

(CONTINUED)

## Make the crust

1. Preheat the oven to 350°F. Process the shortbread cookies in the bowl of a food processor until finely ground. Add the sugar and process until blended. Add the melted butter and process until combined. Transfer the mixture to a 9-inch deep-dish pie pan and press it evenly against the bottom and sides. Bake the crust for 7 to 9 minutes, until set and just barely beginning to turn light brown around the edges. Let cool on a wire rack.

## Make the filling

2. Place the thawed raspberries in the bowl of a food processor and process until pureed. Pass the puree through a fine-mesh sieve into a bowl, pressing down on it with a rubber spatula again and again until you have mostly just seeds left in the sieve. Discard the seeds. Stir the lemon juice into the puree. Place the blackberry preserves in a small microwave-safe cup and microwave on high power for about 10 seconds, until the preserves are liquefied. Stir the preserves into the raspberry puree. Cover the bowl and set the puree aside.

3. In the bowl of an electric mixer fitted with the whisk attachment, whip the cream at high speed until soft peaks form. Transfer the whipped cream to a medium bowl, cover with plastic wrap, and refrigerate until ready to use.

4. Clean and dry the mixer bowl and whisk attachment. Place the egg yolks and ¼ cup (50 g/1.76 oz) of the sugar in the bowl and

1½ cups (170 g/6 oz) fresh raspberries

1½ cups (195 g/6.8 oz) fresh blackberries

1 to 2 tablespoons (12 g/ 0.4 oz to 25 g/0.9 oz) granulated sugar, depending on the sweetness of the berries

1 teaspoon (5 g/0.17 oz) freshly squeezed lemon juice

whip on medium speed while you make the sugar syrup, scraping down the sides of the bowl once or twice with a rubber spatula to make sure the sugar is evenly blended with the yolks. Meanwhile, in a small saucepan, combine the remaining ½ cup (100 g/3.5 oz) sugar with the water and place over medium-high heat. Cook, occasionally brushing down the sides of the saucepan with a wet pastry brush to prevent crystallization, until the syrup reaches 248°F on a candy thermometer (watch the syrup carefully, as it heats up quickly). With the mixer still on medium speed, quickly pour the hot syrup into the egg yolks in a continuous stream near the side of the bowl, trying to avoid getting it on the whisk attachment. Add the salt, raise the mixer speed to high, and whip the egg yolk mixture until completely cool, about 5 minutes.

5. Remove the bowl from the mixer stand and fold in the raspberry puree. Fold in one-third of the whipped cream, then fold in the remaining cream until evenly blended. Scrape the filling into the cooled pie crust, piling it up high and swirling the filling on top with a rubber spatula or a small offset metal spatula. Freeze the pie for at least 3 hours before serving.

### *Macerate the berries and serve*

6. Combine the berries, sugar, and lemon juice in a medium bowl. Refrigerate the berries for 1 hour, stirring occasionally, or until they release their juices. Serve slices of the frozen pie topped with the macerated berries.

# Raspberry Almond Tartlets

*These tartlets, which* combine the sharp flavor of raspberries with a sweet almond filling, are among my favorite desserts. The crusts are made from a classic *pâte sucrée* dough, in which a flavorful frangipane filling is baked. Finely chopped pistachios, sprinkled on top of each whipped-cream pouf, give them a polished look that wouldn't be out of place in a fashionable Paris patisserie.

**MAKES EIGHT 3½-INCH TARTLETS**

**SPECIAL EQUIPMENT:**
Eight 3½-inch tartlet pans

**TARTLET CRUSTS**

1½ cups (198 g/7 oz)
all-purpose flour

6 tablespoons (43 g/1.5 oz)
cake flour

1 teaspoon (4 g/0.15 oz)
granulated sugar

¼ teaspoon plus ⅛ teaspoon salt

12 tablespoons (170 g/6 oz)
unsalted butter, cut into
½-inch cubes and frozen for
20 minutes

¼ cup (59 g/2 oz) ice water

**FILLING**

1 cup Almond Cream (page 15)

**TOPPING**

⅓ cup (102 g/3.5 oz) raspberry
preserves

3 cups (340 g/12 oz) fresh
raspberries

1 cup (232 g/8.18 oz) heavy
cream

2 tablespoons (16 g/0.5 oz)
confectioners' sugar, sifted

1 teaspoon (4 g/0.14 oz) vanilla
extract

1 tablespoon (6 g/0.21 oz)
finely chopped pistachios

## Make the tartlet crusts

1. Place the flours, sugar, and salt in the bowl of a food processor and pulse a few times to combine. Add the butter pieces and toss lightly to coat with flour. Blend the butter and flour with about five 1-second pulses, or until the mixture is the texture of coarse meal with some butter pieces the size of peas. Sprinkle the water over the flour mixture and process continuously until the dough begins to clump together. Don't overprocess; the dough should not form a ball. Turn the dough out onto a work surface and shape it into a thick 5-inch-wide disc. Wrap the dough in plastic wrap and refrigerate for at least 1 hour.

2. Place the unwrapped dough on a lightly floured work surface. Roll out the dough to between ⅛ and ¹⁄₁₆ inch thick, lifting and rotating the dough often while dusting the work surface and dough lightly with flour as necessary. Using a 5-inch pastry cutter (or a paring knife with a plate as a guide), cut out as many rounds from the dough as you can, rerolling scraps as necessary; you should be able to cut a total of 8 rounds. Gently press the dough onto the bottom and up the sides of eight 3½-inch tartlet pans. Roll the pin over the top of the pans to trim off the excess dough. Lightly prick the bottom of the dough in each pan with a fork at ½-inch intervals. Refrigerate the dough in the pans for 20 minutes to firm up the dough.

3. Preheat the oven to 350°F. Right before baking, line the dough in each pan with aluminum foil or parchment paper and cover with pie weights or dried beans. Place the tart pans on a baking sheet and bake for 10 minutes. Carefully lift the foil (along with the weights)

out of the tart pans and bake the crusts for 20 to 22 minutes longer, until the crusts are just beginning to turn light brown in spots around the edge. Leave the oven on. Transfer the tartlet pans to a
wire rack and let cool completely.

## Fill the tartlets

**4.** Scrape the Almond Cream into the cooled tartlet crusts, filling each one and smoothing it into an
even layer (depending on the capacity of your tartlet pans, you may have a little Almond Cream left
over). Place the tartlet pans back on a baking sheet and bake for 25 to 30 minutes, until the filling is
golden brown and a toothpick inserted into the center comes out clean. Let cool on a wire rack.

## Finish the tartlets

**5.** Remove the cooled tartlets from the pans. Spread the tartlets with a thin layer of raspberry preserves (about 1 teaspoon/6 g/0.21 oz each). Arrange a circle of raspberries around the edge of each
tartlet. Spoon the remaining raspberry preserves into a small microwave-safe cup and microwave on
high power for 10 seconds. Pass the preserves through a fine-mesh sieve into a small bowl to remove
the seeds. Using a small pastry brush, brush some of the strained preserves onto the raspberries to
make them shiny.

**6.** In the bowl of an electric mixer fitted with the whisk attachment, whip the cream at high
speed until it just begins to form soft peaks. Add the confectioners' sugar and vanilla and whip to
stiff peaks. Transfer to pastry bag fitted with a medium star tip, such as Ateco #6. Pipe a swirl of
whipped cream in the center of each tartlet and garnish with some of the pistachios. Refrigerate the
tartlets until ready to serve, up to 1 day.

# Strawberry Cheesecake Tart

*When strawberries first make* their appearance at the farmers' markets in early June, this tart is the second thing I make (just after strawberry ice cream). It has a buttery puff pastry base, which is topped with a rich cheesecake filling and glistening slices of strawberry. To heighten their sheen, I brush the berries with strained raspberry preserves. Finely chopped pistachio nuts provide a bit of crunch and a lovely color contrast. Because its shelf life is relatively short, the tart shouldn't be assembled more than four hours before serving. But you can certainly prepare its components — the pastry base and the filling — up to a day ahead.

MAKES ONE 8-BY-13-INCH TART, SERVING 8

### CHEESECAKE FILLING

¾ cup (181 g/6.4 oz) whole milk

6 tablespoons (75 g/2.6 oz) granulated sugar, divided

3 large egg yolks

1 tablespoon plus 2½ teaspoons (14 g/0.5 oz) cornstarch

½ cup (113 g/4 oz) cream cheese, softened and cut into 4 chunks

½ teaspoon (2 g/0.07 oz) vanilla extract

1 tablespoon (15 g/0.5 oz) sour cream

½ cup (121 g/4.3 oz) heavy cream

### PUFF PASTRY BASE

½ (17.3-ounce) box (245 g/ 8.65 oz) frozen puff pastry, thawed, or an equivalent amount (¼ recipe) Quick Puff Pastry (page 16)

1 large egg yolk, whisked with 1 teaspoon water, for egg wash

(CONTINUED)

## Begin to make the filling

1. In a small saucepan, combine the milk and about half the sugar and place over medium-high heat. While the milk is heating, whisk the egg yolks with the cornstarch and the remaining sugar in a small bowl until well blended. When the milk comes to a boil, whisk half of it into the yolk mixture until blended. Pour the yolk mixture into the saucepan with the remaining milk and continue to cook, whisking constantly, until the custard comes to a boil and thickens. Remove the pan from the heat and whisk in the cream cheese until it is completely blended in. Whisk in the vanilla. Pass the custard through a fine-mesh sieve into a medium bowl, cover with plastic wrap, and refrigerate while you make the pastry base.

## Make the pastry base

2. Line a baking sheet with a silicone baking mat or piece of parchment paper. Place the unwrapped puff pastry on a lightly floured work surface and roll it out to a rectangle measuring about 10 by 13 inches. Using a large chef's knife, trim the edges so that they are even. (When cutting the pastry, don't drag the knife through it — cut down on the pastry to make a clean cut. This will allow the pastry to rise more evenly.) Neatly cut two 1-by-13-inch strips from the long sides of the rectangle. Place the pastry rectangle on the prepared baking sheet. Brush some of the egg wash on a 1-inch-wide section along one long edge of the rectangle. Lay one of the

½ cup (154 g/5.4 oz) raspberry preserves (with or without seeds)

4 cups (454 g/1 lb) fresh strawberries, hulled

1 tablespoon (7 g/0.25 oz) finely chopped unsalted pistachios

pastry strips on top of the egg wash and press it down lightly to adhere. Repeat on the other side with the other pastry strip. Using a fork, prick the center of the rectangle all over to prevent it from rising. Freeze the pastry on the baking sheet for 30 minutes. Meanwhile, preheat the oven to 400°F. Cover the bowl containing the egg wash and refrigerate it until ready to bake the pastry.

3. Remove the pastry from the freezer and brush the pastry strips well on the edges with the egg wash. For decoration, using the back of a paring knife, lightly mark down the length of the strips with elongated scallop shapes about 1 inch wide. Bake the pastry for 18 to 22 minutes, until it is nicely browned and baked through. Let cool completely on the baking sheet set on a wire rack.

### Finish the filling

4. Whisk the sour cream into the chilled cream cheese–custard mixture. In the bowl of an electric mixer fitted with the whisk attachment, beat the heavy cream at high speed until soft peaks form. Gently fold the whipped cream into the custard one-third at a time. Cover the bowl and return the filling to the refrigerator.

### Assemble the tart

5. Place the preserves in a small heatproof cup and microwave on high power until bubbling, about 45 seconds. Strain the hot preserves through a fine-mesh sieve into another small heatproof bowl. Brush some of the strained jam over the center of the cooled pastry, covering it completely. (You will have some preserves remaining to brush over the strawberries.) Spoon the cheesecake filling into the center of the pastry base and, using a small offset metal spatula, spread it into an even layer.

6. Slice the strawberries ¼ inch thick. Arrange the slices in slightly overlapping rows across the width of the tart, covering the filling completely. Reheat the remaining preserves in the microwave until bubbling, then brush over the strawberries. Sprinkle the strawberries with the pistachios. Serve the tart immediately, or refrigerate until ready to serve, up to 4 hours.

*Berries and Cherries*

# Extra-Crumbly Blueberry Muffins

*There's nothing exceptional* about a blueberry muffin—unless of course, you've got an exceptional recipe, which this happens to be. This is the muffin version of the kind of buttermilk crumb cake my father would pick up from our local bakery every Sunday morning when I was a kid. The cake had a thick crumb topping, which was crunchy and sweet, and it was dusted liberally with confectioners' sugar. These tender buttermilk muffins are very similar to my memory of that cake, except they're packed with juicy blueberries. Make these muffins when blueberries are at their peak, June through August, or use frozen berries. My favorites are frozen wild blueberries from Maine, which are now available in many supermarkets.

MAKES 12 MUFFINS

### CRUMBLE TOPPING

½ cup (66 g/2.3 oz) all-purpose flour

½ teaspoon (1 g/0.03 oz) ground cinnamon

½ cup firmly packed (108 g/ 3.8 oz) light brown sugar

Pinch of fine sea salt

4 tablespoons (56 g/2 oz) unsalted butter, slightly softened and cut into ½-inch pieces

### BLUEBERRY MUFFINS

2 cups (265 g/9.3 oz) all-purpose flour

⅔ cup (133 g/4.7 oz) granulated sugar

2 teaspoons (10 g/0.35 oz) baking powder

¼ teaspoon (1.25 g/0.04 oz) baking soda

½ teaspoon (1 g/0.03 oz) ground cinnamon

¼ teaspoon (1.6 g/0.06 oz) salt

1 large egg

1 cup (242 g/8.5 oz) buttermilk

(CONTINUED)

### *Make the topping*

1. In a medium bowl, stir together the flour, cinnamon, brown sugar, and salt. Add the butter and stir and mash the mixture with a fork until the topping is crumbly.

### *Make the muffins*

2. Preheat the oven to 350°F. Line a standard 12-cup muffin pan with cupcake liners or butter the cups generously.

3. In a large bowl, stir together the flour, granulated sugar, baking powder, baking soda, cinnamon, and salt. Make a well in the center.

4. In a medium bowl, whisk together the egg and buttermilk until combined. Whisk in the lemon zest, vanilla, and melted butter. Pour the buttermilk mixture into the well in the flour mixture. Begin stirring the liquids, gradually drawing the dry ingredients into the well until they are almost, but not quite, combined—there should be a few streaks of flour showing. Add the blueberries and fold in just to distribute evenly. Do not overmix. Evenly divide the batter among the prepared muffin cups. Evenly divide the crumble topping among the muffins, sprinkling it on top. (It will seem like a lot of topping, but that's okay!)

1 teaspoon (2 g/0.07 oz) finely grated lemon zest

½ teaspoon (2 g/0.07 oz) vanilla extract

6 tablespoons (85 g/3 oz) unsalted butter, melted

1 cup (140 g/5 oz) fresh or frozen (unthawed) blueberries

GARNISH

Confectioners' sugar, for dusting

5. Bake the muffins for 35 to 40 minutes, or until a toothpick inserted into the center of a muffin comes out clean. Let cool in the pan set on a wire rack for 10 minutes, then carefully transfer the muffins from the pan to the rack. Serve warm, or let cool completely. Dust the muffins lightly with confectioners' sugar right before serving. Store in an airtight container at room temperature for up to 2 days.

# Cherry Streusel Coffee Cake

*Whenever I visit* friends for a few days, I try to be a good houseguest and bring something sweet for everyone to snack on during my stay. This non-yeasted coffee cake is an ideal gift for such an occasion, as it travels and keeps well and can be eaten throughout the day. The cake is best made with sour cherries, so if you can get ahold of some, or have a stash in your freezer, use them. Happily, the cake is *almost* as delicious with sweet cherries, which are much more readily available.

**MAKES ONE 9-INCH SQUARE CAKE, SERVING 9**

**SPECIAL EQUIPMENT:**
Cherry pitter (if using fresh cherries)

**STREUSEL FILLING AND TOPPING**

1 cup (132 g/4.6 oz) all-purpose flour

⅓ cup firmly packed (71 g/ 2.5 oz) dark brown sugar

¼ cup (50 g/1.76 oz) granulated sugar

1 teaspoon (1 g/0.03 oz) ground cinnamon

⅛ teaspoon (0.8 g/0.03 oz) salt

7 tablespoons (99 g/3.5 oz) unsalted butter, melted

½ cup (42 g/1.5 oz) sliced almonds

**CAKE**

2 cups (265 g/9.3 oz) all-purpose flour

1 teaspoon (5 g/0.17 oz) baking powder

½ teaspoon (2.5 g/0.08 oz) baking soda

½ teaspoon (3.3 g/0.12 oz) salt

1 cup (242 g/8.5 oz) sour cream

1½ teaspoons (6 g/0.2 oz) vanilla extract

(CONTINUED)

1. Preheat the oven to 350°F. Butter the bottom and sides of a 9-inch square baking pan.

### Make the streusel

2. Place the flour, sugars, cinnamon, and salt in the bowl of a food processor and process for a few seconds until blended. With the motor running, add the melted butter through the feed tube in a steady stream and process just until the mixture resembles coarse crumbs. Stir in the almonds by hand and set the mixture aside.

### Make the cake

3. In a medium bowl, whisk together the flour, baking powder, baking soda, and salt. In a small bowl, stir together the sour cream and vanilla.

4. In the bowl of an electric mixer fitted with the paddle attachment, beat the butter at medium speed until creamy, about 1 minute. Gradually add the sugar and beat at high speed until pale and fluffy, about 5 minutes. Reduce the speed to medium and add the eggs one at a time, beating well after each addition. Reduce the speed to low and add the flour mixture in three additions, alternating it with the sour cream in two additions and mixing just until blended. Remove the bowl from the mixer stand and scrape the bowl with a rubber spatula to make sure the batter is evenly blended.

11 tablespoons (155 g/5.5 oz) unsalted butter, softened

1⅓ cups (266 g/9.4 oz) granulated sugar

2 large eggs

1½ cups (186 g/6.5 oz) fresh or frozen (thawed and drained) sour or sweet pitted cherries

GARNISH

Confectioners' sugar, for dusting

**5.** Scrape about two-thirds of the batter into the prepared pan and spread it into an even layer. Sprinkle 1 ⅓ cups of the streusel evenly over the batter. Top with the cherries, spacing them evenly over the streusel. Spoon the remaining batter in large dollops evenly over the cherries and spread it into an even layer — it's okay if the cherries show through the batter. Sprinkle the remaining streusel over the batter, covering it completely.

**6.** Bake the cake for 60 to 70 minutes, until a toothpick inserted into the center of the cake comes out clean. Let the cake cool completely in the pan set on a wire rack.

**7.** To serve, dust the top with confectioners' sugar and cut squares of the cake right from the pan.

# Vanilla Sponge Roll with Strawberries and Cream Filling

*The sponge cake* relies not on chemical leaveners (baking soda or baking powder), but on beaten eggs for its volume. A deft hand is essential when folding in the whipped whites to keep the cake light. Aside from that, there's nothing complicated about this recipe, which can (and should) be made up to a day before serving. Use the best strawberries you can find, preferably local ones from the farmers' market.

MAKES 8 SERVINGS

### SPONGE CAKE ROLL

1 cup (100 g/3.5 oz) sifted cake flour

¼ teaspoon (1.6 g/0.06 oz) salt

5 large eggs, separated, at room temperature

⅛ teaspoon (0.4 g/0.01 oz) cream of tartar

¾ cup (150 g/5.3 oz) granulated sugar, divided

1 teaspoon (4 g/0.14 oz) vanilla bean paste or extract

Confectioners' sugar, for dusting

### STRAWBERRIES AND CREAM FILLING

2 cups (312 g/11 oz) fresh strawberries, rinsed (but not dried) and hulled

¼ cup (50 g/2.1 oz) granulated sugar

1 cup (232 g/8.18 oz) heavy cream

1 teaspoon (4 g/0.14 oz) vanilla bean paste or extract

2 tablespoons (16 g/0.5 oz) confectioners' sugar

### GARNISH

Confectioners' sugar, for dusting

## *Make the cake roll*

1. Preheat the oven to 375°F. Coat the bottom and sides of a 12-by-18-inch rimmed baking sheet (a half sheet pan) with nonstick cooking spray. Line the bottom of the pan with a silicone baking mat or a piece of parchment paper cut to fit, and coat lightly with more nonstick spray.

2. In a medium bowl, sift together the flour and salt and whisk to combine.

3. In the bowl of an electric mixer fitted with the whisk attachment, beat the egg whites at medium speed until foamy. Add the cream of tartar and beat at medium-high speed until soft peaks just begin to form. Gradually add ¼ cup (50 g/1.76 oz) of the granulated sugar and beat at high speed until stiff peaks form. Transfer the whipped whites to a medium bowl and wash and dry the mixer bowl and whisk attachment.

4. Place the egg yolks in the mixer bowl and, using the whisk attachment, beat at medium speed. Add the vanilla and then gradually add the remaining ½ cup (100 g/3.5 oz) granulated sugar. Raise the mixer speed to high and beat until pale, about 5 minutes. Reduce the speed to low and add the flour mixture in three additions, mixing just until combined (the batter will be very thick). Using a rubber spatula, gently fold one-third of the whipped egg whites into

the batter to lighten it. Gently fold in the remaining whites in two additions. Scrape the batter into the prepared pan, spreading it into an even layer.

**5.** Bake the cake for 7 to 9 minutes, until it springs back when you touch the center with your finger. The cake should still be pale. Place the baking sheet on a wire rack, cover the cake with a tea towel, and let cool for 15 minutes.

**6.** Remove the tea towel and dust the top of the cake generously with the confectioners' sugar. Run a paring knife around the edge of the pan to release the cake. Cover with the tea towel again and place an inverted baking sheet on top of the cake. Invert both pans, remove the top pan, and peel off the baking mat or parchment paper. Let the cake cool completely. While the cake is cooling, whip the cream for the filling.

### Make the filling

**7.** Place the strawberries in a bowl and sprinkle with the granulated sugar. Toss to combine and set aside at room temperature for 30 minutes, stirring occasionally, until the strawberries are slightly syrupy.

**8.** In the bowl of an electric mixer fitted with the whisk attachment, whip the cream and vanilla at high speed until soft peaks just begin to form. Add the confectioners' sugar and whip until stiff peaks form.

**9.** Spoon the whipped cream onto the cake. Use an offset metal spatula to spread the filling over the cake, making it slightly thicker near the short end that is closest to you and leaving a ½-inch border around all the edges. Arrange the strawberries, pointed side up, in a row that runs parallel to the short sides of the cake and that is about 3 inches in from the short edge closest to you. Roll the cake up jelly roll–style, starting from the short end that is closest to you and ending so that the seam is on the bottom of the roll. It's okay if a little filling oozes out at the ends. Cover the roll with plastic wrap and refrigerate for at least 4 hours to allow the filling to firm up and the cake to soften a bit and absorb the flavor of the berries. The cake can also be refrigerated overnight.

**10.** Before serving, cut a 1-inch slice from each end of the roll to reveal the filling. Lightly dust the top of the roll with confectioners' sugar and serve.

# French Strawberries and Cream Cake

*Here's my take* on the classic French fraisier cake, which combines an almond sponge cake with a lightened pastry cream and lots of fresh strawberries that peek out alluringly from the sides. Because it has several components, making this cake is a bit of a production, but the end result is, as they say, a real showstopper. Note that you will need an 8½-inch springform pan (a 9-inch springform will be too big) and a 9-inch cake pan to make this cake.

MAKES ONE 8½-INCH CAKE, SERVING 8

SPECIAL EQUIPMENT:
8½-inch springform pan

ALMOND SPONGE CAKE

1 cup (85 g/3 oz) unblanched sliced almonds, divided

½ cup (57 g/2 oz) cake flour

⅛ teaspoon (0.83 g/0.03 oz) salt

4 large eggs, separated, at room temperature

¾ cup (150 g/5.3 oz) granulated sugar, divided

¼ teaspoon (1.25 g/0.04 oz) cream of tartar

2½ tablespoons (35 g/1.2 oz) unsalted butter, melted and still warm

¼ teaspoon (0.5 g/0.02 oz) almond extract

SOAKING SYRUP

⅓ cup (66 g/2.3 oz) granulated sugar

⅓ cup (78 g/2.7 oz) water

1 tablespoon (15 g/0.5 oz) kirsch or Chambord raspberry liqueur

(CONTINUED)

## Make the sponge cake

1. Preheat the oven to 350°F. Grease the bottom and sides of a 9-inch round cake pan. Dust the pan with flour and set aside.

2. Set aside ¼ cup (21 g/0.75 oz) of the almonds for the top of the cake. Scatter the remaining ¾ cup (63 g/2.24 oz) almonds on a rimmed baking sheet and bake until lightly toasted, 6 to 7 minutes. Set aside to cool.

3. In a medium bowl, sift together the flour and salt. Transfer the mixture to the bowl of a food processor and add the cooled almonds. Process until the almonds are finely ground.

4. In the bowl of an electric mixer fitted with the whisk attachment, whip the egg yolks at medium speed while gradually adding ½ cup (100 g/3.5 oz) of the sugar. Raise the mixer speed to high and beat until light and thick, about 3 minutes. Transfer the mixture to a large bowl and wash and dry the mixer bowl and whisk attachment.

5. In the clean, dry bowl of the electric mixer, using the clean whisk attachment, beat the egg whites at medium speed until frothy. Add the cream of tartar and beat at medium-high speed until soft peaks just begin to form. Gradually add the remaining ¼ cup (50 g/1.76 oz) sugar and beat at high speed until the whites form stiff peaks.

6. Using a rubber spatula, gently fold about one-third of the whites into the yolk mixture. Sprinkle about one-third of the flour mixture over the egg yolk mixture and gently fold it in. Continue adding

## PASTRY CREAM FILLING

1½ cups (363 g/12.8 oz) whole milk

3 large egg yolks

⅓ cup plus 2 tablespoons (91 g/3.2 oz) granulated sugar

3 tablespoons plus 1½ teaspoons (26 g/0.9 oz) cornstarch

2 tablespoons (28 g/1 oz) unsalted butter, cut into ½-inch cubes

2 tablespoons (28 g/1 oz) water

¾ teaspoon (2.25 g/0.08 oz) powdered gelatin

½ cup (116 g/4 oz) heavy cream

1 teaspoon (4 g/0.14 oz) vanilla bean paste or extract

## STRAWBERRIES

4 cups (454 g/1 lb) fresh strawberries

1 tablespoon (12 g/0.42 oz) granulated sugar

## GARNISH

Confectioners' sugar, for dusting

the egg whites and flour mixture alternately, in two additions each, folding very gently.

7. In a small bowl, stir together the butter and almond extract. Scoop about ½ cup of the cake batter into the bowl containing the melted butter and stir until blended. Gently fold this mixture into the remaining cake batter. Scrape the batter into the prepared pan and sprinkle with the reserved ¼ cup (21 g/0.75 oz) sliced almonds.

8. Bake the cake for 18 to 24 minutes, until the top springs back when lightly touched and a tester inserted into the center comes out clean. Let the cake cool in the pan for 15 minutes. Invert the cake onto the wire rack and let cool completely.

### Make the syrup

9. In a small saucepan, combine the sugar and water and bring to a boil over high heat, stirring just until the sugar is dissolved. Remove the pan from the heat and let cool completely. Stir in the kirsch.

### Begin the filling

10. Heat the milk in a small saucepan over medium-high heat until just beginning to bubble around the edges of the pan. Remove the pan from the heat.

11. In a medium bowl, whisk the egg yolks and sugar together vigorously until blended. Whisk in the cornstarch until smooth. Whisk about ½ cup (121 g/4.2 oz) of the hot milk into the yolk mixture until blended. Whisk the yolk mixture into the remaining hot milk and cook over medium heat, whisking constantly, until the mixture bubbles and thickens. Remove the pan from the heat and continue to whisk for a few seconds to prevent the pastry cream on the bottom of the pan from scorching. Whisk in the butter until melted. Scrape the pastry cream into a bowl and press a piece of plastic wrap directly against the surface of the pastry cream to prevent a skin from forming. Refrigerate the pastry cream for at least 1½ hours. While the pastry cream is chilling, prepare the strawberries.

## Make the strawberries

**12.** Set aside 11 of the nicest looking berries to place around the side of the cake. Hull the remaining berries and cut them in half vertically. Place the berries in a medium bowl and toss with the sugar. Refrigerate for at least 30 minutes.

## Finish the filling

**13.** Place the water in a small microwave-safe cup and sprinkle the gelatin on top. Set aside to soften for 5 minutes.

**14.** Place the cup of gelatin in the microwave and cook on high power for 10 seconds, until melted. Stir well. Set aside to cool for 5 minutes, until lukewarm.

**15.** Place the pastry cream in the bowl of an electric mixer fitted with the whisk attachment and whip at high speed until smooth, about 1 minute. Drizzle in the cooled melted gelatin and mix until well blended, about a minute. Add the cream and vanilla and whip at high speed until soft peaks form. Assemble the cake right away.

## Assemble the cake

**16.** Using a long, serrated knife, cut the cake in half horizontally to make two layers. Place the bottom layer, cut side up, in the bottom of an 8½-inch springform pan (it should be a snug fit). Brush the cake with half of the syrup. Cut off the stem ends of the reserved strawberries, slicing straight across the top of the berries with a paring knife. Cut the berries in half vertically and arrange them, cut side against the pan, around the edge of the pan with the pointed side up and the berries touching one another (when the cake is unmolded from the pan, the flat sides of the cut berries will be visible around the edge of the cake). Pile the macerated cut strawberries and any liquid that has accumulated in the center of the cake and spread into an even layer. Scrape the pastry cream over the berries and, using a small offset metal spatula, spread the filling into an even layer, pushing it into the spaces between the berries at the edge of the pan. Brush the cut side of the second cake layer with the remaining syrup and place it, cut side down (the top, with the sliced almonds, should be on top) over the filling. Press down lightly and refrigerate the cake for at least 3 hours.

**17.** Remove the side of the springform pan and slide the cake onto a serving plate (a pancake turner is useful here). Right before serving, dust the top of the cake lightly with confectioners' sugar. Use a sharp knife to cut the cake, slicing between the strawberries around the edge.

# Berry-Filled Layer Cake

*This is the cake* to make when you have beautiful ripe berries on hand and want to enjoy them uncooked, as nature intended. The light lemon chiffon cake layers are a nice foil to the rich white chocolate ganache frosting and the sweet-tart berries. Use the best white chocolate you can find for the ganache—my favorite brands are Guittard, Valrhona, and Green & Black's—and don't even consider using those chalky, super-sweet white chocolate morsels from the supermarket. That would be an insult to your berries (not to mention your guests).

MAKE ONE 9-INCH CAKE, SERVING 8

### WHIPPED WHITE CHOCOLATE-SOUR CREAM GANACHE

9 oz (255 g) high-quality white chocolate, chopped

1 cup (232 g/8.18 oz) heavy cream

½ cup (121 g/4.3 oz) sour cream

### LEMON CHIFFON CAKE LAYERS

1 cup (4 oz/115 g) sifted cake flour

¾ cup (5.3 oz/150 g) granulated sugar, divided

1 teaspoon (5 g/0.17 oz) baking powder

¼ teaspoon (1.6 g/0.06 oz) salt

4 large eggs, separated, plus 1 large egg white, at room temperature

¼ cup (52 g/1.8 oz) vegetable oil

1 teaspoon (2 g/0.07 oz) finely grated lemon zest

3 tablespoons (45 g/1.6 oz) freshly squeezed lemon juice

2 tablespoons (30 g/1 oz) water

¼ teaspoon (0.7 g/0.03 oz) cream of tartar

(CONTINUED)

## Make the ganache

1. Place the white chocolate in the bowl of an electric mixer and set aside.

2. In a small saucepan, bring the cream to a gentle boil over medium-high heat. Pour the hot cream over the white chocolate and let it stand for 1 minute to melt the chocolate. Gently whisk by hand until smooth. Allow to cool until lukewarm, stirring occasionally.

3. Whisk in the sour cream. Cover the bowl with plastic wrap and refrigerate the ganache for at least 6 hours, or up to 1 day.

## Make the cake layers

4. Preheat the oven to 350°F. Grease the bottom (but not the sides) of two 9-inch round cake pans. Line the bottom of each pan with a round of parchment paper and grease the paper.

5. In a medium bowl, sift together the flour, ½ cup (100 g/3.5 oz) of the granulated sugar, the baking powder, and salt, and whisk until well blended.

6. In a large bowl, whisk together the egg yolks, oil, lemon zest, lemon juice, and water. Whisk in the flour mixture, one-third at a time, mixing just until blended.

MACERATED BERRIES

1 cup (113 g/4 oz) fresh
strawberries, hulled and sliced
¼ inch thick

1 cup (113 g/4 oz) fresh
raspberries

2 tablespoons (25 g/0.8 oz)
granulated sugar

1 teaspoon (5 g/0.17 oz) freshly
squeezed lemon juice

ASSEMBLY

1 cup (113 g/4 oz) fresh
strawberries, hulled and halved
(or quartered if large)

1 cup (113 g/4 oz) fresh
raspberries

1 cup (130 g/4.5 oz) fresh
blackberries

Confectioners' sugar, for
dusting

Lemon zest curls

**7.** In the bowl of an electric mixer fitted with the whisk attachment, beat the egg whites and cream of tartar at medium speed until soft peaks form. Gradually beat in the remaining ¼ cup (50 g/1.76 oz) sugar, then raise the speed to high and beat until the whites form medium peaks. Using a large rubber spatula, briskly fold about one-third of the whites into the cake batter. Gently fold in the remaining whites. Scrape the batter into the prepared pans.

**8.** Bake the cakes for 20 to 25 minutes, until a toothpick inserted into the center of each comes out clean. Set the pans on wire racks and run a paring knife around the edges of the pans to loosen the cakes. Let the cakes cool in the pans for 15 minutes. Invert onto the racks, peel off the parchment paper, and let cool completely.

### Macerate the berries

**9.** Place the sliced strawberries and the raspberries in a medium bowl. Sprinkle with the sugar and lemon juice and toss the mixture to combine. Set the berries aside at room temperature for 15 minutes to macerate.

### Assemble the cake

**10.** Place the bowl of ganache in the mixer stand and, using the whisk attachment, whip at high speed until the ganache forms soft peaks and is firm enough to spread (be careful not to overwhip it, though, as it can become grainy).

**11.** Place one of the cake layers on a serving plate and top with the macerated berries, including their juice, spreading them in an even layer. Using a metal spatula, to spread about ⅔ cup of the whipped ganache on top of the berries, going right up to the edge of the cake. Top with the other cake layer. Frost the top and sides of the cake with the remaining ganache.

**12.** Arrange the halved strawberries, raspberries, and blackberries on top of the frosted cake, piling them up in the center. Dust the berries liberally with confectioners' sugar and garnish with lemon zest curls. Serve immediately, or refrigerate until ready to serve. The cake should be served the day it's made.

# Apple

✢ ✢

Surely the apple is
the noblest of fruits.

— HENRY DAVID THOREAU,
*Wild Apples*

*The essence of* fall is in the sweet, soft flavor of baked apples. Autumn is when apples are at their peak, a time when markets overflow with an impressive variety of local and imported varieties. As with any produce, local is better, as this means the apples were not bred to be shipped around the world and are bound to have more flavor. The highly polished, waxed apples in the supermarket might look more appealing, but the apples grown at an orchard nearby will taste a whole lot better.

Because of their mellowness, apples are compatible with a variety of flavors, including maple, honey, brown sugar, brandy, and spices (especially cinnamon and ginger). As far as choosing what type of apple to buy, use the recommendations in each recipe as a guideline. Sweet, juicy varieties include Fuji, Gala, Golden Delicious, and Golden Russet. Sweet-tart, less juicy types include Granny Smith, Braeburn, Goldrush, Suncrisp, and Melrose. These varieties also have a denser flesh than the sweeter apples, and will retain their shape better when baked.

When choosing apples, look for fruit that has a smooth skin and is free of blemishes. Unwaxed fruit is always preferable. Store your fruit in a vented plastic bag in the crisper section of your refrigerator for up to two weeks.

# Green Apple Sorbet

*The juice of tart* green apples makes an incredibly refreshing sorbet. The trick to keeping the apples' beautiful green color and fresh flavor is to add a little vitamin C powder (available at pharmacies) to the juice, which prevents it (and the sorbet) from oxidizing and turning brown. If you don't have an electric juicer but do have a Vitamix blender, you can use the Vitamix to juice the apples (the motor of a regular blender won't be strong enough). Just add ¼ cup water to the apple pieces and blend very gradually until smooth. Then strain the mixture through two layers of cheesecloth or a nut milk bag to obtain the precious green juice.

**MAKES 1¼ QUARTS**

**SPECIAL EQUIPMENT:**
Electric juicer or Vitamix blender; ice cream maker

½ teaspoon (1 g/0.03 oz) vitamin C (ascorbic acid) powder, or 1 vitamin C tablet (1,000 mg), crushed with a mortar and pestle or the back of a spoon

5 to 6 large (1.25 kg/2.75 lb) organic Granny Smith apples

⅔ cup (133 g/4.7 oz) granulated sugar

½ cup (118 g/4.16 oz) water

2 teaspoons (10 g/0.35 oz) freshly squeezed lemon juice

1. Place the vitamin C in a 1-quart container and place under the spout of the juicer.

2. Wash the apples well and cut them into chunks that will fit into the juicer's feed tube. Pass the apple chunks through the juicer into the container with the vitamin C. You will need 3 cups juice. Spoon off any foam on top of the juice, and stir it well. Cover the container and refrigerate the juice.

3. In a small saucepan, combine the sugar and water and place over medium heat. Bring to a boil, stirring until the sugar is dissolved. Remove the pan from the heat and let the syrup cool to room temperature.

4. Stir the lemon juice into the sugar syrup and then stir the syrup into the apple juice. Cover and refrigerate for at least 3 hours, until well chilled.

5. Process the sorbet base in an ice cream maker according to the manufacturer's instructions. Transfer the sorbet to a covered container and freeze for at least 2 hours, or up to 1 month.

*Apple*

# Maple-Walnut Caramel Apples

*Eating a gooey* caramel apple is one of those childish pleasures that everyone — from kids to even the stodgiest adult — can enjoy once in a while (assuming you have a good dentist on call). This recipe is more nuanced than most: The caramel coating is made with maple syrup and a little apple juice, and the apples are then coated with toasted walnuts. I suggest using smaller apples, so there's a high ratio of caramel to apple, and prefer ones that are slightly tart, such as Pink Lady, Cameo, Braeburn, and Jonathan.

**MAKES 8 CARAMEL APPLES**

SPECIAL EQUIPMENT:
8 wooden caramel apple sticks; candy thermometer

8 small slightly tart apples, preferably organic

1 cup (242 g/8.5 oz) heavy cream

8 tablespoons (113 g/4 oz) unsalted butter, cut into tablespoons

½ teaspoon (3.3 g/0.19 oz) salt

1 cup (200 g/7 oz) granulated sugar

¼ cup (60 g/2.1 oz) apple juice

½ cup (150 g/5.3 oz) maple syrup (Grade A)

¼ cup (80 g/2.8 oz) light corn syrup

1 cup (100 g/3.5 oz) walnuts, toasted (see page 13) and finely chopped

1. If your apples are not organic, scrub them well under warm water to remove the wax, then dry them thoroughly (this will help to make the caramel stick). Stick a wooden caramel apple stick through the stem end of each apple and place the apples on a baking sheet lined with a silicone baking mat or piece of parchment paper.

2. Combine the cream, butter, and salt in a small saucepan and bring to a gentle boil over medium-high heat. Remove the pan from the heat.

3. Combine the sugar, apple juice, maple syrup, and corn syrup in a medium (3-quart) saucepan and place over medium-high heat. Bring to a boil, stirring just until the sugar is dissolved. Stop stirring and continue to boil the mixture until it turns a dark amber color, 5 to 7 minutes. Remove the pan from the heat and stir in the hot cream mixture. Reduce the heat to medium-low and simmer the syrup until it reaches 248°F on a candy thermometer. Remove the pan from the heat and let the caramel cool for about 1 minute. Dip an apple in the caramel, tilting the pan so the caramel pools at one end and swirling the apple to cover it completely. Let the excess caramel drip off the apple and then place it, stem end up, on the baking sheet. Repeat with remaining apples and caramel. Let the apples stand at room temperature for 15 minutes.

4. Press the chopped walnuts around the sides of each apple, leaving a 1-inch border around the stem. Let the apples stand at room temperature for 1 hour to set the caramel. Store the apples at room temperature, draped with plastic wrap, for up to 2 days.

# Apple Fritters

*At first glance,* these look like flattened doughnuts, but tucked inside the crunchy fried exterior is a warm, soft ring of apple. A coating of cinnamon sugar balances the tartness of the apple, while the rich rum sauce turns this comfort food into a full-fledged and decadent dessert.

MAKES 18 FRITTERS, SERVING 6

SPECIAL EQUIPMENT:
Deep-frying or candy thermometer

CINNAMON SUGAR

½ cup (100 g/3.5 oz) granulated sugar

¾ teaspoon (1.5 g/0.05 oz) ground cinnamon

Pinch of salt

BUTTERMILK FRITTER BATTER

1⅓ cups (176 g/6.2 oz) all-purpose flour

½ cup (100 g/3.5 oz) granulated sugar

¾ teaspoon (1.5 g/0.05 oz) ground cinnamon

¼ teaspoon (1.6 g/0.06 oz) salt

3 large eggs, separated

1 tablespoon (14 g/0.5 oz) unsalted butter, melted, cooled

1 teaspoon (4 g/0.14 oz) vanilla extract

¾ cup (181 g/6.4 oz) buttermilk

APPLES

2 medium (453 g/1 lb) Granny Smith apples

Vegetable oil, for frying

Brown Sugar–Rum Sauce (page 22), for serving

## Make the cinnamon sugar

1. In a wide, shallow bowl, whisk together the sugar, cinnamon, and salt and set aside.

## Make the fritter batter

2. In a medium bowl, stir together the flour, sugar, cinnamon, and salt until evenly blended. In a large bowl, whisk together the egg yolks, melted butter, and vanilla. Whisk in the flour mixture in three additions, alternating with the buttermilk in two additions and mixing just until combined. Set the batter aside at room temperature.

3. Peel, core, and slice the apples into ¼-inch-thick rings.

4. In the bowl of an electric mixer fitted with the whisk attachment, beat the egg whites at medium-high speed to soft peaks. Using a spatula, gently fold one-third of the whites into the batter. Fold in the remaining whites.

## Coat the apples and fry the fritters

5. Line a baking sheet with paper towels. Pour enough oil into a large, heavy, high-sided skillet so that it comes about 2 inches up the sides. Heat the oil until it registers 375°F on a deep-fat or candy thermometer. Coat the apple rings in batter, three or four at a time, and fry in the oil until golden brown, about 1½ minutes on each side. Transfer the fritters to the paper towel–lined baking sheet to drain for a few seconds, then toss them in the Cinnamon Sugar and serve warm with the Brown Sugar–Rum Sauce.

*Apple*

# Apple Strudel

*Strudel purists and* natives of Vienna may turn their collective noses up at this recipe, which calls for using store-bought phyllo instead of the traditional homemade strudel dough. But if you don't have the time, space, or patience to devote to making and rolling out the classic paper-thin dough, using flaky phyllo is an excellent alternative, and makes the recipe so much easier to put together. The filling is not overly sweet—apple has the starring role here, with golden raisins, musky cinnamon, and finely chopped almonds enhancing their flavor. Panko crumbs soak up all the lovely juice, preventing it from running out of the strudel during baking. Serve this warm, with a scoop of ice cream or generous spoonful of *schlag* (whipped cream) on the side.

MAKES 6 SERVINGS

### APPLE FILLING

2 tablespoons (28 g/1 oz) unsalted butter

About 3 large (680 g/1½ lbs) Granny Smith apples, peeled, cored, and sliced ¼ inch thick

⅔ cup firmly packed (144 g/ 5 oz) light brown sugar

½ cup (121 g/4.3 oz) apple cider or juice

2 tablespoons (30 g/1 oz) freshly squeezed lemon juice

2 tablespoons (30 g/1 oz) brandy

½ cup (70 g/2.5 oz) golden raisins

¼ teaspoon (0.16 g/0.005 oz) ground cinnamon

### STRUDEL

¼ cup (21 g/0.75 oz) sliced almonds

⅓ cup (28 g/1 oz) panko bread crumbs

8 (9-by-14-inch) sheets phyllo dough

7 tablespoons (99 g/3.5 oz) unsalted butter, melted

## *Make the filling*

1. Melt the butter in a large skillet over medium-high heat. Add the apple slices and cook, stirring, for about 1 minute. Sprinkle the brown sugar over the apples and continue to cook over medium-high heat, stirring constantly, for about another 3 minutes, or until the sugar is dissolved. Add the apple cider, lemon juice, brandy, raisins, and cinnamon and bring the liquid to a boil. Continue to cook, stirring constantly, for 7 to 10 minutes, until the apples are tender and mostly translucent and most of the liquid has cooked off. The remaining liquid should be thick and syrupy. Cool the apples, then transfer them to a covered shallow container and refrigerate for at least 1 hour.

## *Assemble the strudel*

2. Preheat the oven to 375°F. Line a baking sheet with a silicone baking mat or piece of parchment paper.

3. Place the almonds in the bowl of a food processor and process until finely ground. Transfer them to a small bowl and combine with the bread crumbs.

4. Unroll the phyllo sheets and place them on a work surface. Cover them with a piece of plastic wrap and then a damp kitchen towel to prevent them from drying out as you work. Place one of the sheets

on a piece of parchment paper or waxed paper and brush it all over
with some of the melted butter. Sprinkle the phyllo sheet with
1 tablespoon of the crumb mixture. Top with another phyllo sheet
and repeat, using all 8 phyllo sheets, as much butter as you need,
and the remaining crumb mixture (use all of the remaining crumb
mixture for the final layer).

**5.** Spoon the chilled apple filling along one long side of the phyllo,
leaving a ½-inch border on the long side and the short sides of the
phyllo and allowing it to spread about 3 inches toward the center.
Fold ½ inch of the short sides in toward the center. Fold the long
edge over the filling and roll up the strudel jelly roll–style, using the
paper as a guide and arranging the strudel so that the seam side is
down. Transfer the strudel to the prepared baking sheet and brush it
with the remaining butter.

**6.** Bake for 25 minutes, until golden brown all over. Let cool on the
baking sheet for 15 minutes.

**7.** The strudel is best served warm. Transfer the warm strudel to a
cutting surface. Dust with sifted confectioners' sugar right before
serving. Using a serrated knife, cut into 2-inch slices.

# Apple Croissant Bread Pudding

*Originally a thrifty* and simple way to use up stale bread, bread pudding has evolved into a dessert sophisticated enough to be served in upscale restaurants, where it's frequently made with brioche or croissants. This version features croissants coated with apple butter and layered with apple cubes that have been sautéed in butter and sugar. Baking the pudding in a water bath ensures a creamy texture—without it, the custard will break, and it won't be pretty. If you don't have time to make your own apple butter, feel free to use a high-quality jarred one.

**MAKES 6 SERVINGS**

2 tablespoons (28 g/1 oz) unsalted butter

2 medium (453 g/1 lb) Granny Smith or Braeburn apples, peeled, cored, and cut into ½-inch cubes

¾ cup (150 g/5.3 oz) granulated sugar, divided

6 tablespoons (114 g/4 oz) Apple Butter (page 14), divided

1½ cups (363 g/12.8 oz) whole milk

1⅓ cups (309 g/10.9 oz) heavy cream

1 cinnamon stick

3 large all-butter croissants, either fresh or 1 day old

3 large eggs

1 teaspoon (4 g/0.14 oz) vanilla extract

2 tablespoons plus 1½ teaspoons (37 g/1.3 oz) brandy or dark rum

1. Butter the interior of a shallow 1½-quart baking dish (I used a 12-by-8-inch oval).

2. In a large skillet, heat the butter over high heat until melted and foamy. Add the apples and cook, stirring, for about 1 minute. Sprinkle ¼ cup (50 g/1.76 oz) of the sugar on top of the apples and add 1 tablespoon of the apple butter; continue to cook, stirring frequently, until the apples are slightly tender, about 4 minutes. Remove the skillet from the heat and set aside to cool.

3. Combine the milk, cream, and cinnamon stick in a small saucepan and cook over medium-high heat until the mixture just begins to boil. Remove the pan from the heat.

4. Using a serrated knife, cut each croissant in half crosswise (as if you were going to use them for a sandwich). Spread each cut side of 2 bottom halves and 3 top halves with 1 tablespoon apple butter. Cut the remaining bottom half into ½-inch cubes. Arrange the apple butter–coated bottom halves of the croissants in the bottom of the prepared baking dish. Scatter the croissant cubes in the empty areas of the pan. Scatter the cooked apple cubes on top of the croissants. Cut each of the croissant tops in half to make half-crescent shapes and arrange them, cut side down, over the apples.

5. In a medium bowl, whisk the eggs with the remaining ½ cup (100 g/3.5 oz) sugar until well blended. Remove the cinnamon stick from the warm milk mixture and gradually whisk the liquid into the egg mixture. Whisk in the vanilla and brandy. Slowly pour

the liquid into the baking dish, over the croissants. Spoon the custard mixture over the croissant tops so they will be glazed when baked. Allow the unbaked pudding to stand at room temperature for 30 minutes before baking. Meanwhile, preheat the oven to 325°F.

**6.** Place the pan of bread pudding into a larger pan, such as a roasting pan. Pour enough hot water into the roasting pan so that it comes about 1 inch up the sides of the baking dish. Cover the pan with a piece of buttered aluminum foil and bake for 30 minutes. Remove the foil and bake for another 15 to 20 minutes, until the pudding is just set and slightly puffed around the edges. Let cool on a wire rack for at least 15 minutes before serving. Cover any leftover pudding and refrigerate for up to 5 days.

# Apple Crostata with Whole Wheat–Rosemary Crust

*A cousin of* the French galette, the Italian *crostata* is a rustic, open-faced tart. I've emphasized the "rustic" by adding whole wheat flour and fresh rosemary to the crust, which gives it a subtle, woodsy flavor that works nicely with the sweet-tart apples. Sprinkling panko crumbs over the dough before baking is a trick I use to sop up some of the liquid from the apples, preventing the crust from getting soggy and heavy. The *crostata* does not keep well, but, happily, you won't have any trouble finishing it off in a day.

MAKES ONE 10-INCH *CROSTATA*, SERVING 6

## WHOLE WHEAT-ROSEMARY DOUGH

1 cup plus 2 tablespoons (150 g/5.3 oz) all-purpose flour

¼ cup (31 g/1 oz) whole wheat flour

1 teaspoon (1 g/0.03 oz) chopped fresh rosemary leaves

2 teaspoons (8 g/0.3 oz) granulated sugar

¼ teaspoon (1.6 g/0.06 oz) salt

9 tablespoons (127 g/4.5 oz) unsalted butter, cut into ½-inch pieces and frozen for 20 minutes

3 tablespoons (44 g/1.5 oz) ice-cold water

½ teaspoon (2.5 g/0.09 oz) white vinegar

## STREUSEL TOPPING

¼ cup (33 g/1.16 oz) all-purpose flour

2 tablespoons (14 g/0.5 oz) chopped walnuts

2 tablespoons firmly packed (27 g/1 oz) light brown sugar

(CONTINUED)

### Make the dough

1. Place the flours, rosemary, sugar, and salt in the bowl of a food processor and pulse a few times to combine. Add the butter pieces and toss lightly with a spoon to coat them with flour. Blend the butter and flour with about five 1-second pulses, or until the mixture is the texture of coarse meal with some butter pieces the size of peas. Sprinkle the water and vinegar over the flour mixture and process continuously until the dough begins to clump together. Do not overprocess; the dough should not form a ball on the blade. Turn the dough out onto a work surface and shape it into a thick 4-inch-wide disc. Wrap the dough in plastic wrap and refrigerate until firm enough to roll, about 1 hour.

2. Place the unwrapped dough on a lightly floured work surface. Roll out the dough into a 12-inch circle, lifting and rotating the dough often and dusting the work surface and dough lightly with flour as necessary. Roll the dough up on the rolling pin and unroll it onto a baking sheet. Refrigerate the dough on the sheet while you make the topping and filling.

### Make the topping

3. In the bowl of a food processor, combine the flour, walnuts, brown sugar, cinnamon, and salt and process until the walnuts are

⅛ teaspoon (0.25 g/0.009 oz) ground cinnamon

Pinch of salt

2 tablespoons (28 g/1 oz) unsalted butter, melted

APPLE FILLING

2 tablespoons (28 g/1 oz) unsalted butter

½ cup firmly packed (108 g/ 3.8 oz) light brown sugar

¼ cup (60 g/2.1 oz) apple juice or water

3 medium (680 g/1.5 lb) Granny Smith or Braeburn apples, peeled, cored, and sliced into ½-inch wedges

½ teaspoon (1 g/0.03 oz) ground cinnamon

¾ cup (75 g/2.6 oz) walnuts, toasted (see page 13) and coarsely chopped

½ cup (70 g/2.5 oz) raisins

1 teaspoon (2 g/0.07 oz) finely grated lemon zest

Pinch of salt

2 tablespoons (30 g/1 oz) Calvados or brandy (optional)

ASSEMBLY

1 large egg, whisked with 1 teaspoon water, for egg wash

⅔ cup (56 g/2 oz) panko bread crumbs

finely ground. Add the melted butter and pulse the machine until the mixture is crumbly. Set the topping aside.

## Make the filling

4. Preheat the oven to 375°F. Melt the butter over medium-high heat in a large skillet. Add the brown sugar, apple juice, apples, and cinnamon and cook, stirring, until the apples have softened but still offer a slight resistance when pierced with a fork and the liquid is reduced to a syrup, about 5 minutes. Remove the skillet from the heat and stir in the walnuts, raisins, lemon zest, salt, and Calvados, if using. Set aside to cool for 10 minutes.

## Assemble and bake the crostata

5. Brush the egg wash around about 1 inch of the outer edge of the chilled dough round. Sprinkle the bread crumbs in the center of the dough, up to the egg-washed border. Spoon the apple filling over the crumbs. Fold the egg-washed edge of dough over the filling. Sprinkle the apple filling with the streusel topping. Brush the edge of the dough well with the egg wash.

6. Bake the *crostata* for 25 to 30 minutes, until the pastry is golden brown around the edges. Let cool on the baking sheet for 10 minutes, then transfer the *crostata* to a serving plate and cut into wedges to serve.

*Apple*

# Apple and Almond Tart

*I love this classic* French tart. A buttery almond crust is filled with a very almond-y cream filling and then topped off with thin slices of apple. Because it's made with almonds, the tart dough is a little delicate to work with, but it can easily be patched, if necessary. The apricot glaze, brushed on after baking, makes this tart look like it came straight from a Paris pastry shop.

MAKE ONE 11-INCH TART, SERVING 10

## ALMOND TART CRUST

¾ cup (64 g/2.24 oz) unblanched sliced almonds

2 tablespoons (25 g/0.88 oz) granulated sugar

1 cup (132 g/4.6 oz) all-purpose flour

⅛ teaspoon (0.83 g/0.03 oz) salt

8 tablespoons (113 g/4 oz) unsalted butter, cut into ½-inch cubes and frozen for at least 20 minutes

1 large egg yolk

2 tablespoons (30 g/1 oz) ice-cold water

## ALMOND CREAM AND APPLE FILLING

Almond Cream (page 15)

2 medium (453 g/1 lb) Granny Smith apples

2 teaspoons (30 g/1 oz) freshly squeezed lemon juice

¼ cup firmly packed (54 g/ 1.9 oz) light brown sugar, divided

## GARNISH

⅓ cup (100 g/3.5 oz) apricot preserves

⅓ cup (28 g/1 oz) unblanched sliced almonds (optional)

## *Make the crust*

**1.** In the bowl of a food processor, pulse the almonds and sugar until the nuts are finely ground. Add the flour and salt and pulse to combine. Add the butter and, using a fork, toss with the flour until coated. Pulse the mixture until the butter pieces are about the size of small peas. In a small bowl, stir together the egg yolk and water with a fork. Add the yolk mixture to the processor and pulse until the mixture just starts to come together. Transfer the dough to a work surface, gather together, and shape into a 5-inch disc. Wrap in plastic wrap and refrigerate for at least 1 hour before rolling out.

**2.** Place the unwrapped dough on a lightly floured work surface. Roll out the dough to a 13-inch circle, lifting and rotating the dough often and dusting the work surface and dough lightly with flour as necessary. Roll the dough up on the rolling pin and unroll it over an 11-inch fluted tart pan with a removable bottom. Gently press the dough onto the bottom and up the sides of the pan. Roll the pin over the top of the pan to trim off the excess dough. Prick the bottom of the tart shell with a fork at ½-inch intervals. Refrigerate the tart shell for 30 minutes.

**3.** Preheat the oven to 375°F. Spray the dull side of a 12-inch square of aluminum foil with nonstick cooking spray. Line the tart shell with the foil, dull side down, and fill with pie weights or dried beans. Place the tart pan on a baking sheet and bake for 15 minutes. Carefully lift the foil (along with the weights) out of the tart pan and bake the crust for about 7 minutes longer, until just beginning to brown lightly. Leave the oven on. Transfer the tart pan to a wire rack and let cool completely.

## Fill the tart

**4.** Spread the Almond Cream into the cooled tart shell in an even layer. Refrigerate the tart while you prepare the apple filling.

## Prepare the filling and bake the tart

**5.** Peel and core the apples and cut them in half. Cut each half into ¼-inch slices and place the slices in a medium bowl. Sprinkle the lemon juice over the apples and toss to coat. Toss 3 tablespoons (40 g/ 1.4 oz) of the brown sugar with the apple slices.

**6.** Arrange the apple slices in concentric circles over the almond cream in the tart, overlapping the slices slightly and covering the cream. Sprinkle the apples with the remaining 1 tablespoon (13.5 g/ 0.5 oz) brown sugar. Place the tart pan on a baking sheet and bake for 40 to 45 minutes, until the filling and apples are nicely browned. Cool the tart in the pan set on a wire rack for 30 minutes.

## Garnish the tart

**7.** Place the apricot preserves in a heatproof glass measuring cup and microwave on high power for about 30 seconds, or until bubbling. Strain the hot preserves through a fine-mesh sieve into a small bowl. Brush the strained apricot preserves over the top of the tart.

**8.** If you want to garnish the tart with almonds, cook them in a skillet over medium heat, tossing or stirring frequently, until lightly toasted. Cool completely.

**9.** Sprinkle the top of the tart with the toasted almonds. Serve the tart at room temperature.

# Classic Tarte Tatin

*Warm and comforting,* this French tart features chunks of juicy, caramel-coated apples clinging to a base of buttery puff pastry. To ensure success, you'll need either a 9½- or 10-inch ovenproof skillet, such as a cast iron or enamel-coated one, or a tarte tatin pan. A tarte tatin pan has two handles on opposite sides, making unmolding the hot tart relatively easy. For the apples, I like to use either Granny Smith or Braeburn, because they hold their shape and are slightly tart. The sprinkling of pistachios on top is not classic, but I like the color and texture they bring to the tart.

MAKES ONE 9½- OR 10-INCH TART, SERVING 8

SPECIAL EQUIPMENT:
Tarte tatin pan or 9½- or 10-inch ovenproof skillet

1 sheet (227 g/8 oz) puff pastry (homemade, page 16, or store-bought frozen, thawed)

8 tablespoons (113 g/4 oz) unsalted butter, cut into tablespoons

⅔ cup (133 g/4.7 oz) granulated sugar

4 medium apples (907 g/2 lb), peeled, cored, and quartered lengthwise

½ teaspoon (1 g/0.03 oz) finely grated lemon zest

¼ cup (38 g/1.3 oz) unsalted shelled pistachios, chopped

1. Preheat the oven to 375°F. On a lightly floured work surface, roll out the puff pastry to a thickness of ⅛ inch (if you are using store-bought pastry, you may have to roll it a little thinner to make a large enough circle). Using a plate as a guide, cut a circle from the dough 1 inch larger than the diameter of your skillet. Transfer the round to a baking sheet that has been lined with waxed or parchment paper, cover with plastic wrap, and refrigerate until ready to use.

2. In a 9½- or 10-inch ovenproof skillet or tarte tatin pan, melt the butter over medium-low heat. Remove from the heat and stir in the sugar over the butter. Add the apple quarters, placing them cut side up and arranging them snugly in concentric circles to cover the bottom of the pan (you may have some left over). Cook over medium-high heat until the sugar mixture turns golden brown, 6 to 7 minutes. Remove from the heat and let cool for 5 minutes.

3. Sprinkle the lemon zest over the apples and place the dough circle on top, tucking the edges down between the side of the pan and the apples so that they are encased. Place the pan on a baking sheet and bake for 25 to 30 minutes, until the dough has risen and is golden brown. Let the tart cool for 5 minutes.

4. Put on potholders and place a large rimmed cake plate (or any plate that is larger than the pan and is not a family heirloom) upside down on top of the pan. Holding the pan and plate tightly together, quickly — but carefully, as the caramel is hot — invert both, so that the plate is on the bottom. Carefully remove the pan. Sprinkle the tart with the pistachios and serve warm (within an hour).

# Applesauce Cake with Maple–Cream Cheese Frosting and Candied Walnuts

*The flavors of apple,* maple, and walnut combine harmoniously in this homey cake. It's served straight from the pan and topped with a maple-flavored frosting and lots of crunchy, sugar-crusted walnuts. I use turbinado instead of white sugar for the cake, which gives it a coarser texture and a hint of molasses flavor. For the frosting, try to find pure maple extract — it's available at gourmet stores and from multiple sources online, such as kingarthurflour.com, and it will make all the difference in your cake. If you can't find it locally and prefer not to order it online, you can simply omit it, increase the confectioners' sugar to 1¼ cups, and add 2 tablespoons of Grade B maple syrup (available in supermarkets). The flavor won't be as bold but will still have a mellow hint of maple. To bump up the maple flavor, you can also drizzle a little maple syrup on top of each cake square right before serving.

MAKES ONE 9-INCH CAKE, SERVING 9

## APPLESAUCE CAKE

2 cups (265 g/9.3 oz) all-purpose flour

¾ teaspoon (3.75 g/0.13 oz) baking powder

¼ teaspoon (1.25 g/0.04 oz) baking soda

¼ plus ⅛ teaspoon (2.5 g/ 0.08 oz) salt

¾ teaspoon (1.5 g/0.05 oz) ground cinnamon

½ teaspoon (1 g/0.03 oz) ground ginger

⅛ teaspoon (0.25 g/0.009 oz) ground cloves

11 tablespoons (155 g/5.4 oz) unsalted butter, softened

1¼ cups (250 g/8.8 oz) turbinado sugar

2 large eggs

1 teaspoon (4 g/0.14 oz) vanilla extract

(CONTINUED)

## Make the cake

1. Preheat the oven to 350°F. Butter the bottom and sides of a 9-inch square baking pan and dust the pan with flour.

2. In a medium bowl, sift together the flour, baking powder, baking soda, salt, cinnamon, ginger, and cloves and whisk to combine.

3. In the bowl of an electric mixer fitted with the paddle attachment, beat the butter at medium-high speed until creamy, about 1 minute. Gradually add the turbinado sugar and beat at high speed until very light, about 6 minutes. Reduce the speed to medium and add the eggs one at a time, mixing well after each addition and stopping to scrape down the sides of the bowl with a rubber spatula as necessary. Add the vanilla and mix until blended. Reduce the speed to low and add the flour mixture in three additions, alternating with the applesauce in two additions and beginning and ending with the flour mixture. Mix just until barely blended. Add the walnuts and mix just until combined. Remove the bowl from the mixer and stir the batter a few times with a rubber spatula to ensure that it is blended. Scrape the batter into the prepared pan and smooth the top.

1 cup (242 g/8.5 oz) unsweetened applesauce

¾ cup (75 g/2.6 oz) walnuts, chopped

MAPLE-CREAM CHEESE FROSTING

1 cup (227 g/8 oz) cream cheese, at room temperature

8 tablespoons (113 g/4 oz) unsalted butter, at room temperature

1 cup (128 g/4.5 oz) confectioners' sugar

½ teaspoon (2 g/0.07 oz) vanilla extract

¼ teaspoon (1 g/0.03 oz) pure maple extract

Pinch of salt

GARNISH

Candied Walnuts (page 13)

**4.** Bake the cake for 40 to 45 minutes, until the top is golden brown and a toothpick inserted into the center of the cake comes out clean. Let the cake cool in the pan set on a wire rack.

## Make the frosting and frost the cake

**5.** In the bowl of an electric mixer fitted with the whisk attachment, beat the cream cheese, butter, confectioners' sugar, vanilla, maple extract, and salt together at medium speed until blended. Raise the speed to high and beat until stiff peaks form, about 5 minutes.

**6.** Swirl the frosting decoratively over the top of the cake in the pan. Sprinkle the Candied Walnuts on top and cut squares of the cake from the pan. Store the cake, loosely covered with plastic wrap, in the refrigerator. Bring the cake to room temperature before serving.

*Apple*

# Sour Cream–Apple Spice Cake with Brandied Cider Glaze

*Everyone should have* an apple cake like this in their baking repertoire. It's versatile enough to be served as is for brunch, or as a more formal dessert with a drizzle of Classic Caramel Sauce (page 252) and a scoop of Caramel Cream (page 18) or vanilla ice cream. Sour cream gives the cake a tender crumb, and a caramel-colored glaze made with apple cider, butter, and a little brandy gives it warm flavor and a glossy sheen. Feel free to substitute walnuts for the pecans, or, if you don't like nuts, leave them out entirely.

MAKES ONE 9-INCH CAKE, SERVING 8 TO 10

## SOUR CREAM-APPLE CAKE

1 teaspoon (15 g/0.5 oz) freshly squeezed lemon juice

2 large (454 g/1 lb) tart apples, such as Granny Smith or Braeburn

14 tablespoons (197 g/7 oz) unsalted butter, softened, divided

1¼ cups plus 2 tablespoons firmly packed (297 g/10.5 oz) light brown sugar, divided

1 cup (132 g/4.6 oz) all-purpose flour

¾ cup (85 g/3 oz) cake flour

1½ teaspoons (7.5 g/0.25 oz) baking powder

½ teaspoon (2.5 g/0.09 oz) baking soda

¼ plus ⅛ teaspoon (2.5 g/ 0.09 oz) salt

1 teaspoon (2 g/0.07 oz) ground cinnamon

¼ teaspoon (0.5 g/0.017 oz) freshly grated nutmeg

¼ teaspoon (0.5 g/0.017 oz) ground cloves

2 large eggs

(CONTINUED)

## Make the cake

1. Preheat the oven to 350°F. Butter the bottom and sides of a 9-inch springform pan well and dust with flour.

2. Place the lemon juice in a medium bowl. Peel and core the apples, then cut them into ¼-inch cubes and toss them with the lemon juice.

3. In a large skillet, melt 2 tablespoons (28 g/1 oz) of the butter over medium-high heat. Add the apples and cook, stirring frequently, for about 2 minutes. Sprinkle 2 tablespoons (27 g/1 oz) of the brown sugar on top and continue to cook, stirring constantly, until the apples have softened but not browned, 3 to 4 minutes. Remove the skillet from the heat and let the apples cool.

4. In a medium bowl, whisk together the flours, baking powder, baking soda, salt, cinnamon, nutmeg, and cloves.

5. In the bowl of an electric mixer fitted with the paddle attachment, beat the remaining 12 tablespoons (170 g/6 oz) butter at medium-high speed until creamy, about 1 minute. Gradually add the remaining 1¼ cups (270 g/9.5 oz) brown sugar and beat at high speed until very light and fluffy, about 4 minutes. Reduce the speed to medium and add the eggs one a time, beating well after each addition and scraping down the sides of the bowl with a rubber

½ cup (121 g/4.3 oz) sour cream

1 teaspoon (4 g/0.14 z) vanilla extract

½ cup (50 g/1.76 oz) pecans, coarsely chopped

**BRANDIED CIDER GLAZE**

3 tablespoons (42 g/1.5 oz) unsalted butter, cut into 3 pieces

½ cup firmly packed (108 g/ 3.8 oz) light brown sugar

¼ cup (60 g/2.1 oz) apple cider

1 tablespoon (15 g/0.5 oz) brandy

spatula as necessary. In a small bowl, stir together the sour cream and vanilla. Reduce the mixer speed to low and add the dry ingredients in three additions, alternating with the sour cream in two additions and mixing just until blended. Remove the bowl from the mixer stand and, using a rubber spatula, blend in the cooled apples. Scrape the batter into the prepared pan and sprinkle with the pecans.

6. Bake the cake for 55 to 65 minutes, until a toothpick inserted into the center comes out clean. Place the pan on a wire rack and let the cake cool while you make the glaze.

## Make the glaze and glaze the cake

7. Melt the butter in a small saucepan over medium-high heat. Add the brown sugar and cook, stirring, until the sugar is dissolved. Stir in the cider and brandy and bring to a boil. Boil for about 1 minute, until slightly thickened. Remove the pan from the heat and let cool for 5 minutes.

8. Run a paring knife around the side of the warm cake and remove the side of the pan. Brush the glaze over the top and sides of the cake.

9. You can either serve the cake warm (in which case you should leave it on the pan bottom), or let it cool completely (then slide it onto a serving plate).

# Streusel-Topped Sour Cream Apple Pie

*Everyone has their own* idea of the perfect apple pie, and here's mine. The filling is flavored with the typical apple pie spices—cinnamon, cloves, and nutmeg—but a handful of chopped crystallized ginger gives it added warmth and zing. Sour cream enriches the filling and offers a tangy complement to the apples. The pie is topped with a delicious layer of almond streusel instead of an upper crust, which has the added bonus of making the pie relatively easy to put together. Serve each slice with a scoop of vanilla ice cream or a drizzle of heavy cream.

MAKES ONE 9-INCH DEEP-DISH PIE, SERVING 8

SPECIAL EQUIPMENT:
9-inch deep-dish pie pan

PIE DOUGH

1¼ cups (165 g/5.8 oz) all-purpose flour

¼ teaspoon (1.6 g/0.06 oz) salt

9 tablespoons (127 g/4.5 oz) unsalted butter, cut into ½-inch chunks and frozen for 15 minutes

1½ teaspoons (7 g/0.25 oz) apple cider vinegar or white vinegar

3 to 4 tablespoons (44 g/ 1.5 oz to 59 g/2 oz) ice-cold water

APPLE FILLING

About 6 medium (1.36 kg/ 3 lb) apples, preferably Granny Smith, peeled, cored, and halved

1 tablespoon (15 g/0.5 oz) freshly squeezed lemon juice

⅓ cup (80 g/2.8 oz) sour cream

⅔ cup firmly packed (144 g/ 5 oz) light brown sugar

⅓ cup (66 g/2.3 oz) granulated sugar

(CONTINUED)

## Make the dough

**1.** Place the flour and salt in the bowl of a food processor and pulse until combined. Scatter the butter pieces over the flour mixture. Pulse until the mixture resembles coarse meal. Mix the vinegar with 3 tablespoons of the water, add it to the flour mixture, and process until the dough just starts to come together. (If the dough seems dry, add the remaining 1 tablespoon water as necessary. Do not allow the dough to form a ball on the blade, or the resulting crust will be tough.)

**2.** Turn the dough out onto a work surface and shape it into a thick disc. Wrap the disc in plastic wrap and refrigerate for at least 2 hours.

**3.** Allow the dough to soften at room temperature just until it is pliable (about 20 minutes). Place the dough on a lightly floured work surface and sprinkle some flour over it. Roll out the dough from the center in every direction, flouring the work surface as necessary to prevent sticking. You want a round about ⅛ inch thick, or slightly less, and about 12 inches in diameter.

**4.** Transfer the crust to a 9-inch deep-dish pie pan by rolling it loosely around the rolling pin and unrolling it carefully over the pan. Press the dough first into the bottom of the pan and then against the sides. Patch any holes or cracks with dough scraps. Trim the edges of the dough with scissors, leaving about ¾ inch

3 tablespoons (30 g/1 oz) chopped crystallized ginger

2 tablespoons plus 1½ teaspoons (19 g/0.66 oz) cornstarch

1 teaspoon (5 g/0.17 oz) finely grated lemon zest

1 teaspoon (2 g/0.07 oz) ground cinnamon

¼ teaspoon (0.5 g/0.017 oz) finely grated nutmeg

¼ teaspoon (0.5 g/0.02 oz) ground cloves

½ teaspoon (3 g/0.12 oz) salt

1 tablespoon (14 g/0.5 oz) cold unsalted butter, cut into ¼-inch pieces

STREUSEL TOPPING

½ cup (66 g/2.3 oz) all-purpose flour

¼ cup (30 g/1 oz) slivered almonds

3 tablespoons firmly packed (40 g/1.4 oz) light brown sugar

½ teaspoon (1 g/0.03 oz) ground cinnamon

Pinch of salt

3 tablespoons (42 g/1.5 oz) unsalted butter, melted

½ teaspoon (2 g/0.07 oz) vanilla extract

of overhang. Fold the dough underneath itself and crimp the edge with your fingers. Refrigerate the dough while you make the filling.

## Make the filling

**5.** Preheat the oven to 375°F. Cut the apple halves into thin slices (about ¼ inch thick) and place them in a large bowl. Sprinkle them with the lemon juice, add the sour cream, and toss to combine. In a small bowl, stir together the sugars, ginger, cornstarch, lemon zest, cinnamon, nutmeg, cloves, and salt. Sprinkle the sugar mixture over the apple slices and toss well to combine. Spoon the filling into the pie dough (it will be piled fairly high) and press it down to compact it a bit. Dot the filling with the butter pieces.

## Make the streusel topping and bake the pie

**6.** In a food processor, pulse together the flour, almonds, brown sugar, cinnamon, and salt until the almonds are finely chopped. Combine the melted butter with the vanilla and add to the flour mixture. Pulse until the mixture is crumbly. Sprinkle the top of the pie evenly with the streusel, so that it covers the apples right up to the edge.

**7.** Place the pie pan on a baking sheet and bake the pie for 30 minutes. Cover the top of the pie with a piece of foil, and continue to bake until the apples are cooked through, about 1 hour longer. Remove the foil and bake for another 15 to 20 minutes, until the top and crust are golden. Remove the pie from the oven and let cool on a wire rack for at least 1 hour before serving.

# Apple Spice Cupcakes with Brown Sugar—Cinnamon Buttercream

*Here are the* flavors of fall, all wrapped up in a powerful little cupcake. Shredded apples and apple juice combine to make a moist, flavorful cupcake, and a generous swirl of cinnamon-spiced buttercream is an irresistible topping. The recipe can easily be doubled.

**MAKES 12 CUPCAKES**

**SPECIAL EQUIPMENT:**
Instant-read thermometer

**APPLE CUPCAKES**

1½ cups (199 g/7 oz) all-purpose flour

¾ teaspoon (3.75 g/0.13 oz) baking soda

¼ teaspoon (1.25 g/0.04 oz) baking powder

½ teaspoon (3.3 g/0.12 oz) salt

1 teaspoon (2 g/0.07 oz) ground cinnamon

½ teaspoon (1 g/0.03 oz) ground ginger

8 tablespoons (113 g/4 oz) unsalted butter, softened

½ cup firmly packed (108 g/3.8 oz) light brown sugar

¼ cup (50 g/1.76 oz) granulated sugar

1 large egg

⅓ cup (80 g/2.8 oz) apple juice or whole milk

1 teaspoon (4 g/0.14 oz) vanilla extract

1 cup (140 g/5 oz) shredded apple, from 1 peeled and cored large tart apple such as Granny Smith, Pink Lady, or Braeburn

(CONTINUED)

## Make the cupcakes

1. Preheat the oven to 350°F. Line a standard 12-cup muffin pan with cupcake liners.

2. In a medium bowl, sift together the flour, baking soda, baking powder, salt, cinnamon, and ginger and gently whisk to combine.

3. In the bowl of an electric mixer fitted with the paddle attachment, beat the butter at medium-high speed until creamy, about 1 minute. Gradually add the sugars and beat at high speed until light and fluffy, about 3 minutes. Reduce the speed to medium and add the egg, beating until completely blended and scraping down the sides of the bowl with a rubber spatula as necessary. In a small bowl, stir together the apple juice and vanilla. Reduce the mixer speed to low and add the flour mixture in three additions, alternating with the apple juice in two additions and mixing just until blended. Remove the bowl from the mixer stand and, using a rubber spatula, blend in the apple and pecans.

4. Divide the batter evenly among the muffins cups and bake for 25 to 28 minutes, until a toothpick inserted into the center of each cupcake comes out clean. Place the muffin pan on a wire rack and let the cupcakes cool completely.

¾ cup (85 g/3 oz) coarsely
chopped pecans or walnuts,
toasted (see page 13)

BROWN SUGAR-CINNAMON
BUTTERCREAM

2 large egg whites

½ cup firmly packed (108 g/
3.8 oz) light brown sugar

1 tablespoon plus 1½ teaspoons
(22 g/0.8 oz) water

12 tablespoons (170 g/6 oz)
unsalted butter, slightly
softened

½ teaspoon (2 g/0.07 oz)
vanilla extract

⅛ teaspoon (0.25 g/0.009 oz)
ground cinnamon

GARNISH

Ground cinnamon

## Make the buttercream and finish the cupcakes

5. Pour enough water into a skillet so that it comes ½ inch up its sides. Bring the water to a simmer; reduce the heat to medium-low to maintain a simmer.

6. In the bowl of an electric mixer, combine the egg whites, brown sugar, and water. Place the bowl in the skillet of water and whisk gently and constantly by hand until the mixture registers 160°F on an instant-read thermometer.

7. Transfer the bowl to the mixer stand and, using the whisk attachment, beat at medium-high speed until the meringue is cool and forms stiff, shiny peaks, about 3 minutes.

8. Reduce the speed to medium and beat in the butter, 1 tablespoon at a time. Beat in the vanilla and cinnamon. Beat at high speed until the buttercream is smooth, about 1 minute.

9. Place the buttercream in a pastry bag fitted with a medium plain tip, such as Ateco #6. Pipe a generous spiral of buttercream on top of each cupcake. Garnish with a sprinkling of ground cinnamon. Serve the cupcakes at room temperature. If not serving right away, refrigerate the cupcakes in a covered container for up to 5 days; bring to room temperature before serving.

*Apple*

# Apple Honey Cake

*Honey cake is* ritually eaten on the Jewish New Year, Rosh Hashanah, with the honey symbolizing hope for a sweet year ahead. Since apples dipped in honey are often served at New Year gatherings, I added shredded apples to this version. It's very moist, with flavors of citrus and warm spices. The black tea balances the sweetness of the honey so the cake is not cloying.

MAKES ONE 9-INCH CAKE, SERVING 9

2½ cups (309 g/10.9 oz) all-purpose flour

1¾ teaspoons (8.75 g/0.3 oz) baking powder

¾ teaspoon (3.75 oz/0.13 oz) baking soda

¼ teaspoon (1.7 g/0.06 oz) salt

2 teaspoons (4 g/0.14 oz) ground cinnamon

½ teaspoon (1 g/0.03 oz) ground ginger

¼ teaspoon (0.5 g/0.02 oz) ground cloves

1 medium (227 g/8 oz) Granny Smith apple, peeled and cored

3 tablespoons (45 g/1.6 oz) orange juice

2 large eggs

⅔ cup (138 g/4.8 oz) vegetable oil

⅔ cup (224 g/7.9 oz) honey

¾ cup (150 g/5.3 oz) granulated sugar

½ cup firmly packed (108 g/3.8 oz) light brown sugar

¾ cup (180 g/6.3 oz) warm brewed black tea

¼ cup (60 g/2.1 oz) dark rum

1 teaspoon (4 g/0.14 oz) vanilla extract

1 teaspoon (2 g/0.07 oz) finely grated orange zest

¾ cup (75 g/2.6 oz) walnuts, chopped

1. Preheat the oven to 350°F. Grease the bottom and sides of a 9-inch square pan.

2. In the bowl of an electric mixer, whisk together the flour, baking powder, baking soda, salt, and spices by hand.

3. Grate the apple into a small bowl (you should have about 1 cup grated apple) and toss it with the orange juice. In a medium bowl, whisk together the eggs, oil, honey, sugars, tea, rum, and vanilla. Stir in the apple mixture and the orange zest. Place the bowl of dry ingredients on the mixer stand and, using the whisk attachment, mix at low speed while adding the egg mixture; mix until just blended. Remove the bowl from the mixer stand and, using a rubber spatula, mix the batter a few times to ensure it is evenly blended. Scrape the batter into the prepared pan and sprinkle the walnuts evenly over the top.

4. Bake for 50 to 60 minutes, or until a toothpick inserted into the center of the cake comes out clean. Let the cake cool completely in the pan set on a wire rack.

5. To serve, cut the cake into squares directly from the pan.

# Apple Crisp with Pecan-Oat Topping

*The apple juice* in the filling of this fall dessert bumps up the fruit flavor and ensures the crisp will be moist. Use any firm-fleshed apple, such as Granny Smith, Braeburn, Honeycrisp, or Fuji. You can also make individual crisps in 8-ounce ramekins — just cut the baking time down to 35 to 45 minutes.

MAKES 6 SERVINGS

APPLE FILLING

5 to 6 medium (1.13 kg/
2.5 lb) apples, peeled, cored,
and sliced ¼ inch thick

⅓ cup (66 g/2.3 oz) granulated
sugar

2 tablespoons (16 g/0.58 oz)
all-purpose flour

½ teaspoon (1 g/0.03 oz)
ground cinnamon

⅛ teaspoon (0.8 g/0.03 oz) salt

2 tablespoons (28 g/1 oz)
unsalted butter, cut into ½-inch
cubes

⅓ cup (80 g/2.8 oz) apple juice

1½ teaspoons (7.5 g/0.26 oz)
freshly squeezed lemon juice

½ cup (74 g/2.6 oz) golden
raisins

PECAN-OAT TOPPING

1 cup (132 g/4.6 oz) all-purpose
flour

½ cup (40 g/1.4 oz) old-
fashioned rolled oats

⅓ cup (66 g/2.3 oz) granulated
sugar

½ cup firmly packed (108 g/
3.8 oz) light brown sugar

⅛ teaspoon (0.8 g/0.03 oz) salt

1 cup (100 g/3.5 oz) pecans,
coarsely chopped

8 tablespoons (113 g/4 oz)
unsalted butter, melted

## Make the filling

1. Preheat the oven to 350°F. Butter the bottom and sides of a 9-inch square (preferably glass) baking dish.

2. In a large bowl, toss together the apples, sugar, flour, cinnamon, and salt. Add the butter, apple juice, lemon juice, and raisins and toss again to combine well. Spoon the filling into the prepared baking dish and spread it into an even layer.

## Make the topping and bake the crisp

3. In a medium bowl, stir together the flour, oats, sugars, salt, and pecans. Add the melted butter and stir until the mixture is evenly combined and crumbly. Spoon the topping evenly over the apple filling.

4. Bake the crisp for 45 to 50 minutes, until nicely browned. Cool in the pan set on a wire rack for 10 minutes before serving. The crisp is best served warm. Store in the refrigerator, covered with plastic wrap, for up to 5 days.

# Jacquy Pfeiffer's French Apple Cake

*This recipe comes* from pastry chef Jacquy Pfeiffer, co-founder of the prestigious French Pastry School in Chicago, star of the 2010 documentary *Kings of Pastry* (a must-see film), and author of the award-winning book *The Art of French Pastry*. Jacquy and I have been friends for many years—he was kind enough to make the beautiful pink pulled sugar roses that adorned my wedding cake in 1997, a favor I'm not likely to forget! Jacquy's delicious apple cake is baked in a cast iron skillet or tarte tatin pan, which gives it a beautiful golden brown exterior. The apple wedges on top release their juices during baking, infusing the cake with wonderful flavor, while a generous topping of pecans gives it a nutty crunch. Note that the skillet or pan must be 9 or 9½ inches in diameter; a 12-inch skillet will be too big.

MAKES ONE 9- OR 9½-INCH CAKE, SERVING 6

SPECIAL EQUIPMENT:
9- or 9½-inch cast iron skillet or tarte tatin pan with sides no higher than 2 inches

PECAN TOPPING

½ cup (50 g/1.76 oz) pecans, coarsely chopped

2 teaspoons (10 g/0.34 oz) egg white, from 1 egg

2 teaspoons (10 g/0.34 oz) turbinado sugar

Pinch of fine sea salt

APPLE CAKE

¾ cup (100 g/3.5 oz) all-purpose flour

¼ teaspoon plus a pinch (1.5 g/0.05 oz) baking powder

2 large (550 g/19.4 oz) Braeburn apples

1 teaspoon (4 g/0.14 oz) freshly squeezed lemon juice

8 tablespoons (113 g/4 oz) unsalted butter, at room temperature

(CONTINUED)

## Make the topping

1. In a small bowl, combine the pecans, egg white, turbinado sugar, and salt; set aside.

## Make the cake

2. Preheat the oven to 350°F. Butter the bottom and sides of a 9- or 9½-inch cast iron skillet or tarte tatin pan and dust with flour.

3. Sift the flour and baking powder into a medium bowl and stir to combine.

4. Peel and core the apples, then cut each one into 8 wedges and place in a medium bowl. Drizzle the lemon juice over the apples and toss gently with your hands to coat.

5. In the bowl of an electric mixer fitted with the paddle attachment, beat the butter at medium speed while gradually adding the turbinado sugar, salt, and vanilla. Continue to beat for 5 minutes, until very creamy. Add the eggs, one at a time, beating well after each addition and scraping down the sides of the bowl with a rubber spatula as necessary. Remove the bowl from the mixer stand and very gently fold the flour mixture in one-half at a time with a rubber spatula. Fold in the sour cream. Scrape the batter into the

½ cup (113 g/4 oz) turbinado sugar

¼ teaspoon (1.6 g/0.06 oz) salt

½ teaspoon (2 g/0.07 oz) vanilla bean paste or extract

2 large eggs

¼ cup (60 g/2.1 oz) sour cream

Confectioners' sugar, for dusting

prepared pan and smooth it into an even layer. Arrange the apple wedges, with a cut side down, on top of the batter in a pinwheel pattern around the pan. Toss the pecan topping once again and scatter it over the top of the cake. Sift confectioners' sugar generously over the cake.

6. Bake for 50 to 55 minutes, until the cake and the edges of the apples are nicely browned. A toothpick inserted into the cake should come out clean. Let the cake cool for 10 minutes in the skillet on a wire rack before serving. Right before serving, dust the cake with more sifted confectioners' sugar. Serve the cake warm, preferably with ice cream.

# Citrus

✤ ✤

I love lemon. It's a kick.
It's an intrusion.

— MAGGIE WALDRON,
food writer and editor

*Citrus desserts can* range in flavor from the soft, fruity notes of mildly acidic orange and grapefruit to the mouth-puckering zing of lemons and limes. They can be as timid as an orange-kissed butter cookie or as bold as a French lemon tart. The acidity level in citrus fruits is measured by pH — generally speaking, the lower the pH, the higher the acidity. Lemons and limes, for example, have relatively low pH levels and high acidity compared to grapefruits, oranges, and Meyer lemons. Of course, since desserts include other ingredients, the acidity of the fruit is usually tempered by the addition of butter, sugar, and eggs. Making a citrus dessert is a balancing act — too much acid and you get a dessert that's way too tart, while too much sugar overwhelms the bright notes of the fruit. In this chapter, I've aimed for perfectly balanced recipes that flaunt the flavor of the chosen fruit.

Citrus fruit is at its peak in January, but local produce markets and supermarkets carry a decent selection throughout the year. For oranges, look for fruit that has a rich orange color and smooth skin. If the orange is heavy, it means it's juicy. When choosing lemons, squeeze them lightly; if they yield to pressure it means they have a thinner skin and contain more juice. Lemons with rough skin tend to have a thicker layer of pith and more seeds. The ideal lime will have a partially yellow skin, which indicates that it is ripe. And like the perfect lemon, it should "give" a little when pressed; this means it will be juicy. As for grapefruit, look for fruit with bright, even color and a symmetrical shape. Pick it up — a juicy grapefruit will feel heavier than it looks. And the juicier the grapefruit, the sweeter it will be.

Store citrus fruit in the crisper drawer of your refrigerator, separated from other fruits and vegetables (citrus releases a gas that can cause other produce to spoil). And if your mother in Florida sends you a case or two of oranges, remember that citrus juice and zest can be frozen, well-wrapped, for up to three months.

# Orange-Cardamom Scones

*These delicate, flaky scones* have a subtle orange-cardamom flavor. They are delicious served warm with orange marmalade or raspberry jam and soft French or Irish butter. When shaping the dough, be as gentle as possible — a light touch leads to a tender scone.

MAKES 8 SCONES

2 cups (266 g/9.3 oz) all-purpose flour

3 tablespoons firmly packed (40 g/1.4 oz) light brown sugar

2 teaspoons (10 g/0.35 oz) baking powder

¾ teaspoon (1.5 g/0.05 oz) ground cardamom

¼ teaspoon (1.6 g/0.06 oz) salt

1¼ teaspoons (2.5 g/0.08 oz) finely grated orange zest

6 tablespoons (85 g/3 oz) cold unsalted butter, cut into ½-inch cubes and frozen for 15 minutes

2 tablespoons (30 g/1 oz) freshly squeezed orange juice

½ cup plus 2 tablespoons (145 g/5.1 oz) heavy cream

1 egg, lightly beaten with 1 teaspoon water, for egg wash

Demerara sugar, for sprinkling on top

Butter and jam, for serving

1. Preheat the oven to 400°F. Line a baking sheet with parchment paper or a silicone baking mat.

2. In the bowl of a food processor, combine the flour, brown sugar, baking powder, cardamom, salt, and orange zest and pulse until blended. Add the butter cubes and process until the mixture forms coarse crumbs. Turn the mixture into a medium bowl and form a well in the center. Stir the orange juice into the cream. Add about ½ cup of the cream mixture to the center of the well in the flour mixture and, using a wooden spoon or rubber spatula, gradually stir the flour mixture into the liquid. If the mixture seems dry, add just enough of the remaining cream mixture to form a soft dough. Knead the dough *very lightly* just a few times, just until it comes together. Transfer the dough to a lightly floured work surface and gently pat it into an 8-inch round. Using a chef's knife, cut the round into 8 wedges and arrange them on the prepared baking sheet, spacing them at least 1 inch apart. Brush the scones with the egg wash, then sprinkle them with demerara sugar.

3. Bake the scones for 14 to 18 minutes, until light golden brown. Serve the scones warm with butter and jam. Store in an airtight container at room temperature for up to 3 days.

# Lemon-Blueberry Parfaits

*Lemon and blueberry* has always been one of my favorite flavor combinations. In fact, a lemon-blueberry parfait was one of the first "fancy" desserts I remember making as a kid. The recipe came from *Gourmet* magazine from some time in the 1970s, and it was a meringue-based lemon mousse with blueberries folded into it. My mother and I served it at a dinner party, which was a big deal for me. Here's my own version of that dessert: I amped up the lemon flavor in the mousse (I like my lemon on the tart side) and paired it with a fresh blueberry compote for a striking color contrast. I like to serve the parfait with a gingersnap cookie (I'm including my recipe, but you can use a good store-bought brand if you're short on time) and some whipped cream.

MAKES 6 PARFAITS

### GINGERSNAPS (MAKES ABOUT 50 COOKIES)

2⅔ cups (354 g/12.48 oz) all-purpose flour

1 teaspoon (5 g/0.17 oz) baking soda

¼ teaspoon (1.6 g/0.06 oz) salt

1 tablespoon (6 g/0.21 oz) ground ginger

1 teaspoon (2 g/0.07 oz) ground cinnamon

¼ teaspoon (0.5 oz/0.02 oz) ground cloves

8 tablespoons (113 g/4 oz) unsalted butter, softened

¼ cup (50 g/1.76 oz) vegetable shortening

1⅓ cups (466 g/16.43 oz) granulated sugar

1 tablespoon (10 g/0.35 oz) finely chopped crystallized ginger

2 large eggs, at room temperature

¼ cup (80 g/2.8 oz) unsulphured molasses

(CONTINUED)

## Make the gingersnaps

1. In a large bowl, whisk together the flour, baking soda, salt, ground ginger, cinnamon, and cloves.

2. In the bowl of an electric mixer fitted with the paddle attachment, beat together the butter, shortening, sugar, and crystallized ginger at medium speed until light, about 2 minutes. Beat in the eggs, one at a time, scraping down the sides of the bowl after each addition and beating until well blended. Add the molasses and lemon zest and beat until combined. Add the flour mixture and mix on low speed just until blended and smooth. Cover the bowl and refrigerate the dough for at least 1 hour, until firm enough to handle.

3. Preheat to 350°F. Line two baking sheets with parchment paper or silicone baking mats.

4. Place the dipping sugar in a shallow dish. Roll the dough into 1-inch balls and dip one side in the sugar. Arrange each ball, sugar side up, on one of the sheets. Using your palm, slightly flatten the balls. Repeat with the remaining dough and second baking sheet. Bake one sheet at a time for 9 to 12 minutes, or until the cookies are puffed and browned. Let the cookies cool on the sheet set on a wire rack for 5 minutes, then transfer the cookies to the rack to cool completely.

¼ teaspoon (0.5 g/0.02 oz) finely grated lemon zest

Granulated sugar, for dipping cookie tops

**FRESH BLUEBERRY COMPOTE**

1 pint (276 g/9.7 oz) fresh blueberries, divided

¼ cup (50 g/1.76 oz) granulated sugar

¼ cup (59 g/2 oz) water

1 teaspoon (5 g/0.17 oz) freshly squeezed lemon juice

**LEMON MOUSSE**

3 tablespoons cold water

1¼ teaspoons (3.9 g/0.14 oz) unflavored powdered gelatin

8 large egg yolks

1 cup plus 2 tablespoons (225 g/8 oz) granulated sugar

2 teaspoons (4 g/0.14 oz) finely grated lemon zest

⅔ cup (161 g/5.6 oz) freshly squeezed lemon juice

Pinch of salt

8 tablespoons (113 g/4 oz) unsalted butter, cut into tablespoons

1 cup (232 g/8.18 oz) heavy cream

**ASSEMBLY**

Sweetened whipped cream

6 gingersnap cookies, homemade or store-bought

## *Make the compote*

**5.** In a small saucepan, combine 1 cup (138 g/4.8 oz) of the blueberries with the sugar and water. Bring to a boil over medium heat, then reduce the heat to medium low and simmer, stirring frequently, until the berries burst, about 5 minutes. Remove the pan from the heat and stir in the remaining 1 cup blueberries and the lemon juice. Let the mixture cool until just warm. Transfer the compote to a small bowl, cover with plastic wrap, and refrigerate while you make the mousse.

## *Make the mousse*

**6.** Place the water in a small, heatproof measuring cup. Sprinkle the gelatin over the water and let the mixture stand for 5 minutes to soften. Set the cup in a pan of simmering water for a few minutes, stirring occasionally, until the gelatin is dissolved and the mixture is clear. Keep the cup of gelatin in the hot water, off the heat, until ready to use.

**7.** Set a fine-mesh sieve over a medium bowl and set aside. In a medium, heavy-bottomed, nonreactive saucepan, whisk together the egg yolks and sugar until blended. Stir in the lemon zest and juice, salt, and butter and cook over medium heat, whisking constantly, until the mixture thickens, 7 to 10 minutes (do not let the mixture boil, or it will curdle). The mixture should leave a path on the back of a wooden spoon when you draw your finger across it. Remove the pan from the heat and stir in the warm gelatin mixture. Immediately strain the mixture through the sieve, pressing it through with a rubber spatula.

**8.** Prepare an ice bath by filling a large bowl one-third full with ice and water and set the bowl containing the lemon mixture in it (be careful that the ice and water doesn't splash into the lemon mixture). Stir the lemon mixture frequently until it is slightly chilled, about 15 minutes. (The lemon curd can be prepared and refrigerated, covered, up to 3 days in advance.)

**9.** Whip the cream to soft peaks. Fold one-third of the whipped cream into the lemon curd, then gently fold in the remaining whipped cream.

### *Assemble the parfaits*

**10.** Spoon 3 rounded tablespoons of the compote into each of 6 serving glasses. Spoon ⅔ cup of the mousse on top of the compote in each glass. Refrigerate, covered with plastic wrap, until ready to serve, up to 1 day.

**11.** Before serving, garnish each parfait with sweetened whipped cream and a gingersnap cookie.

# Lemon-Raspberry Buttermilk Tart

*Here's a variation* on a Southern classic, the buttermilk pie. The buttermilk filling is very similar to cheesecake in flavor, though its texture is much less dense. I added buttermilk to the dough, too, which makes the resulting crust very tender and slightly tangy. A thin layer of raspberry preserves, spread over the baked crust, and a garnish of fresh raspberries add a bright flavor note that works well with the acidic lemon and buttermilk. This tart really needs to be eaten at room temperature, not chilled, and is one of those desserts that's best eaten the day it's made. I also like to serve it with a drizzle of Red Berry Sauce (page 21).

MAKES ONE 9-INCH TART, SERVING 6 TO 8

## TART CRUST

1¼ cups (166 g/5.8 oz) all-purpose flour

1 teaspoon (4 g/0.15 oz) granulated sugar

¼ teaspoon (1.6 g/0.06 oz) salt

8 tablespoons (113 g/4 oz) unsalted butter, cut into ½-inch cubes and frozen for 20 minutes

3 tablespoons (45 g/1.6 oz) cold buttermilk

## OPTIONAL CUTOUTS FOR GARNISH

1 large egg, whisked with 1 teaspoon (5 g/0.17 oz) water, for egg wash

Granulated sugar, for sprinkling

## BUTTERMILK FILLING

¾ cup (150 g/5.3 oz) granulated sugar

1 tablespoon plus 1½ teaspoons (12 g/0.4 oz) all-purpose flour

3 large eggs plus 1 large egg yolk

5 tablespoons (70 g/2.5 oz) unsalted butter, melted and cooled

(CONTINUED)

## *Make the tart crust*

**1.** Place the flour, sugar, and salt in the bowl of a food processor and pulse a few times to combine. Add the butter pieces and toss lightly with a spoon to coat them with flour. Blend the butter and flour with about five 1-second pulses, or until the mixture is the texture of coarse meal with some butter pieces the size of peas. Sprinkle the buttermilk over the flour mixture and process continuously until the dough begins to clump together. Do not overprocess; the dough should not form a ball. Turn the dough out onto a work surface and shape it into a thick 4-inch-wide disc. Wrap the dough in plastic wrap and refrigerate until firm enough to roll, about 30 minutes.

**2.** Place the unwrapped dough on a lightly floured work surface. Roll out the dough into an 11-inch circle, lifting and rotating the dough often while dusting the work surface and dough lightly with flour as necessary. Roll the dough up on the rolling pin and unroll it over a 9-inch fluted tart pan with a removable bottom. Gently press the dough onto the bottom and up the sides of the pan. Roll the pin over the top of the pan to trim off the excess dough. Lightly prick the bottom of the dough with a fork at 1-inch intervals. Refrigerate the dough in the pan for 20 minutes to firm up. (If you like, roll out the dough scraps and, using a 1-inch heart- or flower-shaped aspic cutter or cookie cutter, cut out as many shapes as you can, place them on a small plate, and refrigerate them along with the tart shell. These shapes can be baked later and used to garnish the tart.)

¾ cup (181 g/6.4 oz) buttermilk

¾ teaspoon (3 g/0.1 oz) vanilla extract

1 teaspoon (2 g/0.07 oz) finely grated lemon zest

2 tablespoons (30 g/1 oz) freshly squeezed lemon juice

¼ cup (76 g/2.6 oz) raspberry preserves (with or without seeds)

GARNISH

1½ cups (170 g/6 oz) fresh raspberries

Confectioners' sugar, for sprinkling

**3.** Preheat the oven to 375°F. Right before baking, line the dough with aluminum foil or parchment paper and cover with pie weights or dried beans. Place the tart pan on a baking sheet and bake for 15 minutes. Carefully lift the foil (along with the weights) out of the tart pan and bake the crust for 8 to 10 minutes longer, until it just begins to turn golden brown in spots along the edge. Transfer the tart pan to a wire rack and let cool while you make the filling. (If you've made the pastry hearts or flowers, brush them with the egg wash, sprinkle with sugar, and bake them for about 7 minutes, until they are just beginning to turn golden. Set aside and let cool.) Reduce the oven temperature to 300°F.

## Make the filling

**4.** In a medium bowl, whisk together the sugar and flour. Add the eggs and yolk and whisk until smooth. Whisk in the butter, buttermilk, vanilla, lemon zest, and lemon juice.

**5.** Spread the raspberry preserves onto the baked tart shell (it's okay if the shell is still warm) in an even layer. Place the tart pan on a baking sheet and carefully pour the filling into the tart shell (it will fill the shell).

## Bake and garnish the tart

**6.** Bake the tart for 50 to 60 minutes, until the filling is just set in the center. Let the tart cool on a wire rack.

**7.** You can either garnish the whole tart with the fresh raspberries and pastry shapes (if using), or serve each slice of the tart with a few raspberries and a pastry shape on top. Sprinkle lightly with sifted confectioners' sugar before serving.

# Lemon Buttermilk Ice Cream

*This may be* my favorite ice cream ever. It's very lemony, with the soft, fresh tang of buttermilk. A scoop goes perfectly with fresh berries or just about any berry dessert.

**MAKES ABOUT 1 QUART**

**SPECIAL EQUIPMENT:**
Ice cream maker

2 cups (464 g/16.4 oz) heavy cream

1 cup (200 g/7 oz) granulated sugar, divided

6 large egg yolks

1 cup (242 g/8.5 oz) buttermilk

2 tablespoons (12 g/0.4 oz) finely grated lemon zest

¾ cup (181 g/6.4 oz) freshly squeezed lemon juice

⅛ teaspoon (0.8 g/0.03 oz) salt

1. Fill a large bowl one-third of the way with ice and water and set aside.

2. In a medium, heavy-bottomed saucepan, combine the cream and ½ cup (100 g/3.5 oz) of the sugar and heat over medium-high heat, stirring occasionally, until the sugar is dissolved and the cream begins to bubble around the edges. Remove the pan from the heat.

3. In a medium bowl, whisk together the egg yolks and remaining ½ cup (100 g/3.5 oz) sugar until well combined. Slowly whisk in the hot cream mixture until fully blended. Pour the mixture back into the saucepan, place over medium heat, and cook, stirring constantly with a silicone spatula or wooden spoon, until the mixture thickens enough to leave a path in the back of the spatula or spoon when you drag your finger across it. The mixture should register 185°F on an instant-read thermometer. Strain the mixture through a fine-mesh sieve into a medium bowl. Set the bowl containing the ice cream base into the bowl of ice water. Stir the mixture frequently until it is cool, about 10 minutes. Stir in the buttermilk, lemon zest and juice, and salt. Cover the bowl with plastic wrap and refrigerate the ice cream base for at least 6 hours, or overnight.

4. Strain the ice cream base into the bowl of an ice cream maker to remove the zest, and process according to the manufacturer's instructions. Transfer the ice cream to an airtight container and freeze for at least 2 hours before serving, or for up to 1 month.

*Ingredient Notes*

# Red Grapefruit–White Tea Sorbet

*White tea is made* with tea leaves and buds that are dried in natural sunlight and processed before they oxidize. This yields a delicate, pale yellow brew that goes beautifully with grapefruit, as in this pale pink sorbet. Serve it alone, or with a scoop of vanilla ice cream for a grapefruit Creamsicle flavor.

**MAKES ABOUT 1 QUART**

**SPECIAL EQUIPMENT:**
Ice cream maker

1½ cups (354 g/12.5 oz) water

1 cup (200 g/7 oz) granulated sugar

1½ teaspoons (3 g/0.1 oz) finely grated grapefruit zest

1½ teaspoons (3 g/0.1 oz) loose white tea leaves

2 cups (483 g/17 oz) freshly squeezed grapefruit juice (about 3 grapefruits)

1 teaspoon (5 g/0.17 oz) freshly squeezed lemon juice

**1.** In a small saucepan, combine the water, sugar, and grapefruit zest and place over high heat. Bring to a boil, stirring just until the sugar dissolves. Remove from the heat and stir in the tea leaves. Cover the pan and allow to infuse for 5 minutes.

**2.** Strain the tea mixture into a medium bowl. Stir in the grapefruit and lemon juice. Cover the bowl and refrigerate for at least 4 hours.

**3.** Process the mixture in an ice cream maker according to the manufacturer's instructions. Transfer the sorbet to a covered container and freeze for at least 2 hours before serving.

# Orange Blossom–Cinnamon Ice Cream with Blood Orange Sorbet

*This harlequin-patterned dessert* makes a nice change from boring single-flavor ice cream or sorbet. The fragrant orange ice cream has just a hint of cinnamon, and is paired with a bright blood orange sorbet: Alternate scoops of both flavors in the serving container to create a two-tone effect.

MAKES ABOUT 2 QUARTS

SPECIAL EQUIPMENT:
Instant-read thermometer; ice cream maker

ORANGE BLOSSOM–CINNAMON ICE CREAM

1⅔ cups (402 g/14.2 oz) whole milk

1⅓ cups (309 g/10.9 oz) heavy cream

¾ cup (150 g/5.3 oz) granulated sugar, divided

2 tablespoons (12 g/0.42 oz) finely grated orange zest (from 3 to 4 oranges)

2 cinnamon sticks

6 large egg yolks

⅛ teaspoon (0.8 g/0.03 oz) salt

½ teaspoon (2 g/0.07 oz) orange blossom water

BLOOD ORANGE SORBET

1½ cups (364 g/12.8 oz) freshly squeezed blood orange juice (from about 7 oranges), divided

¾ cup (150 g/5.3 oz) granulated sugar

2 teaspoons (4 g/0.14 oz) finely grated orange zest

(CONTINUED)

## Make the ice cream

1. In a small saucepan, combine the milk, cream, ½ cup (100 g/ 3.5 oz) of the sugar, the orange zest, and cinnamon sticks. Cook over medium-high heat, stirring to dissolve the sugar, until the mixture begins to bubble around the edge of the pan and steam rises from the surface. Remove the pan from the heat, cover, and allow to infuse for 45 minutes.

2. Once the milk mixture has infused, whisk the remaining ¼ cup (50 g/1.76 oz) sugar, the egg yolks, and salt together vigorously in a medium bowl until well blended. Return the saucepan to medium-high heat and cook, stirring occasionally, until it is heated through and bubbles begin to form around the edges of the pan. Slowly whisk about 1 cup of the hot milk mixture into the yolks. Return the yolk mixture to the saucepan with the remaining milk mixture and cook over medium heat, stirring constantly with a heatproof spatula, until the custard thickens enough to coat the back of a wooden spoon or silicone spatula and registers 185°F on an instant-read thermometer. Remove the pan from the heat and strain the custard through a fine-mesh strainer into a large bowl. Stir in the orange blossom water. Prepare an ice bath by filling a large bowl one-third full with ice and water and set the bowl of custard in it. Allow the custard to chill in the ice bath, stirring occasionally, until cold, about 20 minutes. Remove the bowl of custard from the ice bath and press a piece of plastic wrap directly onto the surface of the custard to prevent a skin from forming. Refrigerate the custard for at least 6 hours, or, preferably, overnight.

1½ cups (364 g/12.8 oz) freshly squeezed regular orange juice (from 4 to 5 oranges)

2 teaspoons (10 g/0.35 oz) freshly squeezed lemon juice

**3.** Process the chilled custard in an ice cream maker according to the manufacturer's instructions. Transfer the ice cream to an airtight container and freeze for at least 3 hours.

## Make the sorbet

**4.** In a small saucepan, combine ¾ cup (182 g/6.4 oz) of the blood orange juice with the sugar. Place over medium-high heat and cook, stirring constantly, until the mixture is hot and the sugar is dissolved. Pour the hot juice into a medium bowl and stir in the remaining ¾ cup (182 g/6.4 oz) blood orange juice, the regular orange zest and juice, and the lemon juice. Cover the bowl with plastic wrap and refrigerate the sorbet base for at least 4 hours, until very well chilled.

**5.** Process the sorbet base in an ice cream maker according to the manufacturer's instructions. Transfer the sorbet to an airtight container and freeze for at least 3 hours.

## Marbleize the ice cream and sorbet

**6.** Remove the ice cream and sorbet from the freezer and check to see how firm each is. They should be soft enough to scoop, but not so soft that they will melt quickly. If either is too firm, leave it out at room temperature for 5 to 10 minutes to soften before scooping. Using a clean, 2-quart container and an ice cream scoop (I use a 2-ounce scoop), scoop the ice cream and sorbet alternately in a checkerboard pattern to cover the bottom of the container. Run a spatula over the scoops to make an even layer. Repeat, alternating the scoops, until the ice cream and sorbet are used up. Cover the container and freeze at least 3 hours (or up to a month) before scooping and serving.

# Orange-Scented Madeleines

*Madeleines are classically* made with browned butter, but I opt to use melted, but not browned, butter in this version, so that the delicate orange flavor is not overwhelmed. I've also taken the liberty of coating the tops with a honey-orange glaze—Proust is probably turning in his grave, but he would undoubtedly forgive me if he tried one of these delicious little cakes.

**MAKES 20 MADELEINES**

**SPECIAL EQUIPMENT:**
Twenty 3-inch madeleine molds

### MADELEINES

9 tablespoons (127 g/ 4.4 oz) unsalted butter, cut into tablespoons

1 cup (132 g/4.6 oz) all-purpose flour

1¼ teaspoons (6 g/0.2 oz) baking powder

⅛ teaspoon (0.8 g/0.03 oz) salt

3 large eggs, at room temperature

¾ cup (150 g/5.3 oz) granulated sugar

1½ teaspoons (6 g/0.2 oz) vanilla extract

2 teaspoons (4 g/0.14 oz) finely grated orange zest

### HONEY-ORANGE GLAZE

½ cup (64 g/2.25 oz) confectioners' sugar

3 tablespoons (45 g/1.6 oz) freshly squeezed orange juice

1 teaspoon (15 g/0.5 oz) freshly squeezed lemon juice

1 teaspoon (7 g/0.25 oz) honey

## Make the madeleines

1. Place the butter in a heatproof glass measuring cup or microwave-safe bowl and microwave at medium power for about 1 minute, or until melted. Set aside to cool.

2. In a medium bowl, whisk together the flour, baking powder, and salt.

3. In the bowl of an electric mixer fitted with the whisk attachment, whip the eggs at medium speed while gradually adding the sugar. Raise the speed to high and whip until the egg mixture is pale and thick, about 3 minutes. Remove the bowl from the mixer stand and fold in the flour mixture in three additions. Stir the vanilla and orange zest into the cooled butter and then fold it into the batter. Cover the bowl and refrigerate the batter for at least 3 hours (or up to 3 days) before baking.

4. Preheat the oven to 400°F. Brush twenty 3-inch madeleine molds well with softened butter. (Since the number of cavities in the pans can vary, you may need to bake the madeleines in batches.) Dust the molds with flour.

5. Spoon the batter into each mold, almost filling each one. Bake, one pan at a time, for 12 to 14 minutes, until golden brown. Place the pan on a wire rack to cool for 2 minutes, then invert the pan onto the rack to release the madeleines. If they stick, run a small paring knife around the edges of the madeleines until they release.

## Make the glaze and glaze the madeleines

6. Combine the confectioners' sugar, orange juice, lemon juice, and honey in a small saucepan and bring to a boil over medium-high heat, stirring frequently. Remove the pan from the heat. Brush the ridged side of each madeleine with the glaze. Let stand until set, about 15 minutes. Store the madeleines in an airtight container at room temperature for up to 3 days.

# Lime Meringue Bars

*Not too sweet* and not too tart, these bars have a tender brown sugar crust and potent lime filling. Each bar is topped with a billowy rosette of meringue, transforming them into an uptown version of the classic lemon bar.

**MAKES 24 BARS**

### SPICED BROWN SUGAR CRUST

1¾ cups (232 g/8.17 oz) all-purpose flour

¼ cup plus 2 tablespoons firmly packed (81 g/2.8 oz) light brown sugar

¼ teaspoon (0.5 g/0.017 oz) ground ginger

¼ teaspoon (0.5 g/0.017 oz) ground cinnamon

¼ teaspoon (1.6 g/0.06 oz) salt

14 tablespoons (197 g/7 oz) cold unsalted butter, cut into ½-inch cubes

2 tablespoons (28 g/1 oz) ice-cold water

### LIME FILLING

1⅔ cups (332 g/11.7 oz) granulated sugar

¼ cup (33 g/1 oz) all-purpose flour

Pinch of salt

5 large eggs

½ cup (121 g/4.3 oz) freshly squeezed lime juice

2 teaspoons (4 g/0.14 oz) finely grated lime zest

(CONTINUED)

## Make the crust

1. Preheat the oven to 350°F. Lightly grease the bottom and sides of a 9-by-13-inch baking pan.

2. Place the flour, brown sugar, ginger, cinnamon, and salt in the bowl of a food processor and process until blended. Add the butter pieces and process until the mixture forms coarse crumbs. Add the water and process until the mixture starts to come together as a dough. Press the dough into an even layer over the bottom of the prepared pan. Bake the crust for 20 to 25 minutes, until it is just beginning to brown. Transfer the pan to a wire rack and let cool completely. Reduce the oven temperature to 325°F.

## Make the filling

3. In a medium bowl, whisk together the sugar, flour, and salt. Add all the eggs at one time and whisk until smooth. Gradually whisk in the lime juice, then the lime zest. Pour the filling over the cooled crust and bake for 30 to 35 minutes, until set in the center. Leave the oven on.

## Make the topping and bake the bars

4. In the bowl of an electric mixer fitted with the whisk attachment, beat the egg whites and salt at medium-high speed until soft peaks begin to form. Gradually beat in the sugar, 1 tablespoon at a time, and beat at high speed until stiff and glossy. Transfer the meringue to a large pastry bag fitted with a medium star tip, such as Ateco #6. Pipe large rosettes of the meringue on top of the lime filling,

## MERINGUE TOPPING

**5 large egg whites, at room temperature**

**Pinch of salt**

**⅔ cup (133 g/4.7 oz) granulated sugar**

## GARNISH

**Confectioners' sugar, for dusting**

6 across lengthwise and 4 down the width of the pan, for a total of 24 meringue rosettes.

**5.** Bake the meringue-topped bars for 8 to 12 minutes, until the meringue rosettes are lightly browned. Let the bars cool completely in the pan set on a wire rack.

**6.** Using a thin, sharp knife, cut the rectangle into 24 bars, each with a meringue rosette on top. Lightly dust the tops of the bars with sifted confectioners' sugar before serving. Store the bars, loosely covered, in the refrigerator for up to 3 days (the meringue begins to break down after that).

*Citrus*

# Lime Cream Tart with Ginger—Cream Cheese Crust

*The silky lime* curd filling in this tart isn't made in the classic way—that is, with everything cooked together in a saucepan. Instead, it's cooked in a double boiler, like a sabayon, and then the softened butter is whisked into it once it has thickened, making it more like a light cream or mousse than a curd. The crust is made with a combination of cream cheese and butter, with freshly grated ginger adding a vibrant, spicy note.

MAKES ONE 11-INCH TART, SERVING 10

### GINGER-CREAM CHEESE CRUST

1 cup (132 g/4.6 oz) all-purpose flour

½ cup (57 g/2 oz) cake flour

1 tablespoon (8 g/0.28 oz) confectioners' sugar

¼ teaspoon (1.6 g/0.06 oz) salt

⅛ teaspoon (0.6 g/0.02 oz) baking powder

6 tablespoons (85 g/3 oz) cream cheese, cut into ½-inch chunks

9 tablespoons (127 g/4.4 oz) unsalted butter, cut into ½-inch cubes and frozen for 30 minutes

2 teaspoons (10 g/0.35 oz) finely grated fresh ginger

1½ teaspoons (7 g/0.25 oz) freshly squeezed lime juice

1 tablespoon plus 1½ teaspoons (22 g/0.8 oz) ice-cold water

### LIME CREAM FILLING

4 large eggs plus 4 large egg yolks

⅔ cup (133 g/4.7 oz) granulated sugar

(CONTINUED)

## Make the crust

1. Place the flours, confectioners' sugar, salt, and baking powder in the bowl of a food processor and pulse to combine. Add the cream cheese chunks and process for a few seconds, until the mixture is crumbly. Sprinkle the butter cubes and ginger on top of the mixture and process for a few more seconds, until the mixture resembles coarse meal. Add the lime juice and water and process until the dough just begins to come together, a few more seconds. Scrape the dough onto a work surface and gather it up into a disc. Wrap the disc in plastic wrap and refrigerate the dough for at least 45 minutes (or up to 3 days).

2. Place the unwrapped dough on a lightly floured work surface. Roll out the dough into a 13-inch round, lifting and rotating the dough often while dusting the work surface and dough lightly with flour as necessary. Roll the dough up onto the rolling pin and unroll it over an 11-inch tart pan with a removable bottom. Press the dough against the sides and bottom of the pan, then run the rolling pin over the top of the pan to trim away the excess dough. Prick the bottom of the crust with a fork all over at 1-inch intervals and refrigerate for 20 minutes before baking. Meanwhile, preheat the oven to 400°F.

3. Line the tart pan with a piece of parchment paper or foil and cover with pie weights or dried beans. Place the tart pan on a baking sheet and bake for 20 minutes. Carefully lift the parchment or

⅔ cup (161 g/5.6 oz) freshly squeezed lime juice

Pinch of salt

10 tablespoons (141 g/5 oz) unsalted butter, cut into tablespoons and softened

2 tablespoons (12 g/0.4 oz) finely grated lime zest

SERVING

Sweetened whipped cream

foil (along with the weights) from the tart pan and bake the crust for 5 to 10 minutes more, until it is just beginning to brown lightly in spots. Let the crust cool on a wire rack while you make the filling.

## Make the filling and assemble the tart

**4.** Fill a medium saucepan one-third full with water and bring the water to a simmer. In a medium bowl, whisk together the eggs, egg yolks, sugar, lime juice, and salt until blended. Place the bowl over the saucepan and heat the mixture, whisking constantly, until it is uniformly pale and thickened to the consistency of thin mayonnaise, 8 to 10 minutes. Remove the bowl from over the saucepan and whisk in the butter, 1 tablespoon at a time, whisking until each piece is incorporated before adding the next. Whisk in the lime zest.

**5.** Scrape the filling into the cooled crust and refrigerate the tart for at least 3 hours. Serve the tart with sweetened whipped cream. Store the tart in the refrigerator for up to 5 days.

*Citrus*

# Frozen Lime Meringue Cheesecake Pie

*Though this pie* is really a frozen cheesecake, its taste and texture are similar to that of a frozen Key lime pie, which is why I have it in this chapter and not the Sweet Cheese chapter (beginning on page 181). The addition of egg yolks gives the filling its creamy texture, which never gets rock-hard after freezing. When you scorch the chiffony meringue topping with a blow torch, the filling softens even more, melting seductively at the edges into the crumbly gingersnap crust.

**MAKES ONE 9-INCH DEEP-DISH PIE, SERVING 8 TO 10**

**SPECIAL EQUIPMENT:**
9-inch deep-dish pie pan;
butane or propane blow torch
(optional)

**GINGERSNAP CRUST**

1⅓ cups (185 g/6.5 oz)
gingersnap crumbs (from
about 24 cookies; see recipe,
page 145)

¼ cup (50 g/1.76 oz)
granulated sugar

4 tablespoons (56 g/2 oz)
unsalted butter, melted

**LIME CHEESECAKE FILLING**

1 cup (227 g/8 oz) cream
cheese, at room temperature

1 cup (200 g/7 oz) granulated
sugar, divided

¾ cup (181 g/6.4 oz) sour
cream

½ teaspoon (2 g/0.07 oz)
vanilla extract

3 large egg yolks

¼ cup (60 g/2.1 oz) freshly
squeezed lime juice

⅔ cup (155 g/5.4 oz) heavy
cream

(CONTINUED)

## Make the crust

1. In a bowl, combine the gingersnap crumbs, sugar, and melted butter until evenly blended. Scrape the mixture into a 9-inch deep-dish pie pan and press it evenly over the bottom and sides with your fingers. Freeze the crust while you make the filling.

## Make the filling

2. In the bowl of an electric mixer fitted with the paddle attachment, beat the cream cheese at medium speed while gradually adding ½ cup (100 g/3.5 oz) of the sugar. Continue to beat at medium speed until well blended, about 2 minutes. Beat in the sour cream and vanilla. Turn the mixer off while you heat the yolks.

3. In a medium bowl, whisk the egg yolks with the remaining ½ cup (100 g/3.5 oz) sugar and the lime juice. Place the bowl over a pot half filled with barely simmering water and heat, whisking vigorously, until the mixture thickens slightly and is foamy, about 5 minutes. Remove the bowl from the heat and gently fold the yolk mixture into the cream cheese mixture.

4. In a clean mixer bowl, using the whisk attachment (or by hand with a whisk), whip the cream at high speed until it holds soft peaks. Gently fold the whipped cream into the cream cheese mixture. Scrape the filling into the frozen pie crust and freeze for at least 1 hour before piping the meringue on top.

## MERINGUE TOPPING

¾ cup (150 g/5.3 oz) granulated sugar

¼ cup (82 g/2.9 oz) light corn syrup

¼ cup (59 g/2.1 oz) water

5 large egg whites

⅛ teaspoon (0.4 g/0.01 oz) cream of tartar

## *Make the meringue topping and top the pie*

**5.** In a small saucepan, combine the sugar, corn syrup, and water and place over high heat. Cook, stirring constantly, until the sugar dissolves. Stop stirring and bring the mixture to a full boil. Remove from the heat.

**6.** In the bowl of an electric mixer fitted with the whisk attachment, beat the egg whites at medium-high speed until foamy. Add the cream of tartar and beat until soft peaks begin to form. Reduce the speed to medium and add the hot sugar syrup in a steady stream while beating. Raise the speed to high and whip until the whites are stiff and glossy, about 7 minutes.

**7.** Scrape the whites into a large pastry bag fitted with a large plain tip, such as Ateco #8. Pipe pointed dollops of meringue over the top of the pie, covering it completely. Freeze the pie until ready to serve (cover the pie with plastic wrap once the meringue is frozen, after about an hour). The pie can be frozen, covered, for up to 3 weeks.

**8.** Right before serving, lightly brown the meringue with a blow torch or under a preheated broiler. Serve immediately.

# My Favorite Key Lime Pie

*Almost every restaurant* in South Florida serves Key lime pie, and it's shocking just how dreadful most versions of this classic dessert can be. The problems are varied: too tart, too sweet, too dense, too dry, tough crust, weepy meringue, overly sweet whipped cream. . . . Every atrocity you can imagine has been perpetrated on this simple pie. In my mind, there are two factors that are important in executing the perfect Key lime pie: First is to have the correct balance of sweet to tart. I like my pie a little on the tart side, but not *too* tart, and to temper its acidity, I top it with sweetened whipped cream (which I prefer to meringue). The second factor is to make a filling with a silky texture, as opposed to one that is yolky and dense. To ensure the perfect texture, I fold a hand-whipped egg white into the filling before baking. The result is a Key lime pie with a perfectly balanced, luxurious filling and cloud of cream on top, the ideal South Florida dessert.

MAKES ONE 9-INCH PIE, SERVING 8

### GRAHAM CRACKER CRUST

1½ cups (180 g/6.3 oz) graham cracker crumbs (from about 12 whole graham crackers)

2 tablespoons (25 g/0.88 oz) granulated sugar

6 tablespoons (85 g/3 oz) unsalted butter, melted

### KEY LIME FILLING

4 large egg yolks plus 1 large egg white

1¼ cups (397 g/14 oz) sweetened condensed milk

2 teaspoons (4 g/0.14 oz) finely grated lime zest

⅔ cup (161 g/5.6 oz) strained Key lime or Persian lime juice

⅛ teaspoon (0.38 g/0.01 oz) cream of tartar

(CONTINUED)

## Make the crust

1. Preheat the oven to 350°F. In a medium bowl, combine the graham cracker crumbs and sugar until well blended. Add the melted butter and stir until blended. Pat the mixture into the bottom and up the sides of a 9-inch pie pan. Bake the crust for about 8 minutes, until lightly browned. Set the pan on a wire rack and let the crust cool completely. Reduce the oven temperature to 325°F.

## Make the filling

2. In a medium bowl, whisk the egg yolks until smooth. Add the sweetened condensed milk and lime zest and juice and mix until blended.

3. In a medium bowl, using a hand whisk or handheld electric mixer, beat the egg white until foamy. Add the cream of tartar and whip until shiny and stiff peaks form. Gently fold the egg white into the yolk mixture.

4. Scrape the filling into the cooled crust. Place the pie on a baking sheet and bake for 13 to 16 minutes, until the filling is just set. Transfer the pie pan to a wire rack to cool completely. Refrigerate the pie for at least 2 hours before making the topping.

1 cup (232 g/8.18 oz) heavy cream

½ teaspoon (2 g/0.07 oz) vanilla extract

¼ cup (32 g/1.1 oz) confectioners' sugar, sifted

½ teaspoon (1 g/0.03 oz) finely grated lime zest

## *Make the topping and top the pie*

**5.** In the bowl of an electric mixer fitted with the whisk attachment, whip the cream with the vanilla at high speed until soft mounds begin to form. Add the confectioners' sugar and whip at high speed until firm peaks form. Scrape the whipped cream on top of the chilled pie and swirl it decoratively into an even layer. Sprinkle the lime zest on top and refrigerate the pie until ready to serve.

# Lemon Buttermilk Cupcakes with White Chocolate–Lemon Frosting

*The acidity of lemon* cuts through the richness of white chocolate and is a counterpoint to its sweetness, making these cupcakes indulgent yet refreshing. I used to turn my nose up at white chocolate — I found it cloyingly sweet and slightly chalky. These days, however, you can buy excellent-quality white chocolate that is smooth and creamy, with a subtle hint of vanilla. My favorite brands include Guittard, Valrhona, and Green & Black's.

MAKES 12 CUPCAKES

### LEMON BUTTERMILK CUPCAKES

1⅓ cups (176 g/6.2 oz) all-purpose flour

¼ teaspoon (1.25 g/0.04 oz) baking soda

⅛ teaspoon (0.83 g/0.03 oz) salt

9 tablespoons (127 g/4.5 oz) unsalted butter, softened

¾ cup (150 g/5.3 oz) granulated sugar

2 teaspoons (4 g/0.14 oz) finely grated lemon zest

2 large eggs

⅔ cup (161 g/5.7 oz) buttermilk

1 tablespoon plus 1½ teaspoons (23 g/0.8 oz) freshly squeezed lemon juice

### WHITE CHOCOLATE–LEMON FROSTING

6 oz (170 g) high-quality white chocolate, chopped

12 tablespoons (170 g/6 oz) unsalted butter, at room temperature

1 cup (227 g/8 oz) cream cheese, at room temperature

(CONTINUED)

## Make the cupcakes

1. Preheat the oven to 350°F. Line a standard 12-cup muffin pan with cupcake liners.

2. In a medium bowl, sift together the flour, baking soda, and salt. Whisk to combine and set aside.

3. In the bowl of an electric mixer fitted with the paddle attachment, beat the butter at medium-high speed until creamy, about 30 seconds. Gradually add the sugar and lemon zest and beat at high speed until light and fluffy, about 3 minutes. Reduce the speed to medium and add the eggs one at a time, mixing well after each addition and scraping down the sides of the bowl with a rubber spatula as necessary. Reduce the speed to low and add the flour mixture in three additions, alternating with the buttermilk in two additions and mixing just until blended. Add the lemon juice and mix until just combined. Remove the bowl from the mixer stand and stir the batter a few times with a rubber spatula to make sure it's fully blended. Divide the batter among the prepared cups.

4. Bake for 23 to 28 minutes, until a toothpick inserted into the center of the lightest cupcake comes out clean and the cupcakes are lightly browned around the edges. Set the pan on a wire rack and let cool completely.

2 teaspoons (4 g/0.14 oz) finely
grated lemon zest

2 teaspoons (4 g/0.14 oz) finely
grated lemon zest

## *Make the frosting*

**5.** Place the white chocolate in a medium bowl and set the bowl
over a medium saucepan half filled with barely simmering water.
Heat, stirring occasionally, until the chocolate is melted and smooth
(watch it carefully — white chocolate scorches easily and should be
heated gently). Remove the bowl from the heat and set aside to cool.

**6.** In the bowl of an electric mixer fitted with the paddle attachment, beat the butter, cream cheese, and lemon zest at medium
speed until smooth and creamy, about 3 minutes. Reduce the speed
to low and add the melted white chocolate, mixing until blended.
Beat at medium speed until smooth and creamy, 1 to 2 minutes. If
you see any lumps in the frosting, whisk the frosting vigorously by
hand until completely smooth. Refrigerate the frosting for 15 to 20
minutes (but not longer), until just firm enough to pipe or spread.

## *Frost the cupcakes*

**7.** Scrape the frosting into a pastry bag fitted with a ½-inch plain
tip, such as Ateco #6, and pipe a generous spiral of frosting on top
of each cupcake. Sprinkle some lemon zest on top of each cupcake.
Serve immediately, or refrigerate in an airtight container until ready
to serve (up to 3 days); bring to room temperature before serving.

# Orange Cupcakes with Mascarpone Frosting

*Sweet and slightly tangy* mascarpone cheese pairs very nicely with orange and its floral under-tones. These tender orange cupcakes are filled with a silky smooth orange curd, then topped with a spiral of vanilla-scented mascarpone frosting and a sprinkling of cake crumbs. I like to use vanilla paste in the frosting so it's speckled with tiny vanilla seeds.

MAKES 12 CUPCAKES

### ORANGE CURD

4 large egg yolks

6 tablespoons (75 g/2.6 oz) granulated sugar

1 teaspoon (2 g/0.07 oz) finely grated lemon zest

1 teaspoon (2 g/0.07 oz) finely grated orange zest

6 tablespoons (90 g/3.2 oz) freshly squeezed orange juice

Pinch of salt

8 tablespoons (113 g/4 oz) unsalted butter, cut into tablespoons

1 teaspoon (5 g/0.17 oz) Cointreau or Grand Marnier (optional)

### ORANGE CUPCAKES

1½ cups (182 g/6.4 oz) cake flour

1¼ teaspoons (6 g/0.2 oz) baking powder

¼ teaspoon (1.7 g/0.06 oz) salt

8 tablespoons (113 g/4 oz) unsalted butter, softened

1 cup (200 g/7 oz) granulated sugar

2 large eggs

(CONTINUED)

## Make the orange curd

1. Set a fine-mesh sieve over a medium bowl and set aside. In a medium, heavy, nonreactive saucepan, whisk together the egg yolks and sugar until blended. Stir in the citrus zests, orange juice, salt, and butter and cook over medium heat, whisking constantly, until the mixture thickens, 3 to 5 minutes (do not let the mixture boil, or it will curdle). The mixture should leave a path on the back of a wooden spoon when you draw your finger across it. Immediately strain the mixture through the sieve, pressing it through with a rubber spatula.

2. Prepare an ice bath by filling a larger bowl one-third full with ice and water, and place the bowl of curd in it. Stir frequently until the curd is slightly chilled, about 10 minutes. Stir in the Cointreau, if using. Press a piece of plastic wrap directly on the surface of the curd and refrigerate until ready to use (up to 3 days).

## Make the cupcakes

3. Preheat the oven to 350°F. Line a standard 12-cup muffin pan with cupcake liners.

4. In a medium bowl, sift together the flour, baking powder, and salt and whisk to combine.

5. In the bowl of an electric mixer fitted with the paddle attachment, beat the butter at medium speed until creamy, about 30 seconds.

2 teaspoons (4 g/0.14 oz) finely grated orange zest

3 tablespoons (45 g/1.6 oz) strained freshly squeezed orange juice

⅓ cup (80 g/2.8 oz) whole milk

MASCARPONE FROSTING

⅔ cup (170 g/6 oz) mascarpone cheese

¾ cup (174 g/6.13 oz) heavy cream

2 tablespoons (25 g/0.88 oz) granulated sugar

1 teaspoon (4 g/0.14 oz) vanilla bean paste or extract

GARNISH

Orange zest (optional)

Gradually add the sugar and beat at high speed for 3 minutes, until well blended and light. Scrape down the sides of the bowl with a rubber spatula, reduce the speed to medium, and add the eggs one at a time, beating well after each addition and mixing until blended. Beat in the orange zest and the orange juice until blended (the batter may look curdled at this point, depending on the temperature of your eggs). Reduce the speed to low and add the flour mixture in three additions, alternating with the milk in two additions. Mix just until blended. Scrape the batter into the prepared muffin cups, dividing it evenly.

6. Bake the cupcakes for 18 to 22 minutes, until they are a light golden brown and a toothpick inserted into the center of a cupcake comes out clean. Let cool in the pan on a wire rack for 5 minutes. Transfer the cupcakes to the wire rack to cool completely.

### Fill the cupcakes

7. Using a paring knife, cut out a cone-shaped piece, about 1 inch in diameter and ¾ inch deep, from the center of each cupcake. Set the pieces aside for snacking, or discard them. Fill the center of each cupcake with a scant tablespoon of the orange curd, letting it spread out over the surface of the cupcake to about ¼ inch from the edge. Refrigerate the cupcakes while you make the frosting.

### Make the frosting and finish the cupcakes

8. Combine all the frosting ingredients in a large bowl and whisk by hand just until soft peaks form — don't overbeat, or the frosting will become grainy. Scrape the frosting into a pastry bag fitted with a medium star tip, such as Ateco #6. Pipe a generous swirl of frosting on top of the orange curd on each cupcake. Sprinkle with the orange zest, if using. Refrigerate the cupcakes in an airtight container until ready to serve, up to 3 days. Serve slightly chilled.

# Light Lemon Layer Cake

*Here's a vintage American* chiffon cake, frosted with a classic French buttercream. A lemon syrup lends extra tang to the cake and toasted almonds sprinkled on top add a nice crunch.

MAKES ONE 9-INCH LAYER CAKE, SERVING 10

SPECIAL EQUIPMENT:
Candy thermometer

### LEMON CHIFFON CAKE

1 cup (114 g/4 oz) cake flour

¾ cup (150 g/5.3 oz) granulated sugar, divided

1 teaspoon (5 g/0.17 oz) baking powder

¼ teaspoon (1.6 g/0.06 oz) salt

4 large eggs, separated, at room temperature

⅓ cup (68 g/2.4 oz) vegetable oil

2 tablespoons (12 g/0.42 oz) finely grated lemon zest

3 tablespoons (45 g/1.6 oz) freshly squeezed lemon juice

2 tablespoons (30 g/1 oz) whole milk

½ teaspoon (2 g/0.07 oz) vanilla extract

¼ teaspoon (0.77 g/0.027 oz) cream of tartar

### LEMON SYRUP

⅓ cup (80 g/2.8 oz) freshly squeezed lemon juice

½ cup (100 g/3.5 oz) granulated sugar

(CONTINUED)

## Make the cake

1. Preheat the oven to 325°F. Grease and flour the bottom of a 9-inch springform pan.

2. In a medium bowl, sift together the flour, ½ cup (100 g/3.5 oz) of the sugar, the baking powder, and salt and whisk to combine.

3. In the bowl of an electric mixer fitted with the paddle attachment, beat the yolks, oil, lemon zest and juice, milk, and vanilla at medium speed until blended, 1 minute. Reduce the speed to low and add the flour mixture, one-quarter at a time, mixing just until blended.

4. Place the egg whites and the cream of tartar in a clean mixer bowl and, using the whisk attachment, beat at medium speed until soft peaks form. Gradually beat in the remaining ¼ cup (50 g/1.76 oz) sugar; raise the speed to high and beat until the whites are stiff but not dry. Using a rubber spatula, briskly fold about one-quarter of the whites into the cake batter. Gently fold in the remaining whites. Scrape the batter into the prepared pan and smooth the top.

5. Bake the cake for 22 to 28 minutes, until golden brown and a toothpick inserted into the center of the cake comes out clean. Let the cake cool in the pan on a wire rack for 10 minutes. Invert the cake onto the rack and let cool, upside down, completely.

## Make the syrup

6. Combine the lemon juice and sugar in a small nonreactive saucepan and cook over medium heat, stirring, until the sugar is dissolved. Remove the pan from the heat.

⅔ cup (156 g/5.5 oz) water

½ cup (100 g/3.5 oz) granulated sugar

One ½-inch piece (9 g/0.32 oz) fresh ginger, peeled and thinly sliced

LIME MOUSSE

2 tablespoons (30 g/1 oz) water

1 teaspoon (3 g/0.1 oz) unflavored powdered gelatin

8 large egg yolks

1¼ cups (250 g/8.8 oz) granulated sugar

½ cup (121 g/4.3 oz) lime juice

2 tablespoons (30 g/1 oz) freshly squeezed lemon juice

⅛ teaspoon (0.8 g/0.03 oz) salt

10 tablespoons (142 g/5 oz) unsalted butter, cut into tablespoons

1 cup plus 2 tablespoons (261 g/9.2 oz) heavy cream

GARNISH

3 tablespoons (17 g/0.6 oz) unsweetened shredded coconut

1 cup (232 g/8.18 oz) heavy cream

3 tablespoons (24 g/0.84 oz) confectioners' sugar

½ teaspoon (2 g/0.07 oz) vanilla extract

10 minutes. Invert the pan onto the rack and let the cake cool, upside-down, completely.

## *Make the ginger syrup*

**6.** In a small saucepan, combine the water and sugar and bring to a boil over medium-high heat, stirring occasionally just to dissolve the sugar. Remove from the heat and add the ginger. Let stand at room temperature until ready to use.

## *Make the mousse*

**7.** Place the water in a small, heatproof measuring cup. Sprinkle the gelatin over the water and let the mixture stand for 5 minutes to soften. Set the cup in a pan of simmering water for a few minutes, stirring occasionally, until the gelatin is dissolved and the mixture is clear. Keep the cup of gelatin in the hot water, off the heat, until ready to use.

**8.** Set a fine-mesh sieve over a medium bowl and set aside. In a medium, heavy-bottomed, nonreactive saucepan, whisk together the egg yolks and sugar until blended. Stir in the lime and lemon juices, salt, and butter and cook over medium heat, whisking constantly, until the mixture thickens, 7 to 10 minutes (do not let the mixture boil, or it will curdle). The mixture should leave a path on the back of a wooden spoon when you draw your finger across it. Remove the pan from the heat and stir in the warm gelatin mixture. Immediately strain the mixture through the sieve, pressing it through with a rubber spatula.

**9.** Prepare an ice bath by filling a large bowl one-third full with ice and water and set the bowl containing the lime mixture in it. Stir the lime mixture frequently until it is slightly cooler than room temperature, about 10 minutes.

**10.** In the bowl of an electric mixer fitted with the whisk attachment, beat the cream at high speed until medium-firm peaks form. Fold a large spoonful of the whipped cream into the lime mixture to lighten it. Gently fold in the remaining cream.

*The desserts in* this chapter all feature the flavor of sweet cheese. Most are made with American cream cheese, but a few feature either mascarpone or ricotta cheese. Sweet and slightly tangy, cream cheese adds a distinctive flavor and wonderful texture to desserts. It is rich, smooth, and creamy, particularly when combined with heavy cream or sour cream. This chapter includes several cheesecakes: Crème Fraîche Cheesecake (made with a combination of cream cheese and crème fraîche), Raspberry Swirl Cheesecake, Orange-Kissed Ricotta Cheesecake Bars, Japanese-Style Cheesecake, and Whipped Vanilla Bean Cheesecake. Other desserts were inspired by cheesecake: Cheesecake and Berry Trifles, Cheesecake Mousse Crêpes, Raspberry Cheesecake Cupcakes, and Cheesecake Tart with Ginger–Lemon Curd Topping.

For consistent results, I recommend you use Philadelphia brand cream cheese, which has added stabilizers — carob bean gum and carrageenan — that give cheesecake filling its firm texture. When using cream cheese, pay attention to any recipe instructions, if given, regarding what temperature it should be: Using ice-cold cream cheese in a batter can lead to a lumpy cheesecake. Some of my recipes will direct you to melt the cream cheese with the liquids before mixing it with other ingredients, a process that ensures an ultra-smooth filling.

You can find mascarpone cheese in the dairy section of gourmet stores and good supermarkets. It is sold in 8.8-ounce tubs and is usually imported from Italy, which makes it expensive, but there's nothing in the world like this sweet, rich, and incredibly luxurious cheese. For ricotta cheese, use fresh if available. It is sometimes sold at the deli counter at supermarkets or in clear plastic containers in the cheese section of gourmet shops.

# Lemon Cheesecake Ice Cream

*This ice cream* was inspired by a frozen lemon cheesecake pie I was served many years ago on a visit to my great aunt Hattie in Montreal. The pie was made by Hattie's housekeeper, who was kind enough to write out the recipe for me. The ice cream base (an ice cream mixture is referred to as a "base" before it's churned) has a bright lemon flavor tempered by the tangy flavors of classic American cheesecake. I love to eat this right out of the ice cream maker, when it's soft and creamy. Slivers of candied ginger or crumbled amaretti cookies would be welcome additions; simply add them during the final minute of processing.

**MAKE ABOUT 1½ QUARTS**

**SPECIAL EQUIPMENT:**
Ice cream maker

1 cup (242 g/8.4 oz) whole milk

1 cup (232 g/8 oz) heavy cream

1½ cups (300 g/10.5 oz) granulated sugar

2 cups (454 g/1 lb) cream cheese

1½ cups (362 g/12.8 oz) sour cream

2 teaspoons (4 g/0.14 oz) finely grated lemon zest

⅔ cup (160 g/5.6 oz) freshly squeezed lemon juice

1 teaspoon (4 g/0.14 oz) vanilla extract

1. Combine the milk, cream, and sugar in a small saucepan and place over medium-high heat. Cook, stirring frequently, until the sugar dissolves and the liquid begins to boil. Remove from the heat.

2. Place the cream cheese in a blender and, while blending at low speed, slowly add the hot milk mixture and blend until smooth. Transfer the mixture to a medium bowl and whisk in the sour cream, lemon zest and juice, and vanilla until smooth. Cover the bowl and refrigerate the ice cream base for at least 6 hours or overnight.

3. When you're ready to make the ice cream, whisk the chilled base well, then process in an ice cream maker according to the manufacturer's instructions. Transfer the ice cream to an airtight container and freeze until ready to serve (or up to a month).

# Cheesecake Mousse Crêpes with Mixed Berries

*Mixed berries are* a bright complement to the vanilla-scented cheesecake mousse that fills these buttery crêpes. When you make your first crêpe, you'll soon be able to tell if the batter is the correct consistency. If it's on the thick side (which will make your crêpes heavy), just add a little more milk, one teaspoon at a time, until the batter forms a perfect, delicately thin crêpe. Although you only need eight crêpes, the batter makes ten, so there will be a couple left over for the cook to nibble on.

MAKES 8 CRÊPES

### CRÊPES (MAKES ABOUT TEN 8-INCH CRÊPES)

1 cup (132 g/4.6 oz) all-purpose flour

1 tablespoon (12 g/0.42 oz) granulated sugar

Pinch of salt

2 large eggs

1⅓ cups (322 g/11.36 oz) whole milk

3 tablespoons (42 g/1.5 oz) unsalted butter, melted

¼ teaspoon (0.5 g/0.02 oz) finely grated lemon zest

Vegetable oil or melted butter, for cooking the crêpes

### CHEESECAKE MOUSSE FILLING

1½ cups (348 g/12.3 oz) heavy cream, divided

¾ cup (150 g/5.3 oz) granulated sugar, divided

½ cup (113 g/4 oz) cream cheese, cut into 1-inch chunks

(CONTINUED)

## Make the crêpes

1. In a medium bowl, whisk together the flour, sugar, and salt. Whisk in the eggs along with ⅔ cup (161 g/5.7 oz) of the milk until smooth. Gradually whisk in the remaining ⅔ cup (161 g/5.7 oz) milk, the melted butter, and lemon zest. Transfer the batter to a pitcher or container with a pouring lip. Cover the container and refrigerate the batter for at least 2 hours (or up to 3 days). Don't skip this step—chilling the batter will allow the flour to absorb the liquid and the gluten to relax.

2. Place a 10-inch nonstick skillet over medium heat and allow it to get hot. Brush the pan with a little vegetable oil or melted butter, then pour in a scant ¼ cup crêpe batter, rolling the pan from side to side to coat it evenly. When the bottom of the crêpe has begun to brown, after 30 seconds to 1 minute, turn the crêpe (I use a long, nonstick offset spatula to flip it, but you can use a silicone spatula to lift up an end, then turn the crêpe over with your fingers or, if you're really competent, you can flip it over in the air) and cook on the other side for another 10 to 15 seconds. Place the cooked crêpe on a piece of parchment paper on a plate. Continue cooking the crêpes until all the batter has been used, stacking the crêpes one on top of another as they are finished.

⅓ cup (80 g/2.8 oz) sour cream or plain Greek yogurt (either full-fat or low-fat)

1 teaspoon (4 g/0.14 oz) vanilla extract

MIXED BERRIES

2 cups (227 g/8 oz) fresh strawberries, hulled and sliced lengthwise

3 tablespoons (37 g/1.3 oz) granulated sugar

1 teaspoon (4 g/0.14 oz) freshly squeezed lemon juice

½ cup (56 g/2 oz) fresh raspberries

½ cup (70 g/2.4 oz) fresh blueberries or blackberries

ASSEMBLY

Confectioners' sugar, for dusting

## *Make the mousse filling*

**3.** In a small saucepan, heat ½ cup (116 g/4 oz) of the cream, ½ cup (100 g/3.5 oz) of the sugar, and the cream cheese over medium heat, whisking frequently, until the cream cheese is melted and the mixture is smooth. Transfer the mixture to a medium bowl and set aside to cool to room temperature.

**4.** In the bowl of an electric mixer fitted with the whisk attachment, beat the remaining 1 cup (232 g/8 oz) cream, the remaining ¼ cup (50 g/1.75 oz) sugar, the sour cream (or yogurt), and vanilla at high speed until the cream forms medium peaks. Gently fold the whipped cream into the cream cheese mixture one-third at a time. Cover the bowl and refrigerate the mousse until ready to serve the crêpes.

## *Prepare the berries*

**5.** In a medium bowl, toss together the strawberries, sugar, and lemon juice. Cover the bowl and let macerate for 45 minutes in the refrigerator.

**6.** Gently stir in the raspberries and blueberries.

## *Assemble the crêpes*

**7.** Place a crêpe on a plate and spoon a little less than ½ cup of the cheesecake mousse filling over one half. Spoon some of the mixed berries on top and fold the crêpe over, leaving some of the filling exposed. Dust with confectioners' sugar and serve immediately.

*Sweet Cheese*

# Tiramisu Parfaits

*At first I* couldn't decide if this recipe was more at home in the coffee or the cheese chapter, but finally settled on cheese, because for me, the mascarpone filling is the star attraction of these indulgent parfaits. As in a classic tiramisu, a layer of sponge cake — in this case, genoise — is soaked with sweetened espresso and then layered with a dark rum–spiked mascarpone cream. A light dusting of cocoa powder decorates the top. These can be made up to a day ahead and, in fact, are better after chilling in the refrigerator for a few hours.

**MAKES 6 PARFAITS**

### CLASSIC GENOISE

1 cup (100 g/3.5 oz) sifted cake flour

¼ teaspoon (1.6 g/0.06 oz) salt

6 large eggs

¾ cup (150 g/5.2 oz) granulated sugar

½ teaspoon (1 g/0.03 oz) finely grated lemon zest

1 teaspoon (4 g/0.14 oz) vanilla extract

6 tablespoons (85 g/3 oz) unsalted butter, melted and cooled

### ESPRESSO SYRUP

1 cup (240 g/8.4 oz) hot espresso or strongly brewed coffee

¼ cup (50 g/1.7 oz) granulated sugar

½ teaspoon (2 g/0.07 oz) vanilla extract

### MASCARPONE CREAM

6 large egg yolks

¾ cup (150 g/5.3 oz) granulated sugar

1 tablespoon (15 g/0.5 oz) water

(CONTINUED)

## Make the genoise

1. Preheat the oven to 350°F. Grease the bottom and sides of two 9-inch round cake pans, then dust the pans with flour.

2. In a medium bowl, sift together the flour and salt and whisk to combine.

3. In the bowl of an electric mixer, whisk together the eggs and sugar by hand. Set the bowl over a saucepan of simmering water, making sure that the bottom of the bowl does not touch the water. Heat the egg mixture, whisking constantly, until the eggs are just warm to the touch. Transfer the bowl to the electric mixer stand and, using the whisk attachment, beat on high speed until the mixture has tripled in volume, about 4 minutes. Reduce the speed to low and beat in the lemon zest and vanilla.

4. Sift one-third of the flour mixture over the batter and gently fold it in with a rubber spatula. In two more additions, sift in the remaining flour mixture, again folding gently. Have the melted butter in a small bowl. Scoop about ¾ cup of the cake batter into the bowl with the butter and stir until blended. Fold this mixture into the remaining cake batter. Scrape the batter into the prepared pans, dividing it equally.

5. Bake the cakes for 12 to 15 minutes, until the tops spring back when lightly touched and a tester inserted into the centers comes

⅓ cup (80 g/2.8 oz) sour cream

1 teaspoon (4 g/0.14 oz) vanilla extract

SAUCY BERRY LAYER

3 cups (340 g/12 oz) fresh strawberries, hulled

1⅔ cups (170 g/6 oz) fresh raspberries

3 tablespoons (37 g/1.3 oz) granulated sugar

1 teaspoon (5 g/0.17 oz) freshly squeezed lemon juice

1 tablespoon (15 g/0.5 oz) Cointreau (optional)

## Make the cheesecake layer

5. Combine ½ cup (116 g/4 oz) of the cream with ⅓ cup (67 g/ 2.35 oz) of the sugar in a small saucepan and place over medium-high heat. Cook, stirring frequently, until the sugar is dissolved and the cream comes to a gentle boil. Remove from the heat.

6. In the bowl of an electric mixer fitted with the paddle attachment, beat the cream cheese at medium speed until smooth, about 1 minute. Gradually add the remaining ⅓ cup (67 g/2.35 oz) sugar and beat for 2 minutes. Remove the bowl from the mixer stand and gradually whisk in the hot cream mixture by hand, mixing until perfectly smooth. Whisk in the sour cream and vanilla. Cover the bowl and refrigerate the mixture until well chilled, about 2 hours.

7. In the bowl of an electric mixer fitted with the whisk attachment, whip the remaining ¾ cup (174 g/6 oz) cream at high speed to medium peaks. Gently fold the whipped cream in two additions into the chilled cream cheese mixture. Cover the bowl and refrigerate the mousse for at least 2 hours.

## Make the berry layer

8. Slice 1½ cups (170 g/6 oz) of the strawberries and place them in a medium bowl with the raspberries. Place the remaining strawberries in the bowl of a food processor along with the sugar, lemon juice, and Cointreau, if using, and process until smooth. Scrape the puree over the berries in the bowl and toss to coat. Cover the bowl and refrigerate until ready to assemble the trifles.

## Assemble the trifles

9. Cut enough of the cake into ½-inch cubes to measure 2⅔ cups (save the leftover cake for snacking). Place ⅓ cup of the cake cubes in the bottom of each of 4 parfait glasses. Top with ⅓ cup of the berry mixture, then ⅓ cup of the cheesecake layer. Repeat layering the cake cubes, berries, and cheesecake once more. Refrigerate, covered with plastic wrap, until ready to serve.

# Mascarpone Custard Tart

*Though it's frequently* labeled as and referred to as cheese (including in this book), mascarpone is really a curdled cream that comes from the Lombardy region of Italy. With a delicate flavor and soft texture, it makes a luscious addition to this custard tart, which I like to serve with fresh berries scattered over the top. For a showier presentation, you can chill the tart, sprinkle the top with a thin layer of demerara sugar, and caramelize it with a blowtorch. Or you could swirl or pipe whipped cream that has been sweetened with brown sugar all over the top and garnish with sliced strawberries or assorted berries.

MAKES ONE 11-INCH TART, SERVING 8 TO 10

### TART CRUST

1 cup (132 g/4.6 oz) all-purpose flour

½ cup (57 g/2 oz) cake flour

¾ teaspoon (3.1 g/0.1 oz) granulated sugar

¼ teaspoon (1.6 g/0.06 oz) salt

9 tablespoons (127 g/4.5 oz) unsalted butter, cut into ½-inch cubes and frozen for 20 minutes

2 tablespoons (30 g/1 oz) ice-cold water

### MASCARPONE CUSTARD FILLING

4 large eggs

½ cup firmly packed (108 g/ 3.8 oz) light brown sugar

1 cup (247 g/8.7 oz) mascarpone cheese

¾ cup (174 g/6.13 oz) heavy cream

1½ teaspoons (6 g/0.21 oz) vanilla bean paste or extract

¼ teaspoon (1.6 g/0.06 oz) salt

### SERVING

Fresh berries

### Make the tart crust

1. Place the flours, sugar, and salt in the bowl of a food processor and pulse a few times to combine. Add the butter pieces and toss lightly to coat with flour. Blend the butter and flour with about five 1-second pulses, or until the mixture is the texture of coarse meal with some butter pieces the size of peas. Sprinkle the water over the flour mixture and process continuously until the dough begins to clump together. Do not overprocess; the dough should not form a ball. Turn the dough out onto a work surface and shape it into a thick 4-inch-wide disc. Wrap the dough in plastic wrap and refrigerate until firm enough to roll, about 30 minutes.

2. Place the unwrapped dough on a lightly floured work surface. Using a rolling pin, roll the dough out to a 14-inch circle, lifting and rotating the dough often and dusting the work surface and dough lightly with flour as necessary. Lay the dough on top of an 11-inch tart pan with a removable bottom and gently press the dough onto the bottom and up the sides of the pan. Roll the pin over the top of the pan to trim off the excess dough. Lightly prick the bottom of the dough in the pan with a fork at ½-inch intervals. Refrigerate the dough in the pan for 20 minutes to firm it up.

3. Preheat the oven to 400°F. Right before baking, line the dough with aluminum foil or parchment paper and fill with pie weights or dried beans. Place the tart pan on a baking sheet and bake for 15 minutes. Carefully lift the foil (along with the weights) out of the

tart pan and bake the crust for 5 to 8 minutes longer, until it is beginning to brown lightly around the edges. Reduce the oven temperature to 350°F. Transfer the tart pan to a wire rack and let the tart shell cool completely.

### *Make the filling and bake the tart*

**4.** In a medium bowl, whisk together the eggs and brown sugar until well blended. Whisk in the mascarpone, cream, vanilla, and salt. Place the cooled tart shell on a baking sheet and slowly pour the custard filling into it. Bake for 30 to 35 minutes, until the filling is set and lightly browned. Let the tart cool completely on a wire rack.

### *Serve the tart*

**5.** Once cool, serve the tart immediately with fresh berries scattered on top of each slice, or refrigerate, loosely covered with plastic wrap, for up to 3 days. Bring to room temperature before serving.

# Ginger–Lemon Cheesecake Tart

*This lovely tart* combines a creamy cheesecake filling with a sharp, ginger-infused lemon curd topping. A subtle note of ginger reappears in the crust, which is made from gingersnap cookie crumbs. It is, in my opinion, the perfect dessert, particularly when served with ripe, farmstand berries and a spoonful of whipped cream.

MAKES ONE 11-INCH TART, SERVING 8

### GINGERSNAP CRUST

1¾ cups (216 g/7.6 oz) gingersnap crumbs (about 30 cookies; see recipe, page 145)

3 tablespoons (37 g/1.3 oz) granulated sugar

4 tablespoons (56 g/2 oz) unsalted butter, melted

### CHEESECAKE FILLING

2 cups plus 2 tablespoons (454 g/1 lb) cream cheese, at room temperature

¾ cup (150 g/5.3 oz) granulated sugar

1 large egg

2 teaspoons (10 g/0.35 oz) freshly squeezed lemon juice

½ teaspoon (2 g/0.07 oz) vanilla extract

⅛ teaspoon (0.83 g/0.03 oz) salt

⅓ cup (80 g/2.8 oz) sour cream

3 tablespoons (43 g/1.5 oz) heavy cream

### GINGER-LEMON CURD TOPPING

One 3-inch piece (35 g/1.2 oz) fresh ginger

2 large eggs plus 2 large egg yolks

(CONTINUED)

## Make the crust

1. In a medium bowl, toss together the gingersnap crumbs, sugar, and melted butter until combined. Pat the mixture into the bottom and up the sides of an 11-inch tart pan with a removable bottom. Refrigerate the crust while you make the filling.

## Make the filling and bake the tart

2. Preheat the oven to 350°F. In the bowl of an electric mixer fitted with the paddle attachment, beat the cream cheese on medium-high speed until light and creamy, about 2 minutes. Gradually add the sugar and beat until well combined, about 2 minutes longer. Reduce the speed to medium-low and add the egg, beating until well blended. Add the lemon juice, vanilla, and salt and beat just until combined. Add the sour cream and heavy cream and beat until blended. Remove the bowl from the mixer stand and stir with a rubber spatula to make sure the batter doesn't have any lumps and is well blended.

3. Scrape the batter into the prepared crust and bake the tart until the filling is puffed around the edges and the center is set, 25 to 30 minutes. Place the tart on a wire rack and let cool completely.

## Make the topping

4. Peel the ginger and finely grate it. Place it in a fine-mesh sieve over a bowl and press it with a spatula to extract as much juice as possible. You will need 1 tablespoon of juice, but you should get more from the ginger. Set the ginger juice aside.

*Sweet Cheese*

½ cup plus 1 tablespoon
(112 g/4 oz) granulated sugar

⅛ teaspoon (0.8 g/0.03 oz) salt

1½ teaspoons (3 g/0.1 oz) finely
grated lemon zest

½ cup (125 g/4.4 oz) freshly
squeezed lemon juice

4 tablespoons (56 g/2 oz)
unsalted butter, cut into
tablespoons

SERVING

Sweetened whipped cream

Fresh berries

5. In a medium heatproof bowl (preferably stainless steel), whisk together the eggs, egg yolks, sugar, and salt until blended. Stir in the lemon zest and juice, and butter. Place the bowl over a saucepan filled one-third full with barely simmering water over low heat and cook, stirring constantly with a wooden spoon or silicone spatula, until the butter is completely melted and the curd thickens, 4 to 6 minutes. Remove from the heat and strain the curd through a fine-mesh sieve into a medium bowl. Stir in the reserved 1 tablespoon ginger juice. Cover the surface of the curd with a piece of plastic wrap and let it cool until tepid.

6. Pour the cooled curd on top of the cheesecake tart, spreading it to the edges of the filling with a small offset metal spatula. Refrigerate the tart for at least 2 hours before serving.

### Serve the tart

7. Serve slices of the tart topped with sweetened whipped cream and fresh berries.

# Orange-Kissed Ricotta Cheesecake Bars

*Made with a combination* of ricotta cheese, cream cheese, and sour cream, these cheesecake bars have a creamy texture and luscious, slightly tangy flavor with just a hint of orange. The bars are baked in a water bath, a necessary precaution since direct heat can cause the delicate filling to curdle. Though you may be tempted to eat them right out of the oven, the bars need to be chilled for at least four hours before they are cut. The bonus is that they can be made up to three days in advance. If you like, garnish each bar with a twist of orange zest.

MAKES 8 BARS

### GRAHAM CRACKER CRUST

1½ cups (185 g/6.5 oz) honey graham cracker crumbs (from about 12 whole graham crackers)

2 tablespoons (25 g/0.88 oz) granulated sugar

5 tablespoons (70 g/2.5 oz) unsalted butter, melted

### ORANGE-RICOTTA FILLING

1 cup (242 g/8.5 oz) whole-milk ricotta cheese

1 cup (228 g/8 oz) cream cheese, at room temperature

⅔ cup (133 g/4.7 oz) granulated sugar

2 large eggs plus 1 large egg yolk

1 cup (242 g/8.5 oz) sour cream or heavy cream

1 teaspoon (2 g/0.07 oz) finely grated orange zest

¼ cup (60 g/2.1 oz) freshly squeezed orange juice

2 teaspoons (10 g/0.35 oz) freshly squeezed lemon juice

2 teaspoons (5 g/0.17 oz) cornstarch

1 teaspoon (4 g/0.14 oz) vanilla extract

¼ teaspoon (1.6 g/0.05 oz) salt

### Make the crust

1. Preheat the oven to 350°F. Line a 9-inch square baking pan with aluminum foil, leaving a 3-inch overhang on two opposite sides. Brush the foil with butter or coat it with nonstick cooking spray.

2. In a medium bowl, combine the graham cracker crumbs, sugar, and melted butter. Press the mixture evenly over the bottom of the prepared pan. Bake for 12 to 15 minutes, or until the crust is just lightly browned and fragrant. Transfer to a wire rack and let cool. Leave the oven on.

### Make the filling and bake the bars

3. Place the ricotta in the bowl of a food processor and process until smooth, about 30 seconds.

4. In the bowl of an electric mixer fitted with the paddle attachment, beat the cream cheese on medium-high speed until light and creamy, about 2 minutes. Gradually add the sugar and beat until well combined, about 2 minutes longer. Reduce the speed to medium-low and add the eggs and egg yolk one at a time, beating well after each addition and scraping down the sides of the bowl with a rubber spatula once or twice. Add the ricotta, sour cream or heavy cream, orange zest and juice, lemon juice, cornstarch, vanilla, and salt and mix just until blended.

**5.** Scrape the batter over the prepared crust. Place the pan in a roasting pan and pour enough very hot water into the roasting pan so that it comes about halfway up the sides of the baking pan. Bake until the filling is set and is no longer wobbly, about 45 minutes. Remove the baking pan from the water bath and let the bars cool completely on a wire rack.

**6.** Refrigerate the bars for at least 4 hours or overnight before serving.

**7.** Carefully lift the bars out of the pan using the foil overhang as handles. Using a sharp knife, cut the block in half, then cut each half into 4 bars, making eight 2¼-by-4½-inch rectangles.

# Raspberry Cheesecake Cupcakes

*There's a lot* to be said for portable, individual-sized cheesecakes, especially when they're topped with a trio of shiny, ruby-colored raspberries. While most standard-size cheesecakes require several hours of chilling before they can be served, these cupcakes only need to be chilled for an hour before they can be garnished and served.

MAKES 12 CUPCAKES

### GRAHAM CRACKER CRUSTS

1 cup (120 g/4.2 oz) graham cracker crumbs (from about 8 whole graham crackers)

2 tablespoons (25 g/0.88 oz) granulated sugar

3 tablespoons (42 g/1.5 oz) unsalted butter, melted

### CHEESECAKE FILLING

1½ cups (340 g/12 oz) cream cheese, at room temperature

⅔ cup (133 g/4.7 oz) granulated sugar

1 teaspoon (4 g/0.14 oz) vanilla extract

⅛ teaspoon (0.83 g/0.03 oz) salt

2 large eggs, at room temperature

⅓ cup (80 g/2.8 oz) sour cream

1½ teaspoons (3.5 g/0.125 oz) cornstarch

1 teaspoon (2 g/0.07 oz) finely grated lemon zest

### SOUR CREAM TOPPING

¾ cup (181 g/6.4 oz) sour cream

2 teaspoons (8 g/0.28 oz) granulated sugar

½ teaspoon vanilla extract

(CONTINUED)

## Make the crusts

1. Preheat the oven to 325°F. Line a 12-cup standard muffin pan with cupcake liners.

2. In a medium bowl, stir together the graham cracker crumbs, sugar, and melted butter. Set aside 2 tablespoons of the mixture in a small bowl. Divide the remaining mixture among the muffin cups (a rounded tablespoon or so per cup) and, using your fingers, pat it into an even layer on the bottom of each cup. Bake the crusts until very lightly browned and fragrant, 7 to 9 minutes. Let the crusts cool on a wire rack while you make the filling. Leave the oven on.

## Make the filling and bake the cupcakes

3. In the bowl of an electric mixer fitted with the paddle attachment, beat the cream cheese at low speed until creamy and smooth, about 1 minute. Gradually add the sugar and beat for another minute, until well blended. Beat in the vanilla and salt. Add the eggs one at a time, scraping down the sides of the bowl as necessary and mixing until well blended. Add the sour cream and cornstarch and mix until combined. Remove the bowl from the mixer stand and stir the filling a few times by hand to make sure it is smooth and well blended. Pass the batter through a fine-mesh sieve into a large glass measuring cup with a pouring spout, pressing the batter against the sieve with a rubber spatula to get all of it. Stir the lemon zest into the strained batter. Pour the filling into the muffin cups, filling each almost to the top.

**RASPBERRY GARNISH**

⅓ cup (100 g/3.5 oz) raspberry preserves (with or without seeds)

½ teaspoon (2.5 g/0.08 oz) water

1½ cups (170 g/6 oz) fresh raspberries

**4.** Bake the cheesecake cups for 20 to 25 minutes, until the tops begin to crack and the centers are set. Set the pan on a wire rack to cool while you make the sour cream topping (the cheesecakes will sink slightly in the center as they cool). Leave the oven on.

## Make the topping and top the cupcakes

**5.** In a small bowl, stir together the sour cream, sugar, and vanilla. Spoon 1 tablespoon of the mixture in the center of each cheesecake and, using the back of a spoon, spread it over the top of each cheesecake, covering it completely. Return the cheesecakes to the oven for another 8 to 10 minutes, just until the topping is set. Place the pan on a wire rack and let cool completely.

**6.** Once the cheesecakes are cool, refrigerate them for at least 1 hour before garnishing.

## Garnish the cupcakes

**7.** Place the raspberry preserves in a microwave-safe bowl and microwave on high power until hot and bubbling, about 20 seconds. Pass the preserves through a fine-mesh sieve into a small bowl and stir in the water. Arrange 3 raspberries in the center of each cheesecake. Brush the raspberries with the glaze. Sprinkle the tops of the raspberries with a little of the reserved graham cracker crumbs. Serve the cheesecakes immediately, or refrigerate in an airtight container until ready to serve, up to 3 days.

*Sweet Cheese*

# Japanese-Style Cheesecake with Fresh Raspberries

*This incredibly light cake* bears little resemblance to dense, American-style cheesecakes. Whipped egg whites give it a soufflé-like texture, but once chilled, the cheese and butter in the cake firm up, turning it into the softest, lightest cheesecake in the world. The recipe comes from my friend Lace Zhang, an amazing baker from Singapore who owns Baked by Lace, a home-based bakery specializing in cakes and cupcakes.

MAKES ONE 9-INCH CAKE, SERVING 8

### JAPANESE-STYLE CHEESECAKE

⅓ cup (38 g/1.3 oz) cake flour

2 tablespoons plus 1½ teaspoons (20 g/0.7 oz) cornstarch

1¾ cups (375 g/13.2 oz) cream cheese, cut into 1-inch chunks

½ cup (125 g/4.4 oz) whole milk

4½ tablespoons (63 g/2.2 oz) unsalted butter, cut into ½-inch cubes

5 large eggs, separated, at room temperature

¼ teaspoon (1.6 g/0.06 oz) salt

¾ cup (150 g/5.3 oz) granulated sugar, divided

1 teaspoon (2 g/0.07 oz) finely grated lemon zest

½ teaspoon (2 g/0.07 oz) vanilla extract

### GARNISH

2 cups (226 g/8 oz) fresh raspberries

Confectioners' sugar, for dusting

## Make the cheesecake

1. Preheat the oven to 300°F. Butter the bottom and sides of a 9-inch springform pan. Line the bottom of the pan with a round of parchment paper and butter the parchment paper. Wrap the outside of the pan with a piece of aluminum foil (18-inch-wide heavy-duty foil is best); this will prevent water from leaking in during baking and making the crust soggy.

2. In a medium bowl, sift together the flour and cornstarch and gently whisk to blend.

3. Place the cream cheese, milk, and butter in a heatproof bowl over a pot of simmering water and whisk until the cream cheese is melted and the mixture is smooth. Remove the bowl from the pot and allow the mixture to cool for 10 minutes.

4. In a medium bowl, whisk together the egg yolks and salt until blended. Gradually whisk in ½ cup (100 g/3.5 oz) of the sugar and whisk vigorously until well blended and pale. Whisk in the cream cheese mixture, lemon zest, and vanilla until combined. Add the flour mixture in three additions, whisking just until blended.

5. In the bowl of an electric mixer fitted with the whisk attachment, whip the egg whites at high speed until they form soft peaks. Gradually add the remaining ¼ cup (50 g/1.76 oz) sugar and continue to whip at high speed until the whites are glossy and form stiff peaks.

Fold one-third of the whipped whites into the cream cheese mixture, then fold the cream cheese mixture into the remaining whites.

**6.** Scrape the batter into the prepared springform pan. Place the pan in a roasting pan and pour enough very hot water into the pan so that it comes about 1 inch up the sides of the springform pan. Bake for 55 to 60 minutes, until the cheesecake is a light golden brown on top, puffed, and set in the center (it should wobble a little, but shouldn't look liquid—jiggle the pan slightly to test). Turn the oven off, prop the door open with a wooden spoon, and let the cake cool in the oven for 1 hour.

**7.** Remove the springform pan from the roasting pan and let the cake cool on a wire rack for 20 minutes.

**8.** Run a sharp knife around the edge of the pan and remove the side of the springform pan. Carefully invert the cake onto a serving plate (the browned top will now be on the bottom). Peel off the parchment paper. Refrigerate the cake for at least 4 hours before serving.

### *Garnish and serve the cheesecake*

**9.** Cover the top of the cake with the fresh raspberries, pointed ends up. Dust the cake lightly with sifted confectioners' sugar right before serving.

# Whipped Vanilla Bean Cheesecake with Blueberry Sauce

*The inspiration for* this recipe was a cake I remember from my childhood, although I've transformed it into something entirely new. It came from our local bakery, Miller's, and was an ultralight cheesecake layered with an equally feathery cocoa cake. The cheesecake filling, the part I loved most, was the no-bake variety, and was probably made with quark, a soft, unripened cow's-milk cheese. I decided to try my own version using whipped cream cheese, which is much more readily available, and replaced the cocoa cake with a honey graham crust. The result is an airy, vanilla-speckled cake that's every bit as good as the cake from Miller's. I serve it with a honeyed blueberry sauce drizzled on top.

MAKES ONE 9-INCH CAKE, SERVING 12

### PECAN-GRAHAM CRACKER CRUST

½ cup (50 g/1.76 oz) pecan halves

1½ cups (180 g/6.3 oz) honey graham cracker crumbs (from about 12 whole graham crackers)

2 tablespoons (25 g/0.88 oz) granulated sugar

5 tablespoons (70 g/2.5 oz) unsalted butter, melted

### WHIPPED VANILLA CHEESECAKE FILLING

1 cup (242 g/8.5 oz) whole milk, divided

2½ teaspoons (7.75 g/0.27 oz) unflavored powdered gelatin

1 cup (200 g/7 oz) granulated sugar

2⅔ cups (454 g/1 lb) whipped cream cheese, such as Philadelphia brand, divided

1 cup (242 g/8.5 oz) sour cream

(CONTINUED)

## Make the crust

1. Preheat the oven to 350°F. Butter the bottom and sides of a 9-inch springform pan.

2. Place the pecans in the bowl of a food processor and process until finely ground. Transfer to a medium bowl, add the graham cracker crumbs and sugar, and stir until well blended. Add the melted butter and stir until blended. Pat the mixture into the bottom and about 1 inch up the sides of the prepared pan. Bake the crust for about 8 minutes, until lightly browned. Set the pan on a wire rack and let the crust cool completely.

## Make the cheesecake filling

3. Place ½ cup (121 g/4.26 oz) of the milk in a small bowl. Sprinkle the gelatin over the milk and set aside to soften.

4. Place the remaining ½ cup (121 g/4.26 oz) milk, the sugar, and 1⅓ cups (227 g/8 oz) of the cream cheese in a medium saucepan over medium-low heat. Cook, whisking constantly, until the cream cheese melts and the mixture is smooth, about 3 minutes. Add the gelatin mixture and whisk until the gelatin is dissolved. Pour the

*Sweet Cheese*

refrigerate. Transfer the remaining puree to a plastic squeeze bottle or covered small bowl and refrigerate until ready to use.

**4.** In the bowl of an electric mixer fitted with the paddle attachment, beat the cream cheese at medium speed until very creamy, about 1 minute. Gradually add the remaining 1 cup (200 g/7 oz) sugar and continue to beat until light and creamy, about 2 minutes more. Reduce the speed to medium-low and add the eggs, one at a time, beating well after each addition and scraping down the sides with a rubber spatula once or twice. Add the cornstarch, vanilla, lemon zest, and salt and mix until blended. Add the sour cream and heavy cream and mix until blended, scraping down the bowl again to make sure the mixture is evenly blended. Transfer 3 cups (710 g/25 oz) of the batter to a medium bowl and stir in the reserved ⅓ cup (80 g/2.8 oz) raspberry puree.

### *Bake the cheesecake*

**5.** Pour the raspberry batter into the cooled crust. Using a large spoon, gently spoon the plain batter over the raspberry layer so that it's completely covered. Using a small offset metal spatula, carefully smooth the plain cheesecake batter into an even layer. Using the squeeze bottle and starting at the center of the cheesecake, squeeze out the puree in a spiral pattern to the edge of the cake, leaving about an inch of space between the lines (if you don't have a squeeze bottle, drizzle the puree with a spoon). Using a dinner knife and starting at a point on the edge of the cake, drag the knife through the batter in a figure-eight pattern *just once,* ending where you started. Reserve any remaining puree to serve with the cake.

**6.** Place the cake pan in a roasting pan and add enough very hot water to the roasting pan so that it comes about one-third of the way up the side of the springform pan. Bake for 1 hour—the center will still be a little wobbly. Turn the oven off (don't open the door), and let the cheesecake cool in the oven for another hour.

**7.** Remove the cheesecake from the water bath and let it cool completely on a wire rack.

**8.** Refrigerate the cake for at least 6 hours before serving.

**9.** Garnish the cheesecake with the 12 reserved raspberries and drizzle a little raspberry puree on each plate.

**PEACH TOPPING**

3 ripe medium peaches

⅓ cup (103 g/3.6 oz) apricot preserves

1 tablespoon (15 g/0.5 oz) water

Sliced almonds, for garnish

**4.** Scrape the batter over the prepared crust. Place the pan in a roasting pan and pour enough very hot water into the roasting pan so that it comes about 1 inch up the sides of the springform pan. Bake until the filling is set and only slightly wobbly, 70 to 80 minutes. Turn the oven off and let the cake cool in the turned-off oven for 1 hour. Remove the springform pan from the water bath and let the cheesecake cool completely on a wire rack.

**5.** Refrigerate the cheesecake for at least 4 hours or overnight before topping and serving.

### Make the topping and top the cheesecake

**6.** Cut the peaches in half and discard the stones. Slice the peach halves into ¼-inch wedges. Arrange a circle of peach slices, overlapping them slightly, around the edge of the chilled cheesecake. Continue arranging peach slices in concentric circles, working your way to the center of the cake and covering the cheesecake completely.

**7.** Pass the apricot preserves through a fine-mesh sieve into a small, microwave-safe cup. Stir in the water and microwave on high power for 15 to 30 seconds, until bubbling. Brush the tops of the peaches with the hot glaze and sprinkle with some sliced almonds. Refrigerate the cake, uncovered, for at least 30 minutes (or up to 24 hours) before serving.

# Nuts

❖  ❖

God gives the nuts, but he does
not crack them.

— FRANZ KAFKA

*Each nut has* its own character: Almonds and pistachios have a mellow, rounded flavor, while pecans and walnuts have a slightly bittersweet edge. Some of my favorite flavor partners for pistachio include white chocolate, coconut, and sour cherry; the bold flavor of pecans and walnuts has a natural affinity to sweet apples and pears, and spices such as cinnamon and ginger. Because both nuts are slightly bitter, they also go well with sweet ingredients, such as maple syrup, golden syrup, and brown sugar. The flavors of hazelnuts and peanuts are more intense, and consequently, both stand up well to a strong flavor like chocolate. (Peanuts are technically legumes, not nuts, but because they are such a popular flavor, I am granting them temporary honorary "nut" status and including them in this chapter.)

For most nuts, toasting brings out their depth of flavor. The longer the toasting, the more intense the flavor will be. (See page 13 for toasting guidelines.)

But beyond whole nuts, there are many other options for imparting nutty flavor to desserts, such as nut pastes, butters, and flours. Almond paste, almond butter, and almond flour are all widely available to the home cook. For peanuts, store-bought peanut butter is the best ingredient to use to capture the essence of peanuts in desserts —it's convenient, inexpensive, and easy to store. To add texture, use chopped peanuts in addition to the peanut butter.

Most important, when using any nut product, make sure the nuts are not rancid before adding them to your recipe. Nuts contain unsaturated oils, which spoil faster than saturated oils. The best way to see if your nuts are fresh is to take the plunge and bite into one. If it tastes sour or even slightly off, don't use that batch of nuts (and find yourself a different source). Since baking ingredients tend to be expensive, the last thing you want to do is ruin whatever you're making by adding rancid nuts that you neglected to test. To keep them fresh, store your nuts in an airtight container in the freezer. Store nut butters in the refrigerator for up to three months to ensure freshness. Almond flour should be stored in an airtight container in a cool, dark place.

# Caramelized Chocolate Almonds

*Also known as* givrettes, these are toasted almonds that have been caramelized, coated in tempered chocolate, and then dusted with cocoa powder and confectioners' sugar. Yes, all this is time-consuming and a little messy, but boy oh boy, are these good. I love to make batches of them around the holidays to give as gifts. Since the amount of chocolate is relatively small here, I use a different method of tempering, which works better with small amounts of chocolate, than the one on page 17. This recipe requires some patience, but it's worth it, and that's a guarantee.

**MAKES ABOUT 1 POUND**

**SPECIAL EQUIPMENT:**
Instant-read thermometer

½ cup (100 g/3.5 oz) granulated sugar

2 tablespoons (30 g/1 oz) water

2 cups (300 g/10.5 oz) whole unblanched almonds, toasted (see page 13)

6 ounces (170 g) high-quality semisweet chocolate (62%), preferably Guittard or Valrhona

⅓ cup (37 g/1.3 oz) unsweetened Dutch-processed cocoa powder

½ cup (64 g/2.25 oz) confectioners' sugar, divided

1. Line a baking sheet with a silicone baking mat or piece of parchment paper. Combine the sugar and water in a medium, heavy-bottomed saucepan and bring to a boil over medium-high heat. Add the nuts and stir to coat them evenly with the syrup. Continue to cook, stirring constantly — the sugar will crystallize and turn sandy. Then, as you continue to stir, the sugar crystals will remelt and liquefy, gradually turning to a golden brown caramel. When most of the sandy sugar has melted, remove the pan from the heat.

2. Carefully spread the caramelized nuts onto the prepared baking sheet — they will be extremely hot — trying to separate the nuts as much as possible with a wooden spoon, then use two forks to further separate the nuts. Let the nuts cool completely (if your baking sheet fits in the freezer, freeze the nuts until they are cool).

3. Once cool, break up any remaining clusters of nuts with your hands. Place the nuts in a bowl and place the bowl in the freezer while you temper the chocolate.

4. To temper the chocolate, take 1 ounce (29 g) of the chocolate (make sure that it is shiny and does not have any streaks on its surface) and, using the finest holes on a box grater, grate it onto a piece of parchment. You will need 1 tablespoon, which will be less than 1 ounce (it's easier to grate a larger piece than a smaller one). Place the grated chocolate in a small bowl and set aside in a cool place. Chop the remaining 5 ounces (141 g) chocolate (and any solid chocolate that was left over from grating) and place it in a heatproof bowl. Line a baking sheet with a piece of parchment.

**5.** Place the bowl of chocolate over a saucepan filled one-third of the way with water and turn the heat to medium low. Heat the chocolate slowly, stirring frequently, until it is almost melted. Check the temperature — you want to heat the chocolate just to 110°F, but no higher. When it gets to be about 105°F, turn the heat off and stir the chocolate until it just reaches 110°F. Remove the bowl from the pan, and set aside to let the chocolate cool. Let the chocolate cool gradually, stirring it occasionally so that it cools evenly and checking the temperature often, until it reaches exactly 87°F. When it reaches 87°F, add the reserved grated chocolate and stir to combine. Return the bowl to the pan of water and gently heat the chocolate, stirring constantly, just for a minute or two, until most of the grated chocolate is melted. (Watch it carefully — it is important that you don't heat the chocolate above 90°F.) The chocolate has now been "tempered" and is ready to use.

**6.** Remove the nuts from the freezer. Pour one-third of the tempered chocolate over the nuts and, using a rubber spatula, quickly stir the nuts to coat them. Drizzle the remaining chocolate over the nuts while continuing to stir, then stir until the chocolate begins to set up and harden.

**7.** Sift the cocoa powder and 1 tablespoon (8 g/0.28 oz) of the confectioners' sugar over the nuts in the bowl and, using your hands (this is where things get messy — if you happen to have food-service gloves on hand, now's a good time to wear them!), toss them until they are coated with cocoa powder (break up any remaining clumps of nuts at the same time). Working with small batches, transfer the nuts to a fine-mesh sieve and shake them to remove any excess cocoa powder.

**8.** Place the remaining confectioners' sugar in a bowl and add half the nuts, tossing to coat them. Place them in the sieve over the bowl of confectioners' sugar and shake to remove excess sugar. Transfer them to the prepared baking sheet. Repeat with the remaining nuts and sugar. Store the nuts in an airtight container in a cool place for up to 1 month.

*Nuts*

# Chocolate-Almond Toffee

*I make this classic* confection every year around the holidays, and when I do I probably eat about half of it. I know, not a winning formula, but I just can't resist it, it's that good. The combination of buttery toffee, crunchy toasted almonds, and dark chocolate is totally addictive. It makes a wonderful gift, particularly when wrapped in a cellophane bag that is finished with a pretty ribbon. It's also great coarsely chopped and served over ice cream.

MAKES ABOUT 1½ POUNDS

SPECIAL EQUIPMENT: Candy thermometer

2 cups (240 g/8.4 oz) blanched slivered almonds

7 ounces (198 g) bittersweet chocolate (64% to 70%)

12 tablespoons (170 g/6 oz) unsalted butter

¼ teaspoon (1.6 oz/0.05 oz) fine salt

2 tablespoons (30 g/1 oz) water

1 cup (200 g/7 oz) granulated sugar

¾ cup firmly packed (162 g/5.7 oz) light brown sugar

¼ teaspoon (1.25 g/0.04 oz) baking soda

1 teaspoon (1 g/0.03 oz) vanilla extract

1½ teaspoons (4.5 g/0.15 oz) fleur de sel or Maldon sea salt

1. Preheat the oven to 350°F. Brush the bottom of a 10-by-15-inch rimmed baking sheet with vegetable oil. Use a paper towel to wipe off any excess oil so that the sheet is lightly coated.

2. Place the almonds on a separate baking sheet and bake for 5 to 8 minutes, until lightly golden and fragrant. Let cool.

3. Set aside half of the toasted nuts (these will be stirred into the toffee layer). Place the remaining nuts in the bowl of a food processor and pulse until they are finely chopped. Set aside (these nuts will be used to sprinkle on top of the chocolate layer).

4. Finely chop the chocolate and set aside.

5. Put a small bowl of water and a pastry brush next to the stove (this will be used for washing down the sides of the pan during cooking).

6. In a medium, heavy-bottomed saucepan, combine the butter, salt, water, and sugars and cook over medium heat, stirring gently just until the butter is melted. Increase the heat to medium-high, insert a candy thermometer, and cook, without stirring, until the mixture registers 298°F, occasionally brushing down the sides of the pan with water to prevent sugar crystals from forming. Remove the pan from the heat and immediately stir in the reserved unchopped almonds, then the baking soda and vanilla. Once blended, immediately pour the hot toffee onto the oiled baking sheet, using a small offset metal spatula to spread it evenly into a rectangle that is roughly 8 by 13 inches. While the toffee is hot, sprinkle the choco-

late over it in an even layer. Let the chocolate sit for 2 minutes to melt. Then, using a small offset metal spatula, spread it over the toffee to cover completely. Sprinkle the chopped almonds and the fleur de sel over the melted chocolate. Refrigerate the toffee for 20 minutes, or just until the chocolate is set.

7. Holding it with a piece of waxed paper, break the toffee into shards. Store in an airtight container at room temperature for up to 1 week.

# White Chocolate Holiday Bark and Mendiants

*Green pistachios, red cranberries,* and white chocolate combine festively in these two crunchy and flavorful holiday sweets. Everyone knows what bark is, but you may not be familiar with *mendiants*, little discs of chocolate topped with nuts and dried fruit. I like to package both in small cellophane bags and tie them with ribbon to give as gifts (almost as good as cash!). Make either or both, but be sure to use the best white chocolate you can find—store-brand white chocolate morsels, which have a high melting point and an oily taste and texture, just don't make the grade.

MAKES ABOUT 1⅓ POUNDS BARK OR TWENTY-FOUR 1½-INCH MENDIANTS

## BARK

1 cup (152 g/5.3 oz) unsalted shelled pistachios

17 ounces (482 g) high-quality white chocolate, chopped (I like Guittard, Valrhona, and Scharffen Berger)

¾ cup (90 g/3.17 oz) dried cranberries, divided

## MENDIANTS

¼ cup (38 g/1.3 oz) unsalted shelled pistachios

17 ounces (482 g) high-quality white chocolate, chopped

¼ cup (30 g/1 oz) dried cranberries

## To make bark

1. Preheat the oven to 350°F. Spread the pistachios on a baking sheet and toast in the oven until golden, 5 to 7 minutes, shaking the nuts halfway through the baking time. Let cool completely.

2. Line a 10-by-15-inch rimmed baking sheet with a piece of parchment paper and set aside. In a heatproof bowl over a pot of simmering water, temper the white chocolate according to the instructions on page 17. Remove the pot from the heat and stir half the pistachios and dried cranberries into the white chocolate. Remove the bowl from the pot and carefully wipe the bottom of the bowl dry (even a tiny drop of water can cause the white chocolate to seize and clump up). Pour the white chocolate onto the lined baking sheet and, using a small metal or rubber spatula, spread it into an even layer that covers all but 1 inch around the edges of the sheet. Sprinkle the remaining pistachios and cranberries evenly over the bark. Refrigerate the chocolate for just 20 minutes, until almost set (set your timer—don't refrigerate the chocolate for longer than 20 minutes).

3. Let the chocolate stand at room temperature for another 30 minutes, until completely set. Holding it with a piece of parchment or waxed paper (to avoid smudging the chocolate), break the

block into rugged hunks of bark. Store between layers of parchment or waxed paper in a tightly covered container at room temperature for up to 1 week.

### To make mendiants

1. Preheat the oven to 350°F. Spread the pistachios on a baking sheet and toast in the oven until golden, 5 to 7 minutes, shaking the nuts halfway through the baking time. Let cool completely.

2. Cut each pistachio in half and set aside.

3. Line two baking sheets with silicone baking mats or parchment paper. In a heatproof bowl set over a pot of simmering water, temper the white chocolate according to the instructions on page 17. Remove the bowl from the pot.

4. Scoop up some of the tempered white chocolate in a teaspoon and let it flow onto a prepared baking sheet into a 1½-inch round (hold the spoon very close to the baking sheet for best results). Repeat to make 12 rounds. (If the white chocolate begins to thicken, return the bowl to its position over the hot water to warm it slightly.) Top each round with 2 pistachio halves and 2 dried cranberries, arranging them as you like. Repeat to make 12 more rounds, for a total of 24 mendiants. Let the chocolates stand at room temperature until set, about 1 hour. Store the chocolates in an airtight container at room temperature.

# Toasted Almond—White Chocolate Truffles

*Neutral-tasting white chocolate* ganache is the ideal carrier for the familiar flavor of toasted almonds in these rich, crunchy truffles. The almonds are toasted to a dark brown color and then infused into cream before it is combined with the chocolate—it's the long toasting that gives the truffles their deep almond flavor. The ganache is formed into truffles and then coated with lightly toasted chopped almonds for added flavor and a crunchy finish. I always include these truffles in the assortment of confections I make around the holidays—everyone loves them.

**MAKES ABOUT 30 TRUFFLES**

1¾ cups (210 g/7.4 oz) slivered almonds, divided

½ cup plus 2 tablespoons (145 g/5.1 oz) heavy cream

12 ounces (340 g) high-quality white chocolate, chopped

1 tablespoon (14 g/0.5 oz) unsalted butter, softened

1 teaspoon (7 g/0.25 oz) light corn syrup

1. Preheat the oven to 350°F. Line a 9-inch square baking pan with a piece of parchment paper and set aside. Scatter the nuts on a rimmed baking sheet and bake for 8 minutes, until lightly toasted. Transfer 1¼ cups (126 g/4.44 oz) of the toasted nuts to a plate and set aside to cool. Return the remaining ½ cup (84 g/2.96 oz) nuts to the oven and toast for another 6 minutes, until deeply toasted (but not burnt). Set aside to cool for 5 minutes.

2. Place the cream and the ½ cup of deeply toasted nuts in a small saucepan and bring to a gentle boil over medium-high heat. Remove the pan from the heat, cover, and allow to infuse for 15 minutes.

3. Place the white chocolate and butter in a medium bowl and set aside. Strain the cream mixture through a fine-mesh sieve into a bowl and then return it to the saucepan (discard the nuts). Stir in the corn syrup. Heat the cream over medium-high heat until it just begins to bubble around the edges. Pour the hot cream over the white chocolate and gently whisk the mixture until the chocolate and butter are completely melted and the mixture is smooth. Scrape it into the prepared pan and spread it into an even layer. Cover the pan with plastic wrap and refrigerate for at least 2 hours, until firm enough to roll into truffles.

4. Line a rimmed baking sheet or plate with a piece of parchment paper. Scoop about 1¾ teaspoons of the white chocolate ganache from the pan and roll it into a ball. Place the ball on the prepared

pan and repeat with the remaining ganache (if the ganache softens, return it to the refrigerator for 10 minutes or until firm enough to roll). Refrigerate the ganache balls while you chop the nuts.

5. Place the reserved 1¼ cups lightly toasted nuts on a cutting board and chop so that you have some fine and some medium pieces. Roll the chilled ganache balls in the nuts to coat them. Place each truffle in a small paper truffle cup to serve. Store the truffles in an airtight container at cool room temperature for up to 1 week.

# Peanut Honeycomb

*Honeycomb is a hard,* toffee-flavored confection with an airy texture. When baking soda is added to the cooked toffee mixture, carbon dioxide is released and lots of little air bubbles are formed, resulting in the confection's trademark spongy appearance. This peanut honeycomb comes from Francisco Migoya, the head chef at Modernist Cuisine. Unlike peanut brittle, this honeycomb is easy on the teeth, allowing you to savor the crunch of the salty-sweet, toffee-coated peanuts while avoiding any unscheduled trips to the dentist. You can also dip shards of the honeycomb in tempered chocolate, if you like.

MAKES ABOUT 1½ POUNDS

1 tablespoon (15 g/0.5 oz) baking soda

2 cups (271 g/9.5 oz) lightly salted roasted peanuts

1 cup (200 g/7 oz) granulated sugar

1 cup (328 g/11.5 oz) light corn syrup

1. Line a rimmed baking sheet with a silicone baking mat or parchment paper.

2. Measure out the baking soda and place it in a small cup near the stove. In a 4-quart heavy-bottomed pot (do not use a smaller pot—the sugar mixture may overflow!), stir together the peanuts, sugar, and corn syrup. Place over medium heat and cook, stirring frequently, until the mixture begins to caramelize and turns a tan color. Remove the pot from the heat and sprinkle the baking soda over the hot mixture while stirring vigorously (be very careful, as the sugar is exceptionally hot and the mixture will expand once you add the baking soda, which is why you need a large pot). Immediately pour the mixture onto the prepared baking sheet, but don't try to flatten it or spread it out because that will cause it to lose its volume. Let cool completely.

3. Once cool, break the honeycomb into 1-inch shards. Store in an airtight container in a cool, dry place for up to 1 week.

# Hazelnut Ice Cream Sandwiches

*To achieve maximum flavor* in their hazelnut ice cream or gelato, pastry chefs and frozen dessert professionals typically rely on commercial nut pastes, which can be hard for the home cook to find. Luckily, you can get almost as much flavor simply by roasting unblanched hazelnuts in the oven until their skins turn dark brown, a trick I learned from Meredith Kurtzman, pastry chef of Mario Batali's Otto Pizzeria in New York. Meredith's roasting technique yields an ice cream that is infused with the fragrance of hazelnuts, any bitterness softly mellowed by the sweet cream. Though the ice cream can easily be served on its own, it's even better when sandwiched between two discs of crunchy hazelnut meringue, as it is here.

MAKES TEN 3-INCH ICE CREAM SANDWICHES

**SPECIAL EQUIPMENT:**
Instant-read thermometer; ice cream maker; pastry bag and medium plain tip

**HAZELNUT ICE CREAM**

2 cups (484 g/17 oz) milk, plus up to 1 cup (242 g/8.5 oz) more, as needed

2 cups (464 g/16.36 oz) heavy cream, divided

2 cups (255 g/9 oz) unblanched hazelnuts

1 cup (200 g/7 oz) granulated sugar, divided

7 large egg yolks

¾ teaspoon (5 g/0.17 oz) salt

½ teaspoon (2 g/0.07 oz) vanilla extract

**HAZELNUT MERINGUE COOKIES**

⅔ cup (85 g/3 oz) confectioners' sugar

½ cup (53 g/1.8 oz) unblanched hazelnuts

1 tablespoon plus 1½ teaspoons (12.5 g/0.44 oz) all-purpose flour

(CONTINUED)

## Make the ice cream

1. Preheat the oven to 350°F. Place the 2 cups (484 g/17 oz) milk and 1 cup (232 g/8.18 oz) of the cream in large saucepan.

2. Spread the hazelnuts on a baking sheet and toast in the oven for 20 to 25 minutes, until their skins are dark brown and the hazelnuts are golden brown beneath their skins and very fragrant. Carefully transfer the hot nuts to the bowl of a food processor and process (while still hot) until finely ground.

3. Add the ground nuts to the milk mixture, place the pan over medium heat, and bring to a simmer. Remove the pan from the heat, cover, and set aside to infuse for 40 minutes.

4. Strain the milk mixture through a fine-mesh strainer into a large heatproof glass measuring cup, pressing down on the nuts to extract as much liquid as possible. Discard the nuts. If needed, add enough milk to the hazelnut-infused liquid so that it measures 2¾ cups. Return the hazelnut milk mixture to the saucepan. Stir in the remaining 1 cup (232 g/8.18 oz) cream and ¾ cup (150 g/5.3 oz) of the sugar, and heat until the milk mixture just begins to bubble around the edges.

5. Whisk the remaining ¼ cup (50 g/1.76 oz) sugar, the egg yolks, and salt together in a medium heatproof bowl. Gradually add about

4 large egg whites, at room temperature

⅔ cup (133 g/4.7 oz) granulated sugar

GARNISH

½ cup (71 g/2.5 oz) blanched hazelnuts, toasted (see page 13) and finely chopped

1 cup of the hot milk mixture, whisking constantly, then return the mixture to the saucepan and cook over medium heat, stirring constantly with a heatproof spatula, until the custard registers 185°F on an instant-read thermometer. Immediately strain the custard through a fine-mesh strainer into a heatproof bowl. Stir in the vanilla. Prepare an ice bath by filling a large bowl one-third full with ice and water, and place the bowl of custard in it. Chill, stirring occasionally, until cold. Cover and refrigerate the ice cream base for at least 8 hours, or, preferably, overnight.

6. Freeze the base in an ice cream maker according to the manufacturer's instructions. Transfer the ice cream to an airtight container and freeze until ready to assemble the sandwiches, or up to a month.

## Make the meringue cookies

7. Position two racks near the center of the oven and preheat the oven to 300°F. Cut two pieces of parchment paper to fit two rimmed baking sheets. Using a pencil and a round cookie cutter or coaster as a guide, draw ten 3-inch circles on each sheet of the parchment, spacing the circles at least 2 inches apart. Turn the paper over so that the pencil lines are down and place a piece on each baking sheet.

8. In the bowl of a food processor, combine the confectioners' sugar, hazelnuts, and flour and process until the nuts are finely ground. Sift the mixture through a medium-mesh sieve into a medium bowl. If some of the hazelnut pieces are too large to go through the sieve, just whisk them into the sugar mixture.

9. Place the egg whites in the bowl of an electric mixer fitted with the whisk attachment and begin to whip them on low speed until foamy. Raise the mixer speed to medium and beat until soft peaks just begin to form. Gradually add the granulated sugar, then raise the speed to high and beat until the meringue is glossy and stiff peaks form. Remove the bowl from the machine and gently fold the hazelnut mixture into the meringue one-third at a time. Scrape the mixture into a pastry bag fitted with a ¼-inch plain tip, such as

Ateco #3. Pipe the meringue onto the prepared baking sheets, spiraling it from the outer edge of each circle into the center to form 3-inch discs. Place the baking sheets in the oven and turn off the heat. Leave them in the oven for about 2 hours, checking occasionally, until the meringues are completely dry and crispy. Store the cookies in an airtight container at room temperature until ready to assemble the ice cream sandwiches, up to 1 week.

### Assemble the sandwiches

10. Remove the ice cream from the freezer and allow it to soften for 10 minutes before scooping.

11. Using a ¼-cup (#20) ice cream scoop, place a large scoop of ice cream onto the flat side of one meringue cookie. Place another disc on top of the ice cream and press gently to spread the ice cream to the edges. Sprinkle some of the chopped hazelnuts around the edge, patting them into the ice cream so they stick. Repeat with the remaining ice cream and cookies. Freeze until the ice cream is firm, about 45 minutes. Once frozen, the sandwiches can be individually wrapped or stored in airtight containers and frozen until ready to serve, or up to 2 weeks.

# Pistachio and Walnut Baklava

*Baklava can be* really, *really* sweet, but this version won't send you into sugar shock. While Greek-style baklava is made with lots of honey, Turkish baklava uses a lemony sugar syrup to moisten the layers of baked phyllo and nuts. I prefer the Turkish kind, so I use a lemon syrup flavored with just a little honey. I also add a touch of orange blossom water, the clear, perfumed essence of distilled bitter orange blossoms, which gives the baklava a sweet floral note that complements the pistachios and walnuts so well. My preferred brand is Cortas, which is available in shops that specialize in Middle Eastern products and from several sources online, including amazon.com.

MAKES 16 SERVINGS

### NUT FILLING

1¾ cups (209 g/7.3 oz) unsalted shelled pistachios

1⅓ cups (133 g/4.7 oz) walnuts

¼ cup firmly packed (54 g/1.9 oz) light brown sugar

1 teaspoon (0.66 g/0.02 oz) ground cinnamon

½ teaspoon (0.33 g/0.01 oz) ground cloves

### SOAKING SYRUP

1¾ cups (350 g/12.3 oz) granulated sugar

¾ cup (177 g/6.3 oz) water

3 tablespoons (63 g/2.2 oz) mild honey

1 tablespoon (15 g/0.5 oz) freshly squeezed lemon juice

1 teaspoon (4 g/0.14 oz) orange blossom water

### PHYLLO LAYERS

Twenty 9-by-14-inch sheets (227 g/8 oz) phyllo dough

12 tablespoons (170 g/6 oz) unsalted butter, cut into tablespoons

## Make the filling

1. Preheat the oven to 350°F. Scatter the pistachios on a baking sheet and toast until just fragrant, about 5 minutes. Place the walnuts on a baking sheet and toast until lightly browned and fragrant, about 7 minutes. Cool both types of nuts completely. Leave the oven on.

2. Place the pistachios in the bowl of a food processor and process until most of the nuts are finely chopped (but not ground), with a few larger pieces here and there. Transfer 2 tablespoons of the pistachios to a small bowl and set aside to garnish the top of the baklava. Put the remaining pistachios in a large bowl.

3. Place the walnuts in the bowl of the food processor and process until most of the nuts are finely chopped (but not ground), with a few larger pieces here and there. Add the walnuts to the pistachios in the large bowl. Add the brown sugar, cinnamon, and cloves and stir well to combine. Set the filling aside.

## Make the syrup

4. In a small saucepan, combine the sugar, water, honey, and lemon juice and bring to a boil over medium-high heat, stirring occasionally, until the sugar is dissolved. Reduce the heat to a simmer and cook for 5 minutes more, until the syrup is slightly thickened. Remove the pan from the heat and stir in the orange blossom water.

## *Assemble the baklava*

**5.** Unwrap the phyllo dough and place it on a work surface. Cover the phyllo dough with plastic wrap and then a damp tea towel to prevent it from drying out as you work.

**6.** Place the butter in a glass measuring cup and microwave on 50 percent power until melted, about 2 minutes. Coat the bottom and sides of a 9-inch square baking pan with some of the melted butter. Uncover the phyllo dough and, using a sharp chef's knife, cut the stack into a 9-inch square. Peel one of the sheets off the stack and carefully place it in the bottom of the prepared pan. (Immediately re-cover the phyllo stack with the plastic wrap and tea towel each time you remove a sheet.) Brush the dough in the pan with melted butter and place another phyllo sheet on top. Brush the sheet with butter. Repeat until you have 7 sheets of buttered phyllo dough layered in the pan. Sprinkle one-third (about 1 cup) of the nut filling over the top sheet of phyllo and, using a small offset metal spatula or the back of a spoon, spread it into an even layer. Top with 3 more sheets of phyllo dough, brushing each with melted butter after they have been placed in the pan. Sprinkle another third of the nut filling on top and spread it into an even layer. Top with 3 more phyllo sheets, brushing them again with melted butter. Top with the remaining nut mixture, spreading it evenly in the pan. Finish with another 7 layers of phyllo dough, brushing each sheet with butter. Using a sharp knife, cut the baklava into 16 squares.

**7.** Bake for 25 to 30 minutes, until golden brown. Place the pan on a wire rack and pour the soaking syrup over the baklava, covering it completely. Garnish the top with the reserved chopped pistachios and cool until just warm, about 15 minutes, before serving.

# Pistachio Financiers

*The financier is a small* French cake named for its rectangular shape, which resembles a gold bar. The cakes are traditionally made with ground almonds and butter that is cooked until fragrant and hazelnut brown. This version was adapted from a recipe given to me by François Payard, the great pastry chef and owner of François Payard Bakery and FP Patisserie in New York, Las Vegas, and other spots around the globe. Instead of ground almonds, my version is made with pistachios, and each cake is baked with a fresh raspberry in its center. For convenience, I bake them in mini-muffin cups instead of financier molds. The cakes are crisp on the outside, soft on the inside, and absolutely addictive. Serve them with a cup of hot tea.

MAKES 24 FINANCIERS

¾ cup (114 g/4 oz) salted shelled pistachios

¾ cup (150 g/5.3 oz) granulated sugar, divided

¾ cup plus 2 tablespoons (100 g/3.5 oz/) cake flour

¾ teaspoon (3.75 g/0.13 oz) baking powder

4 large egg whites, at room temperature

1 teaspoon (4 g/0.14 oz) vanilla extract

10 tablespoons (141 g/5 oz) browned butter (page 19), hot

24 small fresh raspberries

1. Preheat the oven to 375°F. Coat 24 mini-muffin cups with non-stick cooking spray.

2. Place the pistachios and ¼ cup (50 g/1.7 oz) of the sugar in the bowl of a food processor and process until the nuts are finely ground. Transfer the mixture to a medium bowl and stir in the remaining ½ cup (100 g/3.5 oz) sugar. Sift the flour and baking powder over the ground nut mixture and whisk to combine.

3. In another bowl, whisk the egg whites just to break them up, then stir them into the nut mixture along with the vanilla. Add the hot browned butter and stir until blended. Let the batter stand for 10 minutes.

4. Scrape the batter into a disposable pastry bag, snip the tip to create a small opening, and pipe the batter into the prepared muffin cups. Arrange a raspberry, pointed side up, in the center of each financier.

5. Bake for 20 to 25 minutes, until lightly browned around the edges. Set the pan on a wire rack to cool for 10 minutes.

6. Invert the pan onto the rack, turn the financiers right side up, and let cool completely. Store in an airtight container at room temperature for up to 3 days.

# Pistachio and Coconut Macaroons

*The partnership of pistachio* and coconut might not be a famous one, but it *is* a good one, especially in these gooey, American-style macaroons. Sweetened coconut flakes and condensed milk make these cookies ultra-moist, while ground pistachios add a subtle nut fragrance and tweedy texture. Delicious just as they are, the cookies can also be gussied up by dipping their bottoms in tempered dark chocolate.

**MAKES 30 MACAROONS**

½ cup (76 g/2.7 oz) unsalted shelled pistachios, plus 2 tablespoons (19 g/0.67 oz) finely chopped unsalted shelled pistachios

½ teaspoon (2 g/0.08 oz) vegetable oil

¾ cup (227 g/8 oz) sweetened condensed milk

1 large egg white

½ teaspoon (2 g/0.07 oz) vanilla extract

⅛ teaspoon (0.8 g/0.03 oz) salt

3 cups (255 g/9 oz) sweetened flaked coconut

1. Preheat the oven to 325°F. Line a baking sheet with a silicone baking mat or piece of parchment paper.

2. Place the ½ cup (76 g/2.7 oz) whole pistachios in the bowl of a food processor and process until they are finely chopped. Add the vegetable oil and process until the pistachios are finely ground and just begin to clump together.

3. In a medium bowl, combine the ground pistachios, condensed milk, egg white, vanilla, and salt. Stir in the coconut. Scoop level tablespoons of the batter (I use a ½-ounce scoop) into mounds on the prepared baking sheet, spacing them about an inch apart. Sprinkle each mound with some of the finely chopped pistachios.

4. Bake the cookies for 20 to 25 minutes, until lightly browned around their bases. Let cool for 5 minutes on the baking sheet, then transfer to a wire rack to cool completely. Store the macaroons in an airtight container at room temperature for up to 5 days.

# Pistachio Linzer Hearts with Sour Cherry Filling

*Linzer dough is classically* made with hazelnuts or almonds, but this version is made with pistachios. The dough is rolled out and cut into heart-shaped cookies, which, after baking, are sandwiched with bright sour cherry preserves. The result is a tender, rich cookie with the soft fragrance of pistachios and a sweet-tart crimson filling. With the colors of Christmas, this cookie is an ideal addition to your holiday baking repertoire.

## MAKES 42 SANDWICH COOKIES

SPECIAL EQUIPMENT:
2-inch heart-shaped cookie cutter; ¾-inch round aspic cutter or pastry tip

### PISTACHIO COOKIES

½ cup (75 g/2.6 oz) unsalted shelled pistachios

½ cup (100 g/3.5 oz) granulated sugar, divided

16 tablespoons (228 g/8 oz) unsalted butter, softened

1 large egg yolk

2 cups (265 g/9.3 oz) all-purpose flour

½ teaspoon (1 g/0.03 oz) finely grated lemon zest

1 teaspoon (4 g/0.14 oz) vanilla extract

⅛ teaspoon (0.8 g/0.03 oz) salt

### ASSEMBLY

½ cup (150 g/5.3 oz) sour cherry preserves

⅓ cup (42 g/1.5 oz) confectioners' sugar

### Make the cookies

1. Place the pistachios and ¼ cup (50 g/1.76 oz) of the sugar in the bowl of a food processor and process until finely ground, about 45 seconds.

2. In an electric mixer fitted with the paddle attachment, beat the butter with the remaining ¼ cup (50 g/1.76 oz) sugar at medium speed until light, about 1 minute. Add the egg yolk and beat until thoroughly blended. Add the pistachio mixture, flour, lemon zest, vanilla, and salt and mix on low speed just until combined. Divide the dough in half and shape into two discs. Wrap each disc in plastic wrap and refrigerate for at least 2 hours, until firm.

3. Arrange two racks near the center of the oven and preheat the oven to 350°F. Place half the dough on a lightly floured work surface. Sprinkle the dough with flour. Roll out the dough to a thickness of ⅛ inch, flouring it as necessary to prevent sticking. Use a 2-inch heart-shaped cookie cutter to cut out as many hearts from the dough as possible, rerolling the scraps until all the dough is used (no need to rechill the dough). Repeat with the remaining dough.

4. Arrange half the cookies on a large ungreased baking sheet. Use a ¾-inch round aspic cutter or pastry tip to cut out the center of these cookies. Place the remaining whole cookies on another baking sheet. Bake the cookies for 11 to 13 minutes, until lightly golden around the edges. Let the cookies cool on the baking sheets set

on wire racks for 15 minutes. Using a metal spatula, gently transfer them to a wire rack to cool completely.

### *Fill and assemble the cookies*

5. Place the sour cherry preserves in a small bowl and stir vigorously until smooth. Spoon about ½ teaspoon of the preserves onto each whole cookie and, with a small offset metal spatula, spread it to within ¼ inch of the edge. Place the confectioners' sugar in a fine-mesh sieve and liberally sprinkle the surfaces of the cut-out cookies. Sandwich the cut-out tops and the bottoms together. Store in an airtight container at room temperature for up to 4 days.

# Pecan Sandwich Cookies

*Made with ground toasted* pecans, this dough makes a very tender, nutty cookie that is then sandwiched with a light cream cheese filling topped with finely chopped pecans. The filling has a very subtle maple flavor — if you want a more pronounced flavor, add ¼ teaspoon natural maple flavoring along with the maple syrup.

**MAKES ABOUT 40 SANDWICH COOKIES**

**SPECIAL EQUIPMENT:**
2-inch flower-shaped or round cookie cutter; ½-inch round pastry tip

**PECAN COOKIES**

1 cup (100 g/3.5 oz) pecans, toasted (see page 13)

⅔ cup plus 2 tablespoons (158 g/5.6 oz) granulated sugar, divided

2½ cups (331 g/11.7 oz) all-purpose flour

¼ teaspoon (1.7 g/0.06 oz) salt

16 tablespoons (226 g/8 oz) unsalted butter, softened

1 large egg

**CREAM CHEESE FILLING**

4 tablespoons (56 g/2 oz) unsalted butter, softened

½ cup (113 g/4 oz) cream cheese, at room temperature

½ cup (64 g/2.2 oz) confectioners' sugar, sifted

1 tablespoon (19 g/0.7 oz) maple syrup

½ teaspoon (2 g/0.07 oz) vanilla extract

Pinch of salt

⅓ cup (33 g/1.16 oz) pecans, toasted (see page 13) and finely chopped

## Make the cookies

**1.** Place the pecans and the 2 tablespoons (25 g/0.9 oz) sugar in the bowl of a food processor and process until the pecans are finely ground. Transfer to a medium bowl and whisk in the flour and salt.

**2.** In the bowl of an electric mixer fitted with the paddle attachment, beat the butter at medium speed until creamy, about 1 minute. Gradually add the remaining ⅔ cup (133 g/4.7 oz) sugar and beat on high speed until very light, about 5 minutes. Reduce the speed to medium and add the egg, mixing until blended and scraping down the sides of the bowl with a rubber spatula as necessary. Reduce the speed to low and add the pecan mixture in three additions, mixing just until blended. Divide the dough in half and shape each piece into a 5-inch square. Wrap each square in plastic wrap and refrigerate for at least 2 hours, until firm enough to roll.

**3.** Preheat the oven to 350°F. Line two baking sheets with silicone baking mats or parchment paper. Unwrap one of the dough squares and place it on a lightly floured work surface. Dust the dough lightly with flour and roll it out to a thickness of ⅛ inch. Slide a long metal spatula underneath the rolled dough to ensure it's not stuck to the work surface. Using a 2-inch flower-shaped or round cookie cutter, cut out as many cookies as possible from the dough. Using a ½-inch round pastry tip, cut out holes from the center of half the cookies. Arrange the cookies on one of the prepared baking sheets, spacing them ½ inch apart. Bake the cookies for 12 to 15 minutes, until they are just lightly browned around the edges. Let the cookies cool completely on the baking sheet. Gather the dough scraps, flatten them into a disc, wrap in plastic, and refrigerate for at least 30 minutes before re-rolling. Repeat the rolling, cutting, and baking process with the remaining square of dough and dough scraps.

## Make the filling

**4.** In the bowl of an electric mixer fitted with the paddle attachment, beat the butter and cream cheese at medium speed. Gradually add the confectioners' sugar, then add the maple syrup, vanilla, and salt. Raise the mixer speed to medium-high and beat until the filling is very smooth and light, about 5 minutes.

## Assemble the sandwich cookies

**5.** Spoon a grape-sized dollop of the filling onto each whole cookie and spread it to within about ¼ inch of the edge. Sprinkle the filling lightly with some of the finely chopped pecans. Top with a cookie with a cut-out center, pressing it down lightly. Refrigerate the cookies for about 20 minutes to set the filling before transferring the cookies to an airtight container. Store the cookies in the refrigerator for up to 5 days. Bring to room temperature before serving.

**4.** Preheat the oven to 325°F. Line two baking sheets with silicone baking mats or parchment paper. Remove one of the dough ovals from the refrigerator. Peel off the top piece of waxed paper. Replace it loosely and flip over the dough. Peel off the other piece of waxed paper. Using a 2-inch flower-shaped cookie cutter, cut out as many cookies as possible from the dough. Using the narrow end of a ½-inch plain pastry tip, such as Ateco #6, cut out a hole in the center of half of the cookies. Transfer the cookies to one of the baking sheets, spacing them ½ inch apart. Bake for 12 to 15 minutes, until they are just beginning to turn a very light brown around the edges. Let them cool on the baking sheet for 10 minutes before transferring to a wire rack to cool completely. Repeat with the remaining dough oval. Gather up the dough scraps, shape them into a disc, and re-roll between sheets of waxed paper to a thickness of ⅛ inch. Chill for at least 30 minutes before cutting out more cookies.

### Assemble the cookies

**5.** Spoon a heaping teaspoon of the ganache onto the flat bottom side of each of the whole cookies, leaving a ¼-inch border around the edge. Top each with a cookie with a hole in the center, pressing down lightly so that the ganache seeps through the hole slightly. Store the cookies in an airtight container in the refrigerator for up to 4 days. Bring to room temperature before serving.

# The Ultimate Pecan Pie

*You're probably thinking* I've got a lot of nerve including something as basic as a pecan pie in this book. After all, there's a decent recipe on the back of the corn syrup label, right? But once you make this recipe, my guess is that all will be forgiven, and you might even silently praise me every year when Thanksgiving rolls around and you need to impress a tableful of cranky relatives with the perfect pie. The basis for a successful pecan pie is a tender crust, and the addition of a little vinegar (which evaporates during baking) ensures this. The secret to the filling is trifold: replacing some of the white sugar with brown sugar, using Lyle's Golden Syrup for flavor (though light corn syrup works in a pinch), and adding just enough dark rum to give it a mysterious sweetness. While I can't promise everything will go smoothly for your Thanksgiving dinner, even if your turkey is overcooked, this pie will guarantee things will end on a good note. Note: Always taste your pecans before adding them to the filling to ensure they're not rancid. I've come across rancid pecans even in freshly opened bags, and they will ruin your pie.

MAKES ONE 9-INCH DEEP-DISH PIE, SERVING 8

SPECIAL EQUIPMENT:
9-inch deep-dish pie pan

PIE DOUGH

1½ cups (198 g/7 oz)
all-purpose flour

¼ teaspoon (1.6 g/0.06 oz) salt

9 tablespoons (127 g/4.5 oz)
unsalted butter, cut into
½-inch chunks and frozen for
15 minutes

1½ teaspoons (7 g/0.25 oz)
apple cider vinegar or white
vinegar

4 to 5 tablespoons (59 g/2 oz
to 74 g/2.6 oz) ice water

PECAN FILLING

4 large eggs

⅔ cup (132 g/4.6 oz)
granulated sugar

⅔ cup firmly packed (144 g/
5 oz) light brown sugar

## Make the pie dough

1. Place the flour and salt in the bowl of a food processor fitted with the metal chopping blade and pulse on and off until combined. Scatter the butter pieces over the flour mixture. Pulse the machine on and off until the mixture is crumbly and resembles coarse meal. Mix the vinegar with 4 tablespoons of the ice water, add it to the flour mixture, and process until the dough just starts to come together. (If the dough seems dry, add the remaining 1 tablespoon water as necessary. Do not allow the dough to form a ball on the blade, or the resulting crust may be tough.)

2. Turn the dough out onto a work surface and shape it into a thick disc. Wrap the disc in plastic wrap and refrigerate for at least 2 hours.

3. Position a rack in the lower third of the oven and preheat the oven to 350°F. Lightly butter the bottom and sides of a 9-inch deep-dish pie pan.

4. Place the unwrapped dough disc on a lightly floured work surface and sprinkle some flour over it. Roll out the dough from the center

1 cup (340 g/12 oz) Lyle's Golden Syrup or light corn syrup

4 tablespoons (56 g/2 oz) unsalted butter, melted

2 tablespoons (30 g/1 oz) dark rum

1 teaspoon (4 g/0.14 oz) vanilla extract

½ teaspoon (3.3 g/0.12 oz) salt

2½ cups (250 g/8.8 oz) pecan halves, coarsely chopped

in every direction, flouring the work surface as necessary to prevent sticking. You want a round about ⅛ inch thick or slightly thinner and about 13 inches in diameter. Transfer the dough to the pie pan by rolling it loosely around the rolling pin and unrolling it carefully over the pan. Press the dough first into the bottom of the pan and then against the sides. Patch any holes or cracks with dough scraps. Trim the edges of the dough with scissors, leaving about ¾ inch of overhang. Tuck the edge underneath itself and crimp the edge decoratively with your fingers. Refrigerate the pie shell while you make the filling.

### Make the filling and bake the pie

5. In a medium bowl, whisk the eggs until the yolks and whites are blended. Whisk in the sugars, breaking up any lumps of brown sugar in the mixture. Whisk in the syrup, melted butter, rum, vanilla, and salt. Stir in the pecans. Pour the filling into the prepared pie crust and place the pan on a baking sheet.

6. Bake the pie for 55 to 65 minutes, until the center is puffed and just set but still slightly quivery. Let the pie cool completely on a wire rack before serving. Store the pie, covered, in the refrigerator for up to 5 days, but bring to room temperature before serving.

# Toasted Almond Crunch Cupcakes

*These mellow almond* cupcakes are topped with a surprisingly light buttercream that's flavored with almond butter. A fine dusting of crunchy almond brittle is sprinkled on top of the cupcakes before and after they're frosted. You'll have some almond brittle crunch left over—it's difficult to make less than this amount—but it makes a great topping for ice cream. Almond butter is sold in supermarkets in the peanut butter aisle.

**MAKES 12 CUPCAKES**

SPECIAL EQUIPMENT:
Instant-read thermometer

**ALMOND CUPCAKES**

1½ cups (171 g/6 oz) cake flour

1½ teaspoons (7.5 g/0.26 oz) baking powder

¼ plus ⅛ teaspoon (2.5 g/ 0.09 oz) salt

9 tablespoons (127 g/4.5 oz) unsalted butter, softened

¾ cup (150 g/5.3 oz) granulated sugar

3 large egg whites

¼ teaspoon (0.5 g/0.02 oz) almond extract

⅔ cup (161 g/5.6 oz) whole milk

**ALMOND BRITTLE CRUNCH**

½ cup (100 g/3.5 oz) granulated sugar

2 tablespoons (30 g/1 oz) water

Pinch of cream of tartar

½ cup (60 g/2.1 oz) blanched slivered almonds, toasted (see page 13)

(CONTINUED)

## Make the cupcakes

1. Preheat the oven to 350°F. Line a 12-cup standard muffin pan with cupcake liners.

2. In a medium bowl, sift together the cake flour, baking powder, and salt and whisk to combine.

3. In the bowl of an electric mixer fitted with the paddle attachment, beat the butter at medium-high speed until creamy, about 30 seconds. Gradually add the sugar and beat at high speed until light, about 2 minutes. Reduce the mixer speed to low and add the egg whites a little at a time, beating well after each addition and scraping down the sides of the bowl occasionally. Beat in the almond extract. With the mixer on low speed, add the flour mixture in three additions, alternating with the milk in two additions. Mix just until the flour is incorporated. Scrape the batter into the prepared muffin cups, dividing it evenly.

4. Bake the cupcakes for 25 to 30 minutes, until lightly browned around the edges. Let the cupcakes cool completely in the pan, set on a wire rack, before frosting.

## Make the crunch

5. Line a baking sheet with a silicone baking mat or brush it lightly with vegetable oil. In a small saucepan, combine the sugar, water, and cream of tartar. Cook over medium heat, stirring, until the sugar is dissolved. Increase the heat to medium high and continue to

*Nuts*

⅓ cup (66 g/2.3 oz) granulated sugar

2 large egg whites

14 tablespoons (197 g/7 oz) unsalted butter, cut into tablespoons

¼ cup (60 g/2.1 oz) almond butter (no sugar or salt added)

¼ teaspoon (0.5 g/0.02 oz) almond extract

Generous pinch of fine sea salt

cook, without stirring, for 4 to 6 minutes, until the syrup caramelizes. Immediately remove the pan from the heat. Quickly stir the almonds into the hot caramel. Pour onto the baking sheet. Let the brittle cool for 30 minutes, or until hard.

**6.** Transfer the brittle to a cutting board and, using a chef's knife, coarsely chop it. Process the brittle in a food processor for 30 to 40 seconds, or until finely ground. Transfer to a small bowl.

## Make the buttercream

**7.** Pour enough water into a skillet so that it comes ½ inch up its sides. Bring the water to a simmer; reduce the heat to medium-low to maintain a simmer.

**8.** In the bowl of an electric mixer, combine the sugar and egg whites. Place the bowl in the skillet of water and whisk gently until the mixture registers 160°F on an instant-read thermometer. Transfer the bowl to the mixer stand and, using the whisk attachment, beat at medium-high speed until the meringue is cool and forms stiff, shiny peaks, about 4 minutes.

**9.** Reduce the speed to medium and beat in the butter, 1 tablespoon at a time. Beat in the almond butter, almond extract, and salt. Beat at high speed until the buttercream is smooth and forms medium peaks, about 3 minutes. If the buttercream seems soft, refrigerate it for 10 to 15 minutes before frosting the cupcakes.

## Frost the cupcakes

**10.** Spread a thin layer of the buttercream on each cupcake and sprinkle with a thin layer of the almond brittle. Scrape the remaining buttercream into a pastry bag fitted with a medium star tip, such as Ateco #6. Pipe the frosting generously on top of each cupcake, swirling it dramatically. Sprinkle the cupcakes with more of the brittle. Store the cupcakes in an airtight container in the refrigerator for up to 5 days; bring to room temperature before serving. Store any leftover almond brittle in an airtight container in a cool, dry place for up to 1 week.

# Walnut Layer Cake with Cream Cheese–Spice Buttercream

**When I worked** at *Chocolatier* magazine, we would occasionally organize "chocolate cruises" to the Caribbean for our readers. On these working cruises, we offered demonstrations, tastings, and special events that were tailored to chocolate lovers. On one such cruise, on the SS *Norway* (formerly the SS *France*), we were served a delicious walnut cake, which inspired this recipe. The cake is lightly flavored with coffee, and the layers are brushed with a Kahlúa-flavored syrup to make them moist. The frosting is an American-style buttercream, with some of the butter replaced by cream cheese. It's incredibly creamy and, unlike most cream cheese frostings, not too tangy.

MAKES ONE 9-INCH LAYER CAKE, SERVING 10 TO 12

## WALNUT CAKE

1½ cups (150 g/5.3 oz) walnut halves

¾ cup (150 g/5.3 oz) granulated sugar, divided

2½ cups (285 g/10 oz) cake flour

2½ teaspoons (12.5 g/0.44 oz) baking powder

¼ teaspoon (1.6 g/0.06 oz) salt

20 tablespoons (282 g/9.9 oz) unsalted butter, softened

1 cup firmly packed (216 g/7.6 oz) light brown sugar

4 large eggs, at room temperature

2 teaspoons (8 g/0.28 oz) vanilla extract

¾ cup (180 g/6.3 oz) brewed coffee, at room temperature

(CONTINUED)

## Make the cake

**1.** Preheat the oven to 350°F. Grease the bottom and sides of two 9-inch round cake pans with shortening. Line the bottom of each pan with a round of parchment paper, brush the paper with shortening, and dust the bottom and sides of the pans with flour.

**2.** Place the walnuts and ¼ cup (50 g/1.76 oz) of the sugar in the bowl of a food processor and pulse until the nuts are finely ground. Transfer to a medium bowl.

**3.** Place a fine-mesh sieve over the bowl containing the nuts and sift the flour, baking powder, and salt over the nuts. Stir to combine well and set aside.

**4.** In the bowl of an electric mixer fitted with the paddle attachment, beat the butter at medium speed until creamy, about 1 minute. Gradually add the remaining ½ cup (100 g/3.5 oz) granulated sugar and the brown sugar and beat at high speed until fluffy, about 4 minutes. Reduce the speed to medium and add the eggs one at a time, beating well after each addition and scraping down the sides of the bowl with a rubber spatula as necessary (if the batter looks curdled at this point, that's okay—it will become smooth after the flour is added). Add the vanilla and mix until blended. Reduce the speed to low and add the flour mixture in three additions,

Nuts

⅓ cup (78 g/2.7 oz) water

¼ cup (50 g/1.76 oz) granulated sugar

¼ cup (60 g/2.1 oz) Kahlúa or dark rum

CREAM CHEESE-SPICE BUTTERCREAM

2 cups (454 g/1 lb) cream cheese, at room temperature

16 tablespoons (226 g/8 oz) unsalted butter, softened

2 cups (256 g/9 oz) confectioners' sugar

1 teaspoon (4 g/0.14 oz) vanilla extract

¼ teaspoon (0.5 g/0.02 oz) ground cinnamon

¼ teaspoon (0.5 g/0.02 oz) ground ginger

⅛ teaspoon (0.8 g/0.03 oz) salt

GARNISH

2 cups (200 g/7 oz) walnuts, toasted (see page 13) and chopped

alternating with the coffee in two additions and mixing just until blended. Divide the batter between the prepared pans.

5. Bake the cake layers for 28 to 32 minutes, until a toothpick inserted into the center of the cake layers comes out clean. Cool the cakes in the pans on wire racks for 15 minutes. Invert the cakes onto the racks, peel off the parchment paper, and let the cakes cool completely.

### Make the syrup

6. In a small saucepan, combine the water and sugar and place over medium-high heat. Cook, stirring frequently, until the mixture boils and the sugar is dissolved. Remove the pan from the heat and stir in the Kahlúa or rum. Let cool completely.

### Make the buttercream

7. In the bowl of an electric mixer fitted with the paddle attachment, beat the cream cheese and butter at medium speed until blended, about 1 minute. Gradually add the confectioners' sugar and beat at medium-high speed until light and very creamy, about 4 minutes. Reduce the speed to medium and add the vanilla, cinnamon, ginger, and salt, mixing until blended.

### Assemble the cake

8. Using a long, serrated knife, cut each cake layer in half horizontally to make a total of 4 layers. Arrange one layer on a cardboard cake round or cake plate and brush with one-third of the soaking syrup. Top with ½ cup of the buttercream, using a metal spatula to spread it into an even layer. Top with another cake layer and brush with another one-third of the syrup, then top with another ½ cup buttercream. Repeat once more, then top with the remaining cake layer, cut side down. Frost the top and sides of the cake with the remaining buttercream. Pat the chopped walnuts around the side of the cake. If you're not serving it immediately, refrigerate the cake for up to 5 days; bring to room temperature before serving.

# Chocolate-Glazed Peanut Butter Mousse Cake

*Genoise, a French sponge cake,* is one of the simplest yet most fickle cakes to make. Poorly done, it can be tough, dry, and sunken in the center. The secret to a moist genoise is to use clarified (instead of melted) butter in the batter. Clarifying removes excess water from the butter that may cause the cake to sink in the center. This chocolaty genoise is especially delicious when layered with a creamy white chocolate–peanut butter mousse filling. The cake is coated with a sleek dark chocolate glaze and, finally, garnished with lots of crunchy sugared peanuts.

MAKES ONE 9-INCH CAKE, SERVING 12

SPECIAL EQUIPMENT:
9-inch-diameter, 3-inch-high springform pan

CHOCOLATE GENOISE

½ cup plus 1 tablespoon (64 g/2.26 oz) sifted cake flour

½ cup (38 g/1.3 oz) sifted unsweetened cocoa powder (preferably Dutch-processed)

½ teaspoon (3.3 g/0.12 oz) salt

6 large eggs

1 cup (200 g/7 oz) granulated sugar

⅓ cup (75 g/2.6 oz) clarified butter (page 19), hot

1 teaspoon (4 g/0.14 oz) vanilla extract

WHITE CHOCOLATE-PEANUT BUTTER MOUSSE

3.5 ounces (100 g) white chocolate, chopped

¾ cup (180 g/6.3 oz) peanut butter (not the natural kind — I prefer Jif brand)

2¼ cups (522 g/18.41) heavy cream, divided

(CONTINUED)

## Make the genoise

1. Preheat the oven to 350°F. Line the bottom of a 9-inch-diameter, 3-inch-high springform pan with a round of parchment paper (don't be tempted to use a standard 9-by-1-inch pan — there will be too much batter).

2. Sift the flour, cocoa, and salt together three times. Return the mixture to the sifter and set aside.

3. In the bowl of an electric mixer, whisk the eggs and sugar together by hand. Place over a saucepan of barely simmering water. Stirring constantly with the whisk (no need to beat air into the eggs at this point), heat the egg mixture until it is hot to the touch and the sugar is dissolved.

4. Remove from the heat, attach the bowl to the mixer stand, and fit the mixer with the whisk attachment. Beat on high speed until the egg mixture triples in volume and is very light, about 8 minutes.

5. Pour the hot clarified butter into a large bowl and stir in the vanilla.

6. Sift about one-third of the flour mixture over the whipped eggs. Using a large rubber spatula, fold together quickly but gently, until nearly combined. Sift in half the remaining flour mixture and fold

Nuts

½ cup (121 g/4.2 oz) whole milk

2 tablespoons (28 g/1 oz) unsalted butter, softened

⅛ teaspoon (0.8 g/0.03 oz) salt

1 teaspoon (4 g/0.14 oz) vanilla extract

QUICK SUGARED PEANUTS

¾ cup (100 g/3.5 oz) lightly salted roasted peanuts

1 tablespoon plus 1½ teaspoons (31 g/1 oz) light corn syrup

1 tablespoon firmly packed (13 g/0.45 oz) light brown sugar

CHOCOLATE GLAZE

6 ounces (170 g) bittersweet chocolate (60% to 62%), finely chopped

¾ cup (174 g/6.13 oz) heavy cream

3 tablespoons (60 g/2.1 oz) light corn syrup

1 teaspoon (4 g/0.14 oz) vanilla extract

again. Repeat with the remaining flour. Scoop about ¾ cup of the batter into the hot butter and fold together until well blended. Pour the butter mixture into the remaining batter and fold it in, being sure it is completely incorporated. Pour into the prepared pan and smooth the top.

**7.** Bake until the cake shrinks slightly from the sides of the pan and the top of the cake springs back when pressed in the center with your fingers, 25 to 30 minutes.

**8.** Transfer the pan to a wire rack and let the cake cool completely in the pan. Run a thin knife around the inside of the pan to release the cake. Unlatch and remove the side of the pan, invert the cake onto the rack, and remove the pan bottom and parchment. Using a long, serrated knife, trim about ⅛ inch off the side of the cake all the way around (this will ensure the mousse will neatly cover the side of the cake when it's assembled). Cut the cake in half horizontally to form two layers. Clean the springform pan to prepare it for the cake assembly.

### *Make the mousse*

**9.** Place the white chocolate and peanut butter in a large bowl. In a small saucepan, heat ½ cup (131 g/4.09 oz) of the cream and the milk over medium-high heat until scalding. Pour the hot cream mixture over the chocolate and peanut butter and gently whisk until smooth. Add the butter and whisk until melted. Whisk in the salt and vanilla. Set the mixture aside to cool completely.

**10.** Place the remaining 1¾ cups cream (391 g/14.32 oz) in the bowl of an electric mixer fitted with the whisk attachment and whip at high speed until soft peaks form. Gently fold the whipped cream into the cooled peanut butter mixture one-third at a time.

### *Assemble the cake*

**11.** Place one of the cake layers in the bottom of the cleaned springform pan, centering it in the pan. Scrape about half the peanut butter mousse over the cake and spread it into an even layer with a spatula, letting it fill the gap between the edge of the cake and the side of the pan. Lay the second cake layer on top, centering it. Scrape the remaining mousse over the cake, spreading it into an even layer with a spatula and letting it fill the gap between the cake and the pan. Freeze the cake for at least 1 hour, until firm.

## Make the peanuts

12. Preheat the oven to 350°F. Line a baking sheet with a silicone baking mat or lightly oil it with vegetable oil.

13. In a medium bowl, stir together the peanuts, corn syrup, and brown sugar. Put the nuts on the prepared baking sheet and use your hands to separate them so they are not in one big mass. Bake, stirring once or twice during baking, until the nuts are nicely browned, about 15 minutes. Place the baking sheet on a wire rack and let the nuts cool completely. Once cool, break the nuts apart with your fingers and then coarsely chop them.

## Make the glaze

14. Place the chocolate in a medium bowl. Heat the cream and corn syrup in a small saucepan over medium-high heat until scalding, stirring occasionally. Pour the hot cream mixture over the chocolate and let it stand for 30 seconds. Gently whisk until smooth. Whisk in the vanilla.

## Glaze the cake

15. Run a thin knife around the edge of the cake pan, wiping it clean as needed, to release the cake. Unlatch and remove the side of the pan. Use a small offset metal spatula to smooth over any uneven spots on the mousse. Place the cake on a cardboard cake round, if you have one, and then place it on a wire rack over a large piece of parchment or waxed paper to catch any drips of glaze. Pour the glaze onto the center of the top of the cake and use a small offset metal spatula to gently nudge the glaze over the edge of the cake, letting it drip over the sides. Use the spatula to spread the glaze carefully over any uncovered spots on the sides of the cake. Sprinkle the nuts over the top of the cake. Let the cake stand at room temperature for at least 30 minutes before serving to allow the mousse to soften. Refrigerate any leftover cake, covered with plastic wrap, for up to 5 days.

# Caramel

✤ ✤

I think love is caramel. Sweet and fragrant; always welcome.

**— JENNY COLGAN,**
*Welcome to Rosie Hopkins'*
*Sweetshop of Dreams*

*While the texture* of caramel can range from gooey to chewy to brittle, its flavor remains sweet, mellow, and complex. The recipes in this chapter all share this irresistible flavor, though each has its own method of imparting it. Some are made with a classic caramel, in which white sugar is cooked with a little water until it liquefies and turns a deep golden-amber hue. Adding cream and butter to this base tempers its bitterness and heightens the buttery notes of the caramel. It also prevents it from becoming brittle as it cools. The caramel can either be used as a component of a dessert (a layer of a tart, for example), or mixed with other ingredients to create a dessert of its own, such as a mousse or pudding.

When making caramel, there are a few rules to keep in mind. First, it's important that your pot and wooden spoon (or silicone spatula) are perfectly clean — sugar crystals tend to form around foreign particles. Second, you'll note in each recipe I've added a little acid, in the form of either cream of tartar or lemon juice, to the sugar and water mixture; the acid helps break down the sucrose molecules and prevents sugar crystals from forming. Stirring tends to splash syrup onto the sides of the pot, where sugar crystals can form, so avoid the temptation to stir once the mixture comes to a boil.

Another way of adding caramel flavor to a dessert is by using a combination of cooked brown sugar, butter, and, sometimes, heavy cream; though not technically caramel, the deep flavor of molasses in the brown sugar is reminiscent of caramel and equally delicious. This mixture can be used as a topping for a cake (Gingered Pear Upside-Down Cake) or pastry (Extra-Sticky Pecan and Raisin Buns), or as a sauce (Sticky Toffee Pudding). Whichever recipe you choose, be assured that the distinctive, complex flavor of caramel in each is bound to make it a resounding success. I mean, is there anyone out there who actually *doesn't like* caramel?

# Chocolate Caramel Sauce

*Buttery caramel and rich,* dark chocolate comingle in this sleek sauce. I like it best on vanilla ice cream, but it works on any dessert with a compatible flavor profile, such as banana, nut (especially peanut butter), vanilla, chocolate, and coffee.

**MAKES 2¼ CUPS**

1 cup (200 g/7 oz) granulated sugar

¼ cup (59 g/2 oz) water

2 tablespoons (41 g/1.4 oz) light corn syrup

1¼ cups (290 g/10.2 oz) heavy cream

5 ounces (142 g) bittersweet chocolate (60% to 62%), finely chopped

1 teaspoon (4 g/0.14 oz) vanilla extract

Pinch of salt

1. Fill a small cup with water and place a pastry brush in it (this will be used for washing down the sides of the pan to prevent crystallization).

2. In a clean, heavy-bottomed 2-quart saucepan, stir together the sugar, water, and corn syrup. Place the saucepan over medium-high heat and cook, occasionally washing down the sides of the pan with the pastry brush to wash away any sugar crystals, until the mixture starts to color around the edges. Gently swirl the pan to ensure that the sugar caramelizes evenly. Continue to cook until the sugar turns a medium amber color. Immediately remove the pan from the heat and very slowly and carefully add the cream (the mixture will bubble up furiously), stirring with a silicone spatula or wooden spoon until smooth. If there are any hardened bits of caramel sticking to the bottom of the pan, place the pan over medium-low heat and stir until they are dissolved. Let the caramel stand off the heat for 2 minutes to cool slightly.

3. Add the chocolate and stir until the chocolate is melted and the sauce is smooth. Stir in the vanilla and salt. Serve the sauce warm, or let cool, cover, and refrigerate until ready to use. Rewarm the sauce in the microwave at medium power for 45 to 60 seconds.

# Classic Caramel Sauce

*Every caramel lover* has his own favorite version of this classic, and here's mine. It's heavy on the cream and butter to temper the bitterness of the caramel. Pure vanilla extract is a must.

MAKES 1¾ CUPS

1 cup (200 g/7 oz) granulated sugar

¼ cup (59 g/2 oz) water

⅛ teaspoon (0.625 g/0.02 oz) freshly squeezed lemon juice

1¼ cups (290 g/10.2 oz) heavy cream

3 tablespoons (42 g/1.5 oz) unsalted butter, cut into tablespoons

1 teaspoon (4 g/0.14 oz) vanilla extract

Large pinch of salt

1. Half fill a small cup with water and place a pastry brush in it (this will be used for washing down the sides of the pan to prevent crystallization).

2. In a clean, heavy-bottomed 2-quart saucepan, stir together the sugar, water, and lemon juice. Place the saucepan over medium-high heat and cook, occasionally washing down the sides of the pan with the pastry brush to wash away any sugar crystals, until the mixture starts to color around the edges. Gently swirl the pan to ensure that the sugar caramelizes evenly. Continue to cook until the sugar turns a medium amber color. Immediately remove the pan from the heat and very slowly and carefully add the cream (the mixture will bubble up furiously), stirring with a silicone spatula or wooden spoon until smooth. If there are any hardened bits of caramel sticking to the bottom of the pan, place the pan over medium-low heat and stir until they are dissolved. Add the butter and stir until melted. Stir in the vanilla and salt. Serve the sauce warm, or let cool, cover, and refrigerate until ready to use. Rewarm the sauce in the microwave at high power for 30 to 45 seconds.

## Coconut Caramel Sauce

Replace ¾ cup (174 g/6.2 oz) of the heavy cream with ¾ cup (180 g/6.3 oz) coconut milk (stir it well before adding). Stir 1 tablespoon (15 g/0.5 oz) dark rum and ⅓ cup (30 g/1 oz) unsweetened shredded coconut, toasted (see page 8), into the finished sauce.

# Banana–Caramel Pudding Parfaits

*Not a dieter's special,* to say the least, but this is a pretty phenomenal treat. It's a variation on a Southern banana pudding and, in my opinion, much better than the original. I've substituted a sensational caramel pudding for the classic vanilla and use homemade vanilla wafers instead of store-bought. The wafer cookies are a snap to make and can be made up to five days in advance (and the pudding up to two days ahead). The parfaits can be assembled up to six hours before serving.

MAKES 6 PARFAITS

CARAMEL PUDDING

3 large egg yolks

3 tablespoons (22 g/0.8 oz) cornstarch

1½ cups (363 g/12.8 oz) whole milk

1 teaspoon (4 g/0.14 oz) vanilla extract

⅛ teaspoon (0.8 g/0.03 oz) fine sea salt

¾ cup (150 g/5.3 oz) granulated sugar

3 tablespoons (44 g/1.5 oz) water

Pinch of cream of tartar

1½ cups (348 g/12.3 oz) heavy cream

2 tablespoons (30 g/1 oz) unsalted butter, cut into ½-inch chunks

(CONTINUED)

## Make the pudding

1. In a medium bowl, whisk together the egg yolks and cornstarch, then gradually whisk in the milk. Whisk in the vanilla and salt.

2. Fill a cup with water and place a pastry brush in it (this will be used for washing down the sides of the pan to prevent crystallization). In a clean, heavy-bottomed 2-quart saucepan, stir together the sugar, water, and cream of tartar. Cook over medium-high heat, occasionally washing down the sides of the pan with the pastry brush, until the mixture starts to color around the edges. Gently swirl the pan to ensure that the sugar caramelizes evenly. Continue to cook until the sugar turns deep amber. Remove the pan from the heat and slowly stir in the cream (the caramel will bubble up furiously). Return the pan to medium heat and cook, stirring, just until any hardened bits of caramel are completely melted.

3. Whisk the egg yolk mixture vigorously until well blended. Whisk about half the caramel into the yolk mixture. Pour this mixture into the remaining caramel in the pan and place over medium heat. Cook, stirring constantly, until the mixture thickens and comes to a boil. Continue to boil for 30 seconds, then remove from the heat and pour the pudding into a medium bowl. Add the butter and whisk until completely melted. Prepare an ice bath by filling a large bowl one-third full with ice and water and set the bowl of pudding in it. Let stand, whisking occasionally, until cool. Press a piece of plastic wrap directly on the surface of the pudding and refrigerate for at least 2 hours, until chilled.

*Caramel*

sides of the pan with the pastry brush to wash away any sugar crystals, until the mixture starts to color around the edges. Gently swirl the pan to ensure that the sugar caramelizes evenly. Continue to cook until the sugar turns deep amber. Remove the pan from the heat and carefully add the remaining 3 tablespoons (44 g/1.5 oz) water (the caramel with bubble up furiously). Stir the caramel gently; if any hardened bits of caramel remain, return the pot to the heat for a few seconds to dissolve them. Immediately pour the hot caramel mixture in a slow stream onto the beating egg yolks, aiming for the gap between the edge of the whisk and the side of the bowl. Once all the caramel has been added, raise the mixer speed to medium-high and continue to mix while you melt the gelatin.

**7.** Microwave the cup of softened gelatin at high power for 10 to 20 seconds, until melted. Reduce the mixer speed to medium low and add the melted gelatin to the beating yolks. Raise the speed to medium-high and continue beating the yolks until they have tripled in volume and are cool. Remove the bowl from the mixer and, using a rubber spatula, gently fold in the whipped cream.

## Assemble the parfaits

**8.** Remove the crispy layer from the freezer and invert it onto a cutting board. Peel off the waxed paper and chop the square into rough ½-inch pieces. Spoon about ¼ cup of the crispy layer pieces into the bottom of each of 6 parfait or serving glasses, then top with a scant ⅓ cup of the mousse. Repeat the layering once more. You should have some of the crispy mixture left over—it can be used to garnish the top of each parfait or for snacking. Refrigerate the parfaits for at least 2 hours before serving. Before serving, garnish each parfait with a dollop of sweetened whipped cream and some chopped peanuts, if desired.

# Sticky Toffee Pudding

*This modern British* dessert ("pudding" is a generic word for dessert in Britain) has become a classic in America, too, and for good reason. It's a super-moist date-spice cake generously blanketed with a caramel-like brown sugar toffee sauce—what's not to like? In my version, the cakes are baked in individual ramekins, so everyone gets a little sugary crust at the edge. In Britain, this would undoubtedly be served with a spoonful of clotted cream, but whipped cream and a few candied pecans are even better accompaniments.

MAKES 8 SERVINGS

### DATE AND GINGER CAKES

¾ cup (141 g/5 oz) finely chopped (¼-inch pieces) pitted dates (preferably Medjool)

1 cup (236 g/8.3 oz) water

1 teaspoon (5 g/0.17 oz) grated fresh ginger

1½ cups (198 g/7 oz) all-purpose flour

¼ teaspoon (1.6 g/0.06 oz) salt

2½ teaspoons (12 g/0.44 oz) baking powder

¼ teaspoon (1.25 g/0.04 oz) baking soda

9 tablespoons (127 g/4.5 oz) unsalted butter, softened

¾ cup firmly packed (162 g/5.7 oz) dark brown sugar

1¼ teaspoons (5 g/0.17 oz) vanilla extract

3 large eggs, at room temperature

### TOFFEE SAUCE

8 tablespoons (113 g/4 oz) unsalted butter, cut into tablespoons

1 cup firmly packed (216 g/7.6 oz) dark brown sugar

½ cup (116 g/4 oz) heavy cream

(CONTINUED)

## *Make the cakes*

1. Preheat the oven to 350°F. Coat the insides of eight 5- or 6-ounce ramekins with softened butter, then coat them with granulated sugar, tapping out the excess. Place the ramekins on a baking sheet and set aside.

2. Place the dates in a small saucepan and add the water. Bring to a boil, reduce the heat to maintain a simmer, and simmer for about 3 minutes. Remove from the heat and add the ginger.

3. In a medium bowl, whisk together the flour, salt, baking powder, and baking soda.

4. In the bowl of an electric mixer fitted with the paddle attachment, cream the butter and brown sugar at high speed until light, about 2 minutes. Add the vanilla and eggs, mixing well after each addition. With the mixer on low speed, add the flour mixture, mixing just until combined. Drain the dates and add them to the batter, stirring gently with a rubber spatula to combine. Scrape the batter into the prepared ramekins, filling them between half and two-thirds full.

5. Bake the cakes on the baking sheet for 30 to 35 minutes, until a toothpick inserted into the center comes out clean. Set the baking sheet on a wire rack to cool slightly while you make the sauce.

1½ teaspoons (6 g/0.21 oz)
vanilla extract

Pinch of salt

GARNISHES

Sweetened whipped cream

Candied Pecans (page 13)

*Make the sauce*

6. In a medium saucepan, melt the butter over medium heat. Add the brown sugar and bring to a boil, stirring to blend. Stir in the cream and return to a boil. Reduce the heat to medium-low and simmer the mixture for about 5 minutes, until slightly thickened. Remove from the heat and stir in the vanilla and salt. Allow the sauce to cool for 5 minutes.

7. Unmold each cake and place domed side up on a dessert plate. Pour a generous amount of the warm sauce on top, and serve with the whipped cream and candied pecans.

# Caramel Cream Puffs

*These are not your typical* cream puffs. Instead of a vanilla pastry cream, they are filled with a silky caramel cream that is rich and utterly delicious. A dusting of confectioners' sugar is the only garnish required.

**MAKES ABOUT 15 CREAM PUFFS**

**SPECIAL EQUIPMENT:**
Pastry bags; small, medium, and large plain tips

**CARAMEL CREAM FILLING**

1 cup (220 g/7 oz) granulated sugar

3 tablespoons (44 g/1.5 oz) water

Pinch of cream of tartar

1¾ cups (406 g/14.3 oz) heavy cream, divided

⅛ teaspoon (0.83 g/0.03 oz) salt

1 teaspoon (4 g/0.14 oz) vanilla extract

**CHOUX PASTE**

⅓ cup (78 g/2.7 oz) water

⅓ cup (80 g/2.8 oz) whole milk

1 tablespoon (12 g/0.42 oz) granulated sugar

¼ teaspoon (1.6 g/0.06 oz) salt

5⅓ tablespoons (75 g/2.6 oz) unsalted butter, cut into tablespoons

⅔ cup (88 g/3 oz) all-purpose flour, sifted

3 large eggs

1 egg, lightly beaten with 1 teaspoon water, for egg wash

**GARNISH**

Confectioners' sugar, for dusting

## Make the caramel for the filling

**1.** Fill a small cup with water and place a pastry brush in it (this will be used for washing down the sides of the pan to prevent crystallization).

**2.** In a clean, heavy-bottomed 2-quart saucepan, stir together the sugar, water, and cream of tartar. Cook over medium-high heat, occasionally washing down the sides of the pan with the pastry brush to wash away any sugar crystals, until the mixture starts to color around the edges. Gently swirl the pan to ensure that the sugar caramelizes evenly and continue to cook until the caramel turns a medium-dark amber color. Remove the pan from the heat and carefully add ¾ cup (174 g/6.13 oz) of the cream (the mixture will bubble up furiously). Once the bubbling has subsided, stir the mixture until it is completely smooth. If there are any hardened bits of caramel in the mixture, return the saucepan to medium heat until they have dissolved. Stir in the salt and vanilla. Pour the hot caramel mixture through a fine-mesh sieve into the bowl of an electric mixer (or a different mixing bowl if you have only one electric mixer bowl; you will need it for the choux) and let cool for 10 minutes.

**3.** Cover the bowl with plastic wrap and refrigerate the caramel until chilled, about 2 hours. Meanwhile, make the choux.

## Make the choux paste

**4.** Preheat the oven to 400°F.

**5.** In a medium saucepan, combine the water, milk, sugar, salt, and butter and bring to a full boil over medium-high heat, stirring frequently. Remove the pan from the heat, add the flour all at once, and stir vigorously with a wooden spoon until the flour is completely incorporated and the mixture pulls away from the side of the pan. Return the pan to the heat and continue to cook for another minute, stirring, to dry out the dough a bit. Transfer the dough to the bowl of an electric mixer fitted with the paddle attachment and let it cool for 2 minutes.

**6.** While mixing on medium speed, add the eggs, one at a time, mixing until the first egg is completely incorporated before adding the next. Mix until you get a smooth, shiny dough that falls heavily from a spoon, about 2 minutes.

## Pipe the cream puffs

**7.** Line two baking sheets with silicone baking mats or pieces of parchment paper. Scrape the choux paste into a large pastry bag fitted with a ⅝-inch plain tip, such as Ateco #7. Pipe out 2-inch mounds of the choux paste onto one baking sheet, leaving 1½ inches between each cream puff. Brush the surface of each cream puff with the egg wash. Use your finger to smooth out the points on the surface of each one. (Leave the remaining choux paste in the pastry bag until the first batch of cream puffs has been baked.) Bake the cream puffs for 15 minutes, then reduce the heat to 350°F degrees and bake until puffed up and light golden brown, 10 to 15 minutes longer. Let cool on the baking sheet. Pipe out and bake more cream puffs with the remaining batter.

## Finish the filling and fill the cream puffs

**8.** Remove the chilled caramel from the refrigerator and gradually stir in the remaining 1 cup (232 g/8.18 oz) cream with a rubber spatula until blended. Place the bowl on the mixer stand (or transfer the cream to a mixer bowl) and, using the whisk attachment, beat the filling on high speed until medium-firm peaks form. Transfer the filling to a pastry bag fitted with a ¼-inch plain tip, such as Ateco #802.

**9.** Use a small, plain pastry tip to make a hole in the center of the bottom of each cream puff. Gently pipe the caramel filling into the hole, filling the puff completely. Lightly dust the cream puffs with sifted confectioners' sugar before serving. If you are not serving the cream puffs immediately, place them in an airtight container and refrigerate. The shells can be made up to 3 days in advance and stored in an airtight container at room temperature, but don't fill them more than 3 hours before serving.

# Caramel-Glazed Cake Doughnuts

*If you've never had* a homemade doughnut, you don't know what you're missing—they're miles above store-bought in taste and texture. I even prefer their homespun look to the just-a-little-too-perfect appearance of machine-made doughnuts. Because these treats are deep-fried, they do take a little more effort than baking, but since their dough is not yeast-based, they are easier than most doughnuts. They have a cakey texture and tender crumb, and the buttery caramel glaze on top is truly amazing.

## MAKES 12 DOUGHNUTS

SPECIAL EQUIPMENT:
Candy thermometer

### CARAMEL GLAZE

1¾ cups (406 g/14.3 oz) heavy cream

1 cup plus 2 tablespoons firmly packed (243 g/8.5 oz) light brown sugar

1 tablespoon plus 1½ teaspoons (30 g/1 oz) light corn syrup

⅛ teaspoon (0.8 g/0.03 oz) salt

3 tablespoons (42 g/1.5 oz) unsalted butter

1 teaspoon (5 g/0.17 oz) vanilla extract

### DOUGHNUTS

1 large egg plus 2 large egg yolks

½ cup (121 g/4.3 oz) buttermilk

4 tablespoons (56 g/2 oz) unsalted butter, melted and cooled slightly

1 teaspoon (4 g/0.14 oz) vanilla extract

2 cups (265 g/9.3 oz) all-purpose flour

1 cup (114 g/4 oz) cake flour

(CONTINUED)

### Make the glaze

**1.** In a 1½-quart saucepan, bring the cream, brown sugar, corn syrup, and salt to a boil over high heat, stirring just until the sugar is dissolved. As soon as it reaches a boil, reduce the heat to low or medium-low, so that the mixture is at a low boil. Continue to boil until the mixture reaches 224°F on a candy thermometer, 10 to 15 minutes. Remove the pan from the heat and add the butter and vanilla, stirring until the butter is melted. Set the glaze aside while you make the doughnuts.

### Make the doughnuts

**2.** In a medium bowl, whisk together the egg, egg yolks, buttermilk, butter, and vanilla.

**3.** In the bowl of an electric mixer fitted with the paddle attachment, mix the flours, sugars, baking powder, baking soda, and salt at low speed until blended. Add the egg mixture and mix at low speed just until the mixture comes together as a dough.

**4.** Transfer the dough to a large sheet of parchment or waxed paper (about 22 by 12 inches). Top with a second sheet of paper and, with a rolling pin, roll the dough out to an oval that is ½ inch thick (the oval will be about 12 by 9 inches). Place the dough and paper on a baking sheet and freeze for 30 minutes, until firm enough to cut.

½ cup (100 g/3.5 oz) granulated sugar

⅓ cup firmly packed (71 g/ 2.5 oz) light brown sugar

1¾ teaspoons (8.75 g/0.3 oz) baking powder

½ teaspoon (2.5 g/0.09 oz) baking soda

¾ teaspoon (5 g/0.17 oz) salt

Vegetable oil, for frying

**5.** Peel the paper off the top of the dough and lightly dust the dough with flour. Replace the paper loosely, flip the dough over, and peel off the other sheet of paper. Spray a baking sheet with nonstick cooking spray. Using a 3-inch round cutter, cut out as many rounds as possible from the dough. Use a 1-inch round cutter to cut out the centers of the rounds (save the centers to fry some "doughnut holes"). Place the doughnuts (and the holes) on the greased baking sheet, cover them loosely with waxed or parchment paper, and refrigerate for 30 minutes.

**6.** Meanwhile, gather up the dough scraps and repeat the rolling, freezing, and cutting process.

### Fry and glaze the doughnuts

**7.** Line a baking sheet with paper towels. Pour enough oil into a wide pot or large, high-sided skillet so that it comes about 2 inches up its side. Heat the oil to 350°F. Fry the doughnuts in batches of three until golden, turning them with a metal spatula halfway through cooking, about 1½ minutes per side. Drain the doughnuts on the paper towel–lined baking sheet. Fry the doughnut holes for about 1 minute, turning them once or twice during frying.

**8.** While the doughnuts are still warm, dip one side in the glaze, letting the excess drip off. Dip all the doughnuts once, then dip them a second time. You can eat the doughnuts immediately or store them in an airtight container in the refrigerator for up to 5 days (bring to room temperature before serving).

*Caramel*

# Extra-Sticky Pecan and Raisin Buns

*A sticky brown sugar* caramel and lots of toasted pecans top sweet raisin buns in my version of this brunch-time favorite. The sweet dough is yeast-based but eggless, which makes it very easy to roll out and work with. I use fast-acting yeast (also known as instant yeast) for the dough, which means you don't have to wake up at the crack of dawn to enjoy these for brunch. Since they are rich, serve the buns with something light, such as an assortment of fresh fruit.

MAKES 9 LARGE BUNS

### SWEET DOUGH

1 cup (242 g/8.5 oz) milk, heated to 115°F

2¼ teaspoons (7 g/0.25 oz) fast-acting dry yeast (such as Fleischmann's RapidRise)

3 cups (397 g/14 oz) all-purpose flour, divided

4 tablespoons (56 g/2 oz) unsalted butter, melted and cooled

¼ cup (50 g/2.1 g) granulated sugar

1 teaspoon (6.7 g/0.23 oz) salt

### FILLING

½ cup (70 g/2.5 oz) golden raisins

⅓ cup (80 g/2.8 oz) dark rum or water

½ cup firmly packed (108 g/3.8 oz) light brown sugar

1 tablespoon (6 g/0.21 oz) ground cinnamon

3 tablespoons (42 g/1.5 oz) unsalted butter, softened

(CONTINUED)

## Make the dough

1. Place the warm milk in the bowl of an electric mixer (or a large bowl if you plan to knead the dough by hand) and stir in the yeast and ⅔ cup (88 g/3.1 oz) of the flour. Let the mixture stand for 15 minutes, until small bubbles have formed on the surface. Stir in the butter, sugar, salt, and the remaining 2⅓ cups (309 g/10.9 oz) flour, mixing until a rough dough forms.

2. If you are kneading the dough by machine, transfer the bowl to the mixer stand and, using the dough hook, knead the dough at medium-low speed for 10 minutes, or until the dough is smooth and elastic. If necessary, you can add a little flour to prevent the dough from sticking to the bowl during kneading, but don't add more than 2 tablespoons (16 g/0.6 oz) of additional flour. If you prefer to knead the dough by hand, knead it on a lightly floured work surface until it is smooth and elastic, 10 to 15 minutes (depending on how vigorously you work the dough).

3. Transfer the dough to a buttered bowl, cover with a tea towel, and allow it to rise in a warm place until doubled in volume, about 30 minutes. While the dough is rising, make the filling and topping.

## Make the filling

4. Place the raisins and rum in a heatproof glass measuring cup and microwave on high power until bubbling, about 1 minute.

8 tablespoons (113 g/4 oz) unsalted butter, cut into tablespoons

1¾ cups firmly packed (378 g/13.33 oz) light brown sugar

½ cup (160 g/5.6 oz) light corn syrup

1 cup (100 g/3.5 oz) pecan halves, toasted (see page 13) and coarsely chopped

**5.** In a small bowl, combine the brown sugar and cinnamon. Set the softened butter aside.

## Make the topping

**6.** In a small saucepan, melt the butter over medium heat. Whisk in the brown sugar and corn syrup and bring to a boil over high heat, whisking occasionally until the sugar is dissolved. Remove the pan from the heat.

## Roll and cut the dough

**7.** Butter the bottom and sides of a 9-inch square baking pan.

**8.** Place the dough on a lightly floured work surface and, using a rolling pin, roll it into a 10-by-14-inch rectangle. With a long side facing you, use a small offset metal spatula to spread the softened butter for the filling over the dough, covering it completely. Sprinkle the dough with the brown sugar mixture. Drain the raisins, discarding the rum, and sprinkle them over the sugar. Starting with the long end closest to you, roll the dough up jelly roll–style into a log, positioning it so that the seam is on the bottom of the roll. Pinch the ends of the log to seal them. Using a serrated knife, trim about ½ inch off the sealed ends of the log. Cut the log into three equal segments, then cut each segment into three slices.

**9.** Pour the warm topping mixture into the bottom of the prepared baking pan. Sprinkle the topping with the pecans. Arrange the nine dough slices, cut side down, in rows of three on top of the nuts, filling the pan. Cover the pan with a tea towel and let the buns rise for another 30 minutes. Meanwhile, preheat the oven to 375°F.

**10.** Line a baking sheet with aluminum foil and place the pan of buns on the sheet (this will prevent any caramel spillover from dripping onto your oven floor and burning). Bake the buns for 22 to 26 minutes, until golden brown. Let cool in the pan set on a wire rack for 5 minutes (but no longer). Using potholders, carefully invert the buns onto a large serving plate or a foil-lined baking sheet and remove the pan. Serve the buns warm or at room temperature. Store in an airtight container at room temperature for up to 1 day.

# Caramel Almond Macarons

*Macarons have been* all the rage for a few years now, supplanting cupcakes as the treat du jour. They can be tricky to make—it's all in the method of folding the dry ingredients into the whipped egg whites (a process known as *macaronage*) until the batter is the correct consistency—but once you've mastered the technique, you'll be impressing friends and family by making them in assorted flavors and colors to suit every occasion (just add paste food coloring to the shells along with the vanilla extract). Store-bought almond flour, which is powder-fine, is available in most supermarkets, often in the "health food" aisle (I like Bob's Red Mill brand best). I make a French meringue (the simplest kind: egg whites and sugar are whipped together to stiff peaks) for the shells, but add the sugar all at once at the beginning of beating, instead of adding it a little at a time, and then gradually increase the speed of the mixer until a stiff meringue forms. This makes a stronger meringue. The egg whites are also "aged" slightly before whipping, which simply means they're separated from the yolks and refrigerated overnight. This reduces their water content, giving the whipped whites more volume. If you're pressed for time you can skip this step, but it does make for a puffier macaron. In some pastry shops, the whites are aged for much longer, frequently at room temperature and well hidden from any unannounced health inspectors that might show up in the kitchen. My lawyer and I, however, do not endorse this method.

## MAKES ABOUT 40 FILLED MACARONS

**SPECIAL EQUIPMENT:**
Pastry bag and medium plain tip

**MACARON SHELLS**

**4 large egg whites**

**1 cup plus 2 tablespoons (5 oz/140 g) almond flour**

**2 cups (256 g/9 oz) confectioners' sugar**

**½ cup (3.5 oz/100 g) granulated sugar**

**1 teaspoon (4 g/0.14 oz) vanilla extract**

**⅓ cup (28 g/1 oz) finely chopped almonds, for sprinkling**

(CONTINUED)

### Make the macaron shells

1. Place the egg whites in a covered container and refrigerate for at least 8 hours or overnight to "age." When you are ready to make the macarons, bring the aged egg whites to room temperature.

2. Position a rack in the lower third of the oven and preheat the oven to 350°F. Line two baking sheets with silicone baking mats or parchment paper. In a food processor, process the almond flour with the confectioners' sugar for a few seconds until well blended. Sift the mixture through a medium-mesh sieve into a medium bowl.

3. In the bowl of an electric mixer, whisk the aged egg whites and granulated sugar together by hand until blended. Place the bowl on the mixer stand and, using the whisk attachment, beat the egg whites on medium speed until they are very foamy, about 2 minutes. Raise the mixer speed to medium-high and beat the whites until they are opaque and form soft peaks, another 2 minutes. Raise

## CARAMEL FILLING

¾ cup (174 g/6.13 oz) heavy cream

1½ cups (10.5 oz/300 g) granulated sugar

6 tablespoons (3.12 oz/88 g) water

⅛ teaspoon (0.4 g/0.013 oz) cream of tartar

¼ teaspoon (1.6 g/0.06 oz) salt

4 tablespoons (57 g/2 oz) unsalted butter, softened

½ teaspoon (2 g/0.07 oz) vanilla extract

the speed to high and beat until the whites are glossy and hold stiff peaks, another 2 minutes. Add the vanilla and beat until blended.

4. Sprinkle half of the sifted almond mixture on top of the meringue and fold it in with a rubber spatula. Add the remaining almond mixture and mix it in a light circular motion. Fold the batter until it drips down from the spatula in a continuous lava-like flow. This can take anywhere from 20 to 40 strokes, depending on how strong your arm is. You don't want the batter to be too thick (the macaron tops won't be smooth) or too thin (the macarons will spread too much and won't puff up). This is undoubtedly the most important step in making macarons.

5. Fit a pastry bag with a ⅜-inch plain tip, such as Ateco #4, and prop it up in a tall glass. Scrape the batter into the bag. Pipe 1-inch rounds of batter onto the prepared baking sheets, spacing them 1 inch apart. Rap the baking sheet firmly against the counter once or twice to remove any air bubbles. Sprinkle the macarons lightly with the chopped almonds. (Place the pastry bag containing any remaining batter back in the glass and cover with plastic wrap to pipe more macarons later.) Bake the macarons, one sheet at a time, for 12 to 14 minutes, until they have puffed up and the tops are set (they should not have colored). Let the macarons cool completely on the baking sheet set on a wire rack.

6. Repeat with the remaining macarons and batter, again baking them one sheet at a time.

### Make the filling

7. Place the cream in a microwave-safe glass measuring cup and microwave on high power until boiling, about 1 minute. Set aside.

8. Fill a cup with water and place a pastry brush in it (this will be used for washing down the sides of the pan to prevent crystallization). In a small, heavy saucepan, combine the sugar, water, and cream of tartar and place over medium heat. Cook, stirring occasionally, just until the sugar is dissolved. Increase the heat to high and cook, without stirring and occasionally brushing down the sides of the pan with the wet pastry brush to prevent crystallization,

until the syrup caramelizes and turns a medium amber color, about 4 minutes. Remove the pan from the heat and slowly add the cream (the mixture will bubble up). Give the caramel a quick stir (avoid overstirring it) and quickly stir in the salt, butter, and vanilla. Transfer the caramel filling to a small bowl or glass measure and let stand, uncovered, at room temperature, without stirring it (stirring will make it grainy), for 2 hours, or until firm enough to spread.

### Fill the macarons

9. Using a small offset metal spatula, spread a grape-sized dollop of the caramel filling onto the underside of a macaron shell. Gently press the underside of another macaron shell against the filling until it spreads almost to the edge. Repeat with the remaining macarons and filling. Place the macarons in an airtight container and refrigerate for at least 4 hours (or up to 5 days) before serving. Serve slightly chilled.

# Caramel Pecan Brownies

*These brownies are* not too rich (they are more cakey than fudgy), so they don't overwhelm the star of the show — the gooey caramel topping. A drizzle of bittersweet chocolate ganache and chopped toasted pecans make the brownies an irresistible indulgence.

MAKES 36 BROWNIES

### BROWNIES

16 tablespoons (227 g/8 oz) unsalted butter, cut into tablespoons

4 ounces (113 g) unsweetened chocolate, coarsely chopped

4 large eggs

1¾ cups (350 g/12.3 oz) granulated sugar

¼ teaspoon (1.6 g/0.06 oz) salt

1½ teaspoons (6 g/0.21 oz) vanilla extract

¾ cup plus 1 tablespoon (108 g/3.8 oz) all-purpose flour

1½ cups (150 g/5.3 oz) pecan halves, toasted (see page 13) and coarsely chopped

### CARAMEL TOPPING

1 cup (200 g/7 oz) granulated sugar

¼ cup (59 g/2 oz) water

⅛ teaspoon (0.65 g/0.02 oz) freshly squeezed lemon juice

½ cup (121 g/4.3 oz) heavy cream

3 tablespoons (42 g/1.5 oz) unsalted butter, cut into tablespoons

⅛ teaspoon (0.8 g/0.03 oz) salt

1 teaspoon (4 g/0.14 oz) vanilla extract

(CONTINUED)

## Make the brownies

1. Preheat the oven to 350°F. Coat the bottom and sides of a 9-by-13-inch baking pan with nonstick cooking spray.

2. Place the butter and chocolate in a medium heavy saucepan and cook over low heat, stirring frequently, until both are melted and the mixture is smooth. Remove from heat and set aside.

3. In a medium bowl, whisk the eggs until well blended. Gradually whisk in the sugar and continue to whisk vigorously until well blended. Whisk in the melted chocolate mixture, salt, and vanilla. Add the flour and whisk until blended. Stir in the pecans.

4. Scrape the batter into the prepared pan. Bake for 22 to 25 minutes, until firm to the touch (the brownies will puff up in spots, but will settle as they cool). Transfer the pan to a wire rack to cool while you make the topping.

## Make the topping and top the brownies

5. Fill a cup with water and place a pastry brush in it (this will be used for washing down the sides of the pan to prevent crystallization). In a clean, heavy-bottomed, small saucepan, stir together the sugar, water, and lemon juice. Place the saucepan over medium-high heat and cook, occasionally washing down the sides of the pan with the pastry brush to prevent crystallization, until the mixture starts to color around the edges. Gently swirl the pan to ensure that the sugar caramelizes evenly. Continue to cook the caramel to a medium amber color. Remove the pan from the heat and slowly add the cream (the mixture will bubble up furiously). Once the bubbling

2 ounces (57 g) bittersweet chocolate (70%), coarsely chopped

1 tablespoon (14 g/0.5 oz) heavy cream

½ cup (50 g/1.7 oz) pecan halves, toasted (see page 13) and chopped

has subsided, add the butter and stir until completely melted. Whisk in the salt and vanilla.

6. Pour the caramel topping over the warm brownies, using a small metal offset spatula to spread it over the entire top. Let the brownies cool on the wire rack for 45 minutes, then refrigerate for at least 1 hour, until the caramel topping is set.

### *Garnish the brownies*

7. Combine the chocolate and cream in a small saucepan and cook over low heat, stirring frequently, until the chocolate is melted and the mixture is smooth. Pour the chocolate into a small sealable plastic bag and seal the bag. Using scissors, snip a small hole in a corner of the bag and drizzle the chocolate diagonally over the brownies. Sprinkle the pecans on top. Refrigerate for 30 minutes, until the chocolate is set.

8. To serve, use a sharp knife to cut the brownies into 36 bars. The brownies can be served chilled or at room temperature. Store the brownies, well covered, in the refrigerator for up to 5 days.

# Gingered Pear Upside-Down Cake

*This unpretentious upside-down* cake is easy to put together yet makes an impressive presentation. Buttery brown sugar caramel is poured into the cake pan and then pear slices and pecans are layered on top. A spiced cake batter goes over the fruit and, after baking, the cake is inverted onto a serving plate. With the caramelized pears now on top, as the cake cools, their juices gradually seep into the cake, making it moist and delicious. I like to use red pears for this, but any type will do, as long as they're ripe.

MAKES ONE 9-INCH CAKE, SERVING 8 TO 10

### CARAMELIZED PEAR AND PECAN TOPPING

3 tablespoons (42 g/1.5 oz) unsalted butter, cut into tablespoons

¾ cup firmly packed (162 g/5.7 oz) light brown sugar

2 large (567 g/20 oz) ripe pears

½ cup (50 g/1.76 oz) pecans, toasted (see page 13) and coarsely chopped

### CAKE

1½ cups (198 g/7 oz) all-purpose flour

1½ teaspoons (7.5 g/0.25 oz) baking powder

¼ teaspoon (1.25 g/0.04 oz) baking soda

½ teaspoon (1 g/0.03 oz) ground ginger

½ teaspoon (1 g/0.03 oz) ground cinnamon

½ teaspoon (3.35 g/0.12 oz) salt

½ cup (121 g/4.3 oz) buttermilk

2 teaspoons (30 g/1 oz) finely grated fresh ginger

(CONTINUED)

## Make the topping

1. Preheat the oven to 350°F. Butter the sides (but not the bottom) of a 9-inch round cake pan. Place the butter in a small saucepan with the brown sugar. Cook over medium-high heat, stirring occasionally, until the butter is melted and the mixture is bubbling. Pour the hot mixture onto the bottom of the cake pan and spread it as evenly as possible.

2. Cut each pear in half and remove its core. Cut each pear half lengthwise into ½-inch slices. Arrange the pear slices in a circle around the edge of the pan with the pointed ends toward the center, overlapping them slightly, on top of the sugar and butter. Sprinkle the pecans over the pears.

## Make the cake

3. Sift together the flour, baking powder, baking soda, ground ginger, cinnamon, and salt into a medium bowl and whisk to combine. In a small bowl, stir together the buttermilk, fresh ginger, vanilla, and orange zest.

4. In the bowl of an electric mixer fitted with the paddle attachment, beat the butter at medium-high speed until creamy, about 1 minute. Gradually add the brown sugar and beat at high speed until the mixture is lightened in texture and color, about 3 minutes. Reduce the speed to medium and add the eggs one at a time, beating well after each addition and scraping down the sides of the bowl

2 teaspoons (8 g/0.28 oz)
vanilla extract

½ teaspoon (1 g/0.03 oz) finely
grated orange zest

8 tablespoons (113 g/4 oz)
unsalted butter, softened

1 cup firmly packed (216 g/
7.6 oz) light brown sugar

2 large eggs

as needed. With the mixer on low speed, add the flour mixture in three additions, alternating with the buttermilk mixture in two additions and mixing just until blended. Spoon the batter in large dollops over the pears, then smooth it into an even layer.

5. Bake for 48 to 52 minutes, until the cake is golden brown and a toothpick inserted into the center comes out clean. Set the pan on a wire rack and let cool for 10 minutes.

6. Run a thin-bladed knife around the edge of the pan. Place a cake plate upside down on top of the cake pan and, using pot holders, very carefully invert the cake pan and plate. Carefully remove the cake pan. Serve the cake warm or at room temperature.

# Banoffee Pie

*Banoffee pie, which combines* bananas with a sticky toffee filling and whipped cream, is an English dessert, and not a very subtle one. It's very sweet, but sometimes a sweet, over-the-top-indulgent cream pie is just the right thing. For the toffee filling — which is simply made by heating unopened cans of condensed milk in simmering water over the course of a couple hours — you'll need to check the cans occasionally while they are cooking to make sure they are covered with water. Just set your timer to ring every 30 minutes and inspect the water level then.

MAKES ONE 9-INCH DEEP-DISH PIE, SERVING 8

SPECIAL EQUIPMENT:
9-inch deep-dish pie pan

### TOFFEE FILLING

Two 14½-ounce (411 g) cans sweetened condensed milk

### PECAN-GRAHAM CRACKER CRUST

½ cup (50 g/1.76 oz) pecans

1½ cups (180 g/6.3 oz) graham cracker crumbs (from about 12 whole graham crackers)

Generous pinch of salt

5 tablespoons (70 g/2.5 oz) unsalted butter, melted

### TOPPING

2 ripe large bananas

3 tablespoons (45 g/1.5 oz) dark rum, divided

1½ cups (348 g/12.27 oz) heavy cream

⅓ cup (42 g/1.5 oz) confectioners' sugar, sifted

½ teaspoon (0.65 g/0.02 oz) instant espresso powder, dissolved in 1 teaspoon (5 g/0.17 oz) hot water and cooled

(CONTINUED)

## Make the filling

1. Remove the labels from the cans of condensed milk. Place the unopened cans on their sides in a medium saucepan and cover with water. Bring the water to a boil over high heat, then reduce it to a simmer and continue to simmer for 2 hours, adding more hot water as necessary to make sure the cans are always covered. Carefully remove the cans from the water with tongs and let them cool completely.

## Make the crust and fill

2. Preheat the oven to 350°F. Butter the bottom and sides of a 9-inch deep-dish pie pan.

3. Place the pecans, graham cracker crumbs, and salt in the bowl of a food processor and process until finely ground. Transfer the mixture to a medium bowl and combine with the butter. Press the mixture onto the bottom and up the sides of the prepared pie pan. Bake for 8 minutes. Let cool completely.

4. Once the condensed milk cans are cool, open them and scrape the toffee filling into the cooled crust, spreading it evenly. Refrigerate for at least 1 hour.

1 teaspoon (4 g/0.14 oz) vanilla
extract

GARNISH

½ cup (57 g/2 oz) chopped
Candied Pecans (page 13)

## Make the topping and finish the pie

**5.** Slice the bananas ¼ inch thick and place in a medium bowl. Pour 2 tablespoons (30 g/1 oz) of the rum over them and gently toss to coat evenly. Arrange the banana slices on top of the toffee layer, covering it completely.

**6.** In the bowl of an electric mixer fitted with the whisk attachment, whip the cream at high speed until soft peaks start to form. Add the remaining 1 tablespoon (15 g/0.5 oz) rum, the confectioners' sugar, espresso mixture, and vanilla and beat until firm peaks form. Scrape the cream over the bananas, spreading it decoratively with a spatula. Garnish the pie with the candied pecans. Serve immediately or refrigerate until ready to serve, up to 1 day.

# Almond Caramels

*While mass-produced caramels* can be hard and overly sweet, these confections are extra creamy and just firm enough to hold their shape. I wrap each caramel in a 2-by-3-inch rectangle of waxed paper to preserve their freshness, and pack them with toasted almonds as a nice counterpoint.

## MAKES 32 CARAMELS

**SPECIAL EQUIPMENT:**
Candy thermometer

¾ cup (174 g/6.13 oz) heavy cream

1½ cups (300 g/10.5 oz) granulated sugar

¼ cup (59 g/2 oz) water

¼ cup (82 g/2.9 oz) light corn syrup

4 tablespoons (56 g/2 oz) unsalted butter, cut into tablespoons and softened

1 teaspoon (4 g/0.14 oz) vanilla extract

¼ teaspoon (1.6 g/0.06 oz) salt

1 cup (120 g/4.2 oz) whole blanched almonds, toasted (see page 13) and coarsely chopped

1. Preheat the oven to 350°F. Line an 8-inch square pan with a piece of parchment paper or aluminum foil, letting the paper or foil extend 2 inches beyond the edge of two opposite sides of the pan. Butter the bottom and sides of the paper or foil.

2. Place the cream in a heatproof glass measuring cup and microwave on high power for 1 minute, until hot. Set aside. Fill a cup with water and place a pastry brush in it (this will be used for washing down the sides of the pan to prevent crystallization).

3. In a clean, heavy-bottomed 3-quart saucepan, stir together the sugar, water, and corn syrup. Place the saucepan over medium-high heat and cook, occasionally washing down the sides of the pan with the pastry brush to wash away any sugar crystals, until the mixture starts to color around the edges. Gently swirl the pan to ensure that the sugar caramelizes evenly. Continue to cook until the sugar turns a medium amber color. Remove the pan from the heat and add the butter, 1 tablespoon at a time, stirring until melted. Stir in the warm cream. Return the pan to medium-high heat and cook, stirring constantly to prevent the mixture from scorching on the bottom, until the mixture registers 250°F on a candy thermometer. Remove the pan from the heat and stir in the vanilla, salt, and almonds. Pour the caramel into the prepared pan and let it stand at room temperature for at least 2 hours or until firm enough to cut.

4. If your kitchen is warm, refrigerate the caramel block for 15 minutes—this will make it easier to cut. Use the paper or foil ends to lift the caramel from the pan. Flip the slab over and peel off the paper. Cut into thirty-two 2- by-1-inch rectangles. Store between sheets of waxed paper in an airtight container or individually wrapped in waxed paper at room temperature for up to 2 weeks.

# Chocolate-Caramel-Almond Tart with Fleur de Sel

*This seductive tart* has a deep, buttery caramel almond filling topped off with a thin ganache glaze and a sprinkling of crunchy fleur de sel. I developed a similar recipe a few years ago; here I've adapted it slightly so that the caramel is slightly firmer and doesn't ooze out of the tart onto your plate (although that is really not such a bad thing). The crust is ultra-simple, and comes together in the food processor in minutes. The dough for the crust can be made up to three days ahead and stored, well wrapped, in the refrigerator.

MAKES ONE 9-INCH TART, SERVING 8

## CRUST

1½ cups (199 g/7 oz) all-purpose flour

3 tablespoons (37 g/1.32 oz) granulated sugar

¼ teaspoon (1.6 g/0.06 oz) salt

9 tablespoons (127 g/4.5 oz) unsalted butter, cut into ½-inch dice and frozen for 15 minutes

3 tablespoons (44 g/1.6 oz) ice-cold water

## CARAMEL ALMOND LAYER

¾ cup (100 g/3.5 oz) blanched slivered almonds

1 cup (200 g/7 oz) granulated sugar

¼ cup (59 g/2 oz) water

2 tablespoons (41 g/1.4 oz) light corn syrup

6 tablespoons (87 g/3 oz) heavy cream

4 tablespoons (56 g/2 oz) unsalted butter

¼ teaspoon (1.67 g/0.06 oz) salt

1 teaspoon (4 g/0.14 oz) vanilla extract

(CONTINUED)

## Make the crust

1. Place the flour, sugar, and salt in the bowl of a food processor and pulse a few times to combine. Add the butter pieces and toss to coat with flour. Blend the butter and flour with about five 1-second pulses, or until the mixture is the texture of coarse meal with some butter pieces the size of peas. Sprinkle the water over the flour mixture and process continuously until the dough begins to clump together. Do not overprocess; the dough should not form a ball.

2. Turn the dough out onto a work surface and shape it into a thick 4-inch-wide disc. Wrap the dough in plastic wrap and refrigerate until firm enough to roll, about 30 minutes.

3. Place the unwrapped dough on a lightly floured work surface. Roll out the dough into an 11-inch circle, lifting and rotating the dough often while dusting the work surface and dough lightly with flour as necessary. Roll the dough up on the rolling pin and unroll it over a 9-inch fluted tart pan with a removable bottom. Gently press the dough onto the bottom and up the sides of the pan. Roll the pin over the top of the pan to trim off the excess dough. Lightly prick the bottom of the dough with a fork at ½-inch intervals. Refrigerate the dough in the pan for 20 minutes to firm up the dough. Meanwhile, preheat the oven to 375°F.

## CHOCOLATE TRUFFLE LAYER

2 ounces (57 g) bittersweet chocolate (60% to 65%), chopped

⅓ cup (77 g/2.7 oz) heavy cream

1 tablespoon (14 g/0.5 oz) unsalted butter, cut into 3 pieces

½ teaspoon (2 g/0.07 oz) vanilla extract

Pinch of fleur de sel or Maldon sea salt, for sprinkling

**4.** Right before baking, line the dough with parchment paper or aluminum foil and cover with pie weights or dried beans. Place the tart pan on a baking sheet and bake for 15 minutes. Carefully lift the paper or foil (along with the weights) out of the tart pan and bake the crust for 8 to 12 minutes longer, until golden brown. Leave the oven on. Transfer the tart pan to a wire rack and let cool completely. Keep the oven on to toast the almonds.

### Make the caramel layer

**5.** Toast the almonds on a baking sheet in the oven for 7 to 9 minutes, until golden. Let the nuts cool.

**6.** Fill a cup with water and place a pastry brush in it (this will be used for washing down the sides of the pan to prevent crystallization). In a clean, heavy-bottomed 2-quart saucepan, stir together the sugar, water, and corn syrup. Place the saucepan over medium-high heat and cook, occasionally washing down the sides of the pan with the pastry brush to wash away any sugar crystals, until the mixture starts to color around the edges. Gently swirl the pan to ensure that the sugar caramelizes evenly and continue to cook until the caramel turns a medium-dark amber color. Remove the pan from the heat and carefully add the cream (the mixture will bubble up furiously). Once the bubbling has subsided, add the butter and stir until completely melted. Whisk in the salt, vanilla, and toasted almonds and stir until the nuts are completely coated. Pour the hot caramel mixture into the cooled tart shell, using a spoon to make sure that the nuts are evenly distributed. Let the caramel cool for 30 minutes, then refrigerate until the caramel is chilled, about 1 hour.

### Make the chocolate truffle layer

**7.** Place the chocolate and cream in a small saucepan over low heat and cook, stirring occasionally, until the chocolate is melted. Add the butter and stir until melted and the mixture is smooth. Stir in the vanilla. Pour the warm mixture over the caramel and smooth it into an even layer. Sprinkle the fleur de sel lightly over the chocolate. Refrigerate for at least 30 minutes, until the chocolate is set. Serve the tart at room temperature or slightly chilled. Store, uncovered, in the refrigerator for up to 5 days.

# Caramel Coconut Cream Pie

*Coconut cream pie* is one of my favorite desserts. Since coconut is so compatible with caramel, I decided to gild the lily by adding a layer of caramel to the classic, and the result is an indulgent pie that every caramel and coconut lover is bound to adore.

MAKES ONE 9-INCH PIE, SERVING 10

### FLAKY COCONUT CRUST

1⅓ cups (176 g/6.2 oz)
all-purpose flour

3 tablespoons (17 g/0.6 oz)
unsweetened shredded
coconut

1 tablespoon (12 g/0.44 oz)
granulated sugar

¼ teaspoon (1.6 g/0.06 oz) salt

8 tablespoons (113 g/4 oz)
unsalted butter, cut into
½-inch cubes and frozen for
30 minutes

1 teaspoon (5 g/0.17 oz) white
vinegar

2 tablespoons (30 g/1 oz)
ice-cold water

½ teaspoon (2 g/0.07 oz)
vanilla bean paste or extract

### CARAMEL LAYER

1 cup (200 g/7 oz) granulated
sugar

1 tablespoon plus 1½ teaspoons
(30 g/1 oz) light corn syrup

3 tablespoons (44 g/1.5 oz)
water

½ cup (116 g/4 oz) heavy cream

3 tablespoons (42 g/1.5 oz)
unsalted butter

Pinch of salt

½ teaspoon (2 g/0.07 oz)
vanilla extract

(CONTINUED)

## Make the crust

1. Place the flour, coconut, sugar, and salt in the bowl of a food processor and pulse until blended. Add the butter cubes and, using a spoon, toss to coat them in the flour. Pulse the machine on and off just until the mixture resembles coarse crumbs. Combine the vinegar with the ice-cold water and vanilla. With the processor on, add the vinegar-water mixture through the feed tube and process until the mixture just starts to come together. Don't allow the dough to form a ball on the blade, or the resulting crust will be tough.

2. Turn the dough out onto a work surface and shape it into a thick disc. Wrap the disc in plastic wrap and refrigerate for at least 1 hour.

3. Place the unwrapped chilled dough disc on a lightly floured surface and sprinkle some flour over it. Roll out the dough from the center in every direction, flouring the work surface as necessary to prevent sticking. You want a round about ⅛ inch thick or slightly thinner and about 12 inches in diameter.

4. Transfer the dough to a 9-inch pie pan by rolling it loosely around the rolling pin and unrolling it carefully over the pan. Press the dough first into the bottom of the pan and then against the sides. Trim the edges of the dough with scissors, leaving about ¾ inch of overhang. (Patch any holes or cracks with dough scraps.) Tuck the overhang underneath itself and, using your thumb and index finger, crimp the edge. Prick the bottom of the crust with a fork at 1-inch intervals. Refrigerate the pie shell for 20 minutes. Meanwhile, preheat the oven to 400°F.

## COCONUT CREAM LAYER

2 large egg yolks

⅔ cup (133 g/4.7 oz) granulated sugar

2 tablespoons plus 1 teaspoon (17 g/0.6 oz) cornstarch

2¾ cups (638 g/22.5 oz) heavy cream, divided

½ teaspoon (4 g/0.14 oz) vanilla extract

¾ cup plus 2 tablespoons (78 g/2.7 oz) unsweetened shredded coconut, divided

5. Right before baking, line the dough with aluminum foil or parchment paper and cover with pie weights or dried beans. Place the pie pan on a baking sheet and bake for 20 minutes. Carefully lift the foil (along with the weights) out of the pan and bake the crust for 5 to 10 minutes longer, until golden brown around the edges. Transfer the pan to a wire rack and let the crust cool completely.

### Make the caramel layer

6. Fill a small cup with water and place a pastry brush in it (this will be used for washing down the sides of the pan to prevent crystallization).

7. In a clean, heavy-bottomed 2-quart saucepan, stir together the sugar, corn syrup, and water. Place the saucepan over medium-high heat and cook, occasionally washing down the sides of the pan with the pastry brush to wash away any sugar crystals, until the mixture starts to color around the edges. Gently swirl the pan to ensure that the sugar caramelizes evenly and continue to cook until the caramel turns a medium-dark amber color. Remove the pan from the heat and carefully add the cream (the mixture will bubble up furiously). Once the bubbling has subsided, add the butter and stir until completely melted. Stir in the salt and vanilla. Pour the hot caramel mixture into the cooled pie shell. Let the caramel cool for 30 minutes, then refrigerate until the caramel is chilled, about 1 hour.

### Make the coconut cream layer

8. In a medium bowl, whisk together the egg yolks with the sugar, cornstarch, and ¼ cup (58 g/2 oz) of the cream until smooth.

9. In a small saucepan, heat 1½ cups (348 g/12.3 oz) of the cream over medium-high heat until it just begins to bubble around the edges. Remove the pan from the heat and whisk about ½ cup of the hot cream into the yolk mixture. Whisk this mixture into the remaining hot cream and cook over medium-high heat, whisking constantly, until the mixture thickens and begins to bubble. Transfer the custard to a medium bowl and whisk in the vanilla. Prepare an ice bath by filling a large bowl one-third full with ice and water and place the bowl of custard in it. Allow the custard to chill in the ice

bath, stirring occasionally, until cold, about 20 minutes. Press a piece of plastic wrap directly on the surface of the custard and refrigerate until well chilled, about 2 hours.

**10.** In a large skillet over medium heat, toast the coconut, tossing constantly, until it is a light golden brown. Set aside to cool completely.

**11.** In the bowl of an electric mixer fitted with the whisk attachment, whip the remaining 1 cup (232 g/8.18 oz) cream on high speed until medium peaks form. Remove the chilled custard from the refrigerator and whisk it by hand until smooth. Gently fold the whipped cream into the custard along with ¾ cup (67 g/2.4 oz) of the toasted coconut. Scrape the custard over the caramel layer in the pie crust and spread it into even layer, swirling the filling with a metal spatula. Garnish the top of the pie with the remaining 2 tablespoons (11 g/0.4 oz) toasted coconut. Refrigerate the pie in an airtight container or loosely covered with plastic wrap for up to 3 days.

# Coffee

✦ ✦

Coffee is a language in itself.

— JACKIE CHAN

*Coffee is one* of life's simple pleasures, and its robust flavor is an enduring favorite in desserts of all kinds. Coffee or espresso flavor can be added to desserts in several ways. The most direct way is to add freshly ground coffee beans to batter, filling, frosting, or whatever you're making. This will also give your dessert a slightly gritty texture and tweedy appearance, which may or may not be appropriate. Another way is to add some strong brewed coffee or espresso. You can also infuse coffee beans into cream or another liquid in the dessert. Or a fourth method is to dissolve instant espresso powder in a small amount of hot water to make a sort of coffee extract. This technique might not give you the purest coffee flavor, but it is convenient and works well in some recipes, such as the buttercream in my Espresso Macarons.

The recipes in this chapter range from subtly to strongly flavored. Coffee-Caramel Mousse Pie and Frozen Café con Miel Parfaits, for example, are as light as cappuccino, while Espresso Granita and Frozen Espresso Crunch Parfaits offer a bracing shot of espresso. Since coffee and chocolate go so well together, several recipes combine the two. Shards of dark chocolate run through the Espresso–Chocolate Chip Semifreddo, while chunks of milk chocolate and chocolate-covered espresso beans enhance the Espresso–Milk Chocolate Chunk Cookies. Many of the recipes in this chapter are either chilled, semi-frozen, or frozen; the bold flavor of coffee shines through even in ice-cold desserts. No matter how you take your coffee, this chapter has a dessert for you.

# Coffee-Cardamom Pots de Crème

*A light coffee flavor* with a cardamom endnote makes this simple pot de crème unusually good. For the topping, ice-cold milk is frothed up with a battery-operated milk frother or stick blender. If you don't have either appliance, use a small whisk and a little elbow grease. Make sure to use lowfat milk; whole milk will not froth up well because of its higher fat content. Serve the pots de crème in small coffee or espresso cups for a faux cappuccino look.

**MAKES 6 POTS DE CRÈME**

**SPECIAL EQUIPMENT:**
Handheld battery-operated milk frother or immersion blender

**COFFEE-CARDAMOM CUSTARD**

2 cups (464 g/16.4 oz) heavy cream

¼ cup (19 g/0.7 oz) coffee beans, coarsely ground (3 or 4 quick spins in a coffee grinder)

3 cardamom pods, lightly crushed

Pinch of salt

6 large egg yolks

⅓ cup (66 g/2.3 oz) granulated sugar

1 teaspoon (4 g/0.14 oz) vanilla extract

**GARNISH**

¾ cup (181 g/6.4 oz) very cold lowfat (1%) milk

Unsweetened Dutch-processed cocoa powder

## Make the custard

1. Preheat the oven to 300°F. Have ready six 4- or 5-ounce oven-safe coffee cups or ramekins in a 9-by-13-inch baking pan.

2. In a small saucepan, combine the cream, coffee beans, cardamom pods, and salt and cook over medium-high heat until the mixture is just beginning to bubble around the edges of the pan. Remove the pan from the heat, cover, and let stand for 15 minutes.

3. In a medium bowl, whisk the egg yolks with the sugar until well blended. While whisking, strain half the hot cream mixture into the yolks. Strain the remaining cream into the yolks, whisking constantly. Whisk in the vanilla. Divide the custard among the coffee cups or ramekins.

4. Pour enough hot water to come halfway up the sides of the cups and bake for 30 to 40 minutes, until the custards are set but still slightly jiggly in the center. Remove the pan from the oven and let the custards cool in the water for 15 minutes. Transfer the custards to a wire rack and let cool completely. Refrigerate the pots de crème until well chilled, at least 3 hours, or up to 3 days.

## Garnish and serve the pots de crème

5. Right before serving, place the milk in a tall glass. Using a handheld milk frother or immersion blender, froth the milk well. Spoon a generous amount of froth onto each custard, sift a little cocoa powder on top, and serve the pots de crème immediately.

# Double-Espresso Panna Cotta with Sambuca Cream

*This dessert was inspired* by the shot of Sambuca with three coffee beans that is served after dinner at old-style Italian restaurants. The tradition is both practical and symbolic: A *digestif*, Sambuca aids the digestion, while the coffee beans represent health, happiness, and prosperity (the beans are not meant to be eaten). The bottom layer of my espresso panna cotta is a latte-colored cream with a flavor to match. The second layer is a dark and sweet espresso gelée. A cloud of Sambuca-spiked whipped cream tops the whole thing off. The single chocolate-covered espresso bean garnish, by the way, *is* meant to be eaten.

MAKES 6 SERVINGS

### ESPRESSO PANNA COTTA

¼ cup (59 g/2 oz) cold water

1 tablespoon (9.36 g/0.33 oz) unflavored powdered gelatin

2½ cups (580 g/20.4 oz) heavy cream

1 cup (242 g/8.5 oz) whole milk

½ cup (38 g/1.3 oz) espresso beans, very coarsely ground (about 3 short spins in a coffee grinder)

½ cup (100 g/3.5 oz) granulated sugar

### ESPRESSO GELÉE

1 cup (240 g/8.5 oz) cold brewed espresso, divided

1⅛ teaspoons (3.5 g/0.12 oz) powdered gelatin

2 tablespoons (25 g/0.88 oz) granulated sugar

(CONTINUED)

## Make the panna cotta

1. Have 6 serving glasses or wineglasses at hand. Place the water in a small cup and sprinkle the gelatin on top in an even layer. Set aside to soften for 5 minutes.

2. In a medium saucepan, combine the cream, milk, espresso beans, and sugar and cook over medium-high heat until bubbles start to form around the edge of the pan. Remove the pan from the heat, cover, and allow to stand for 10 minutes.

3. Stir the softened gelatin mixture into the hot espresso cream and cook over medium heat, stirring until the gelatin is completely dissolved. Strain the mixture through a fine-mesh sieve into a medium bowl. Prepare an ice bath by filling a larger bowl one-third full with ice and water, and set the bowl of espresso cream in it. Let stand, stirring occasionally, until cool, about 10 minutes. Divide the mixture evenly among the serving glasses and refrigerate for at least 3 hours, until set.

## Make the gelée

4. Place ¼ cup (60 g/2.1 oz) of the espresso in a small cup and sprinkle the gelatin evenly on top. Let stand for 5 minutes to soften.

1 cup (232 g/8.18 oz) heavy cream

3 tablespoons (24 g/0.84 oz) confectioners' sugar

1 tablespoon (15 g/0.5 oz) Sambuca liqueur

GARNISH

6 chocolate-covered espresso beans

**5.** Place the remaining ¾ cup (180 g/6.3 oz) espresso in a microwave-safe cup and microwave on high power for 1 minute, or until hot. Stir in the sugar until dissolved. Stir in the gelatin mixture until dissolved. Let the mixture cool, stirring occasionally, until it is at room temperature. Carefully pour a thin layer of the mixture (about 2½ tablespoons) over each espresso panna cotta and refrigerate until set, at least 3 hours.

### Make the Sambuca cream and finish the dessert

**6.** In the bowl of an electric mixer fitted with the whisk attachment, beat the cream at high speed until soft peaks begin to form. Add the confectioners' sugar and Sambuca and whip until firm peaks just begin to form. (The cream should be made no more than 4 hours before serving the dessert.)

**7.** Spoon about ⅓ cup of the Sambuca cream on top of each dessert and garnish with a chocolate-covered espresso bean.

# Frozen Café con Miel Parfaits with Caramel-Walnut Espresso Topping

*This frozen dessert* is based on the Spanish drink *café con miel,* which is coffee flavored with honey and spices. In Spain, it is typically served after dinner, so I thought it made sense to create a dessert with the same flavors. Though honey is more typically associated with tea, it actually goes quite well with coffee. This ultra-smooth parfait is unexpectedly light — much lighter than ice cream — and topped with a walnut-coffee–brown sugar mixture that is crunchy and utterly delicious.

**MAKES 8 PARFAITS**

**SPECIAL EQUIPMENT:**
Candy thermometer

**FROZEN CAFÉ CON MIEL PARFAITS**

⅓ cup (25 g/0.88 oz) dark roast coffee beans, coarsely ground (3 or 4 quick spins in a coffee grinder)

2 cups (464 g/16.3 oz) heavy cream

One 3-inch cinnamon stick

¾ teaspoon (3 g/0.1 oz) vanilla extract

6 large egg whites, at room temperature

⅛ teaspoon (0.4 g/0.013 oz) cream of tartar

⅓ cup (113 g/4 oz) honey

⅓ cup (66 g/2.3 oz) granulated sugar

Pinch of salt

Pinch of freshly grated nutmeg

**CARAMEL-WALNUT ESPRESSO TOPPING**

1 cup (200 g/7 oz) turbinado sugar

(CONTINUED)

## Make the parfaits

1. In a medium saucepan, combine the coffee beans, cream, and cinnamon stick. Place over medium-high heat and bring to a boil, stirring occasionally. Remove the pan from the heat, cover, and allow to infuse for 20 minutes.

2. Strain the cream through a fine-mesh sieve into the bowl of an electric mixer (discard the coffee beans and cinnamon stick). Cover the bowl and refrigerate the cream until chilled, at least 1½ hours.

3. Place the bowl in the mixer stand and stir in the vanilla. Using the whisk attachment, beat at high speed until soft peaks form. Transfer the coffee cream to another bowl, cover, and refrigerate until ready to use.

4. Clean and dry the mixer bowl and whisk attachment. Place the egg whites in the bowl and beat at medium speed until frothy. Add the cream of tartar and beat at medium-high speed until the whites begin to turn opaque. At this point, start heating the honey syrup.

5. Fill a cup with water and place a pastry brush in it (this will be used for washing down the sides of the pan to prevent crystallization). In a small, heavy-bottomed saucepan, combine the honey and sugar and place over medium-high heat. Cook, without stirring, occasionally brushing down the sides of the pan with the wet pastry brush to prevent crystallization, until the syrup reaches 248°F on

1 cup (232 g/8.18 oz) heavy cream

Pinch of salt

⅓ cup (80 g/2.8 oz) brewed espresso or strong coffee

½ teaspoon (2 g/0.07 oz) vanilla extract

1 cup (100 g/3.5 oz) walnuts, toasted (see page 13) and coarsely chopped

a candy thermometer (watch the syrup carefully, as it heats up quickly). With the mixer running on medium speed, quickly pour the hot syrup into the egg whites in a continuous stream near the side of the bowl, trying to avoid getting it on the whisk attachment. Add the salt and nutmeg. Raise the speed to high and whip the egg whites until they are completely cool, about 5 minutes.

6. Scrape the whipped coffee cream into the whites and fold until well combined. Divide the mixture among 8 serving glasses and cover loosely with plastic wrap. Freeze for at least 3 hours.

## Make the topping and finish the dessert

7. In a small saucepan, combine the turbinado sugar, cream, and salt and place over medium-high heat. Bring to a boil, then reduce the heat to low and simmer the mixture for 3 minutes. Remove the pan from the heat and stir in the espresso, vanilla, and walnuts. The topping can be made up to 1 week ahead and stored in a covered container in the refrigerator. Just warm it up over low heat when ready to serve.

8. Right before serving, spoon some of the warm topping over each parfait; serve immediately.

# Frozen Espresso Crunch Parfaits

*This parfait is a celebration* of flavors and textures. A crunchy espresso ice cream, espresso caramel sauce, vanilla gelato, shards of crispy sugar cones, and whipped cream combine to create the ultimate coffee lover's sundae. If you like, you can skip the vanilla ice cream and use two scoops of the espresso ice cream, or store-bought coffee ice cream, instead. Friendly warning: Don't eat this dessert right before bedtime. With all that caffeine, you might just see the sun rise.

**MAKES 4 PARFAITS**

---

**SPECIAL EQUIPMENT:**
Instant-read thermometer; ice cream maker

---

**ESPRESSO CRUNCH ICE CREAM**

1 cup (242 g/8.5 oz) whole milk

2 cups (464 g/16.3 oz) heavy cream, divided

1 cup (75 g/2.6 oz) espresso beans, coarsely ground (1 or 2 quick spins in the grinder)

¾ cup (150 g/5.3 oz) granulated sugar, divided

6 large egg yolks

⅛ teaspoon (0.8 g/0.02 oz) salt

1 teaspoon (4 g/0.14 oz) vanilla extract

½ cup (80 g/2.8 oz) chocolate-covered espresso beans, coarsely chopped

**ESPRESSO CARAMEL SAUCE**

1½ cups (10.5 oz/300 g) granulated sugar

½ cup (118 g/4.16 oz) water

½ cup (116 g/4 oz) heavy cream

½ cup (118 g/4.16 oz) brewed espresso or strong coffee

3 tablespoons (42 g/1.5 oz) unsalted butter

¾ teaspoon (5 g/0.17 oz) salt

(CONTINUED)

## Make the espresso ice cream

**1.** In a medium, heavy-bottomed saucepan, combine the milk, 1 cup (232 g/8.18 oz) of the cream, the ground espresso beans, and ½ cup (100 g/3.5 oz) of the sugar. Cook over medium-high heat, stirring to dissolve the sugar, until the mixture begins to bubble around the edge of the pan and steam rises from the surface.

**2.** Meanwhile, whisk the remaining ¼ cup (50 g/1.76 oz) sugar, the egg yolks, and the salt together vigorously in a medium bowl until well blended. Slowly pour in about 1 cup of the hot milk mixture, whisking constantly. Return the mixture to the saucepan with the remaining milk mixture and cook over medium heat, stirring constantly with a heatproof spatula, until the custard thickens slightly and registers 185°F on an instant-read thermometer. Remove the pan from the heat and stir in the remaining 1 cup (232 g/8.18 oz) cream and the vanilla. Strain the custard through a fine-mesh strainer into a large bowl (discard the espresso beans). Prepare an ice bath by filling a larger bowl one-third full with ice and water and place the bowl of custard in it. Allow the custard to chill in the ice bath, stirring occasionally, until cold, about 20 minutes. Press a piece of plastic wrap directly onto the surface of the custard to prevent a skin from forming. Refrigerate the custard for at least 6 hours, or, preferably, overnight.

**3.** Process the espresso custard in an ice cream maker according to the manufacturer's instructions, adding the chocolate-covered

½ cup (116 g/4 oz) heavy cream

½ teaspoon (2 g/0.07 oz) vanilla extract

2 tablespoons (16 g/0.5 oz) confectioners' sugar

ASSEMBLY

1 pint (454 g/16 oz) Vanilla Gelato (page 30) or store-bought ice cream or gelato

8 sugar cones, coarsely crushed (2 cups total)

4 chocolate-covered espresso beans

espresso beans during the final minute of mixing. Pack into a container and freeze for at least 3 hours before serving. (The ice cream is best served the day it is made.)

### *Make the sauce*

**4.** Fill a cup with water and place a pastry brush in it (this will be used for washing down the sides of the pan to prevent crystallization). In a medium, heavy-bottomed saucepan, combine the sugar and water and place over medium heat. Cook, stirring constantly, until the sugar dissolves. Increase the heat to high and cook, without stirring and occasionally brushing down the sides of the pan with the wet pastry brush, until the syrup caramelizes and turns a deep golden amber color, about 8 minutes.

**5.** Remove the pan from the heat and very slowly and carefully add the cream (the mixture will bubble up furiously) and espresso, stirring until smooth. If there are some hardened bits of caramel sticking to the bottom of the pan, place the pan over medium-low heat and stir until they are dissolved. Add the butter and salt and stir until the butter is melted.

**6.** Pour the sauce into a container, cover, and refrigerate for at least 2 hours before serving.

### *Make the whipped cream*

**7.** In the bowl of an electric mixer fitted with the whisk attachment, whip the cream and vanilla at high speed until soft peaks start to form. Add the confectioners' sugar and whip until stiff peaks just begin to form. Cover the bowl and refrigerate the cream until ready to serve. (The cream should be whipped not more than 2 hours before assembling the parfaits.)

### *Assemble the parfaits*

**8.** Spoon 2 tablespoons of the espresso caramel sauce into the bottom of each of 4 wineglasses or parfait glasses. Top each with a large scoop (about ½ cup) of Vanilla Gelato. Spoon another 2 tablespoons sauce on top, then sprinkle with ¼ cup of the crushed sugar cones. Top with a large scoop (about ½ cup) of the espresso ice cream, then 2 tablespoons of the sauce and another ¼ cup crushed sugar cones. Top with a large dollop of whipped cream and garnish with a chocolate-covered espresso bean. Serve the parfaits immediately with long spoons.

# Espresso Granita with Mascarpone Cream

*I love this combination* of bold, icy espresso granita with sweet mascarpone fluff. It reminds me of tiramisu, but much more refreshing. Perfect for a hot summer evening when you want something light, sweet, and flavorful.

MAKES 6 SERVINGS

ESPRESSO GRANITA

1 cup (200 g/7 oz) granulated sugar

4 cups (960 g/33.8 oz) freshly brewed espresso or very strong coffee, hot

MASCARPONE CREAM

¾ cup (174 g/6.13 oz) heavy cream

½ cup (121 g/4.2 oz) mascarpone cheese

2 tablespoons plus 1½ teaspoons (52 g/1.8 oz) honey

1 teaspoon (4 g/0.14 oz) vanilla extract

GARNISH

Cocoa powder, for dusting

## Make the granita

1. Stir the sugar into the espresso until dissolved. Set aside until tepid.

2. Pour the sweetened espresso into a shallow container that measures about 8 by 12 inches. Freeze, uncovered, until the mixture begins to turn icy around the edges, about 1½ hours. Remove the container from the freezer and, using a fork, scrape any frozen parts of the mixture from the edges into the center, breaking up any large pieces. Return the container to the freezer and continue to scrape as before every hour, until you have nothing but flaky crystals. Cover the container with a lid or plastic wrap and freeze the granita until ready to serve.

## Make the cream and finish the dessert

3. Combine the cream, mascarpone, honey, and vanilla in the bowl of an electric mixer fitted with the whisk attachment. Beat on high speed just until the cream forms soft peaks.

4. Spoon about ⅔ cup of the granita into each of 6 chilled serving glasses (wineglasses or champagne flutes work well). Top the granita in each glass with ⅓ cup of the mascarpone cream. Sift a light dusting of cocoa powder on top of the cream and serve immediately.

# Espresso–Chocolate Chip Semifreddo

*Much less dense* than ice cream or gelato, semifreddo is an Italian dessert that has the texture of frozen mousse. In this rendition, small flecks of dark chocolate punctuate the ultra-light, creamy espresso base. I like to serve this with Chocolate Caramel Sauce (page 251).

**MAKES 8 SERVINGS**

**SPECIAL EQUIPMENT:**
Instant-read thermometer

1 cup (232 g/8.18 oz) heavy cream

1 teaspoon (4 g/0.14 oz) vanilla extract

3 large eggs, separated, plus 1 large egg yolk

¾ cup (150 g/5.3 oz) granulated sugar, divided

⅓ cup (80 g/2.8 oz) brewed espresso or strong coffee, at room temperature

¼ teaspoon (0.8 g/0.03 oz) cream of tartar

2 ounces (57 g) bittersweet chocolate (62%), finely chopped

1. Line an 8-by-4½-inch loaf pan with plastic wrap, letting the wrap extend a few inches beyond each side.

2. In the bowl of an electric mixer fitted with the whisk attachment, whip the cream with the vanilla at high speed until soft peaks form. Transfer the whipped cream to a medium bowl, cover, and refrigerate until ready to use. Clean and dry the mixer bowl and whisk attachment.

3. Fill a medium saucepan one-third of the way with water and heat the water until barely simmering. In a medium bowl, whisk together the 4 egg yolks, ½ cup (100 g/3.5 oz) of the sugar, and the espresso. Place the bowl on top of the saucepan of simmering water and heat, whisking constantly, until the mixture thickens and reaches 160°F on an instant-read thermometer, about 8 minutes. Remove the bowl from over the water and set aside. Leave the water on the heat.

4. In the bowl of an electric mixer, whisk together by hand the egg whites, remaining ¼ cup (50 g/1.7 oz) sugar, and the cream of tartar until combined. Place the bowl over the saucepan of simmering water and heat, whisking constantly, until the whites are foamy and reach 145°F on an instant-read thermometer. Transfer the bowl to the mixer stand and, using the whisk attachment, whip the egg whites at high speed until they are completely cool and form stiff peaks.

5. Using a rubber spatula, gently fold the egg whites into the yolk mixture. Fold in half the whipped cream and half the chocolate, then fold in the remaining whipped cream and chocolate. Scrape the mixture into the prepared pan and smooth it into an even layer (it

should fill the pan). Cover the surface of the semifreddo with a piece of plastic wrap and freeze for at least 6 hours, until firm enough to slice (it will still feel softer than ice cream).

6. To serve, use the plastic wrap as handles to lift the semifreddo from the pan. Peel off the plastic wrap. Using a thin-bladed sharp knife, cut the semifreddo into 1-inch slices. Serve each slice on a plate. The semifreddo can be made up to 3 days ahead.

# Espresso–Milk Chocolate Chunk Cookies

*Made with freshly ground* coffee beans and chopped chocolate-covered espresso beans, these chewy cookies offer a double shot of joe. They have slightly more butter than a traditional chocolate chip cookie recipe, which makes them spread more, but that's what makes them moist. They will puff up during baking and then flatten as they cool. The cookies make a great midafternoon snack, perking you up nicely when you start to show signs of zombie-like behavior. The recipe can easily be doubled.

**MAKES 36 COOKIES**

1 cup plus 2 tablespoons (149 g/5.2 oz) all-purpose flour

½ teaspoon (2.5 g/0.09 oz) baking soda

¼ teaspoon plus ⅛ teaspoon (2.5 g/0.09 oz) salt

9 tablespoons (127 g/4.5 oz) unsalted butter, softened

¼ cup (50 g/1.76 oz) granulated sugar

½ cup firmly packed (108 g/ 3.8 oz) light brown sugar

1 tablespoon plus 1 teaspoon (5 g/0.18 oz) finely ground dark roast coffee beans

½ teaspoon (2 g/0.07 oz) vanilla extract

1 large egg

1 cup (170 g/6 oz) ½-inch chunks good-quality milk chocolate

1 cup (100 g/3.5 oz) walnuts

½ cup (80 g/2.8 oz) coarsely chopped chocolate-covered espresso beans

1. In a medium bowl, gently whisk together the flour, baking soda, and salt until blended.

2. In the bowl of an electric mixer fitted with the paddle attachment, beat the butter at medium speed until creamy, about 2 minutes. Gradually add the sugars and beat at high speed until well blended and light, about 2 minutes. Add the ground coffee, vanilla, and egg and mix at medium speed until blended, scraping down the sides of the bowl as necessary. Reduce the speed to low and add the flour mixture one-third at a time, mixing until almost completely blended. Remove the bowl from the mixer stand and, using a wooden spoon or rubber spatula, stir in the chocolate, walnuts, and chocolate-covered espresso beans. Cover the bowl and refrigerate the dough for at least 2 hours (or overnight) before baking.

3. Preheat the oven to 375°F. Line two baking sheets with silicone baking mats or parchment paper. Remove the dough from the refrigerator and let it soften at room temperature for 15 minutes.

4. Scoop the dough out by well-rounded tablespoonfuls (I use a ½-ounce scoop) onto one of the prepared baking sheets, spacing them 2 inches apart. Wet your palm and use it to flatten the mounds into discs that are about ½ inch high. Bake the cookies for 10 to 12 minutes, until slightly puffed and browned around the edges. While the cookies are baking, scoop dough onto the other baking sheet for the second batch. Let the cookies cool on the baking sheet, set on a wire rack. Store the cookies in an airtight container at room temperature for up to 1 week.

# Coffee Almond Biscotti

*With a hint* of orange and lots of toasted almonds, these coffee-charged biscotti are full of flavor and crunch. Unlike most biscotti, they are made with lots of butter, making them moister than the typical Italian variety. For a double hit of caffeine, serve these cookies with espresso — biscotti are notoriously good dunkers.

MAKES ABOUT 32 BISCOTTI

2¼ cups (298 g/10.5 oz) all-purpose flour

1¼ teaspoons (6.25 g/0.22 oz) baking powder

⅛ teaspoon (0.8 g/0.03 oz) salt

13 tablespoons (183 g/6.5 oz) unsalted butter, softened slightly

1 cup (200 g/7 oz) granulated sugar

2 large eggs

1 teaspoon (2 g/0.07 oz) finely grated orange zest

1 teaspoon (4 g/0.14 oz) vanilla extract

¼ cup (19 g/0.6 oz) coffee beans, ground

1¼ cups (186 g/6.5 oz) blanched whole almonds, toasted (see page 13) and coarsely chopped

1. Position two racks near the center of the oven and preheat the oven to 325°F. Line two baking sheets with parchment paper.

2. Sift together the flour, baking powder, and salt in a medium bowl and whisk to combine well.

3. In the bowl of an electric mixer fitted with the paddle attachment, beat the butter at medium speed and gradually add the sugar. Beat for about 2 minutes, until well blended and creamy, scraping down the sides of the bowl as necessary. Beat in the eggs, one at a time, beating well after each addition. Beat in the orange zest and vanilla. With the mixer on low speed, add the flour mixture, mixing just until blended. Add the coffee beans and mix until blended. Remove the bowl from the mixer stand and stir in the almonds.

4. Divide the dough in half and place one of the dough halves on a floured surface (the dough will be sticky). Sprinkle the dough lightly with flour and gently shape into a log that is 3 inches wide and 12 inches long. Transfer the log to one of the prepared baking sheets using two metal spatulas. Repeat with the remaining dough and place it on the same baking sheet, spacing the logs 3 inches apart (they will spread). Place the baking sheet on the upper of the two racks in the oven and bake for 30 to 35 minutes, until the logs just start to brown lightly. Set the baking sheet on a wire rack and let cool for 15 minutes. Reduce the oven temperature to 300°F.

5. Slide a pancake turner under each log to loosen it from the parchment paper. Carefully transfer the logs to a cutting surface. Replace the parchment paper on the baking sheet on which the logs were baked. Using a serrated knife, cut the logs on the diagonal into

# Two-Tone Milk Chocolate Mousse with Sweet-and-Salty Almonds

*Only two ingredients* are necessary for a good chocolate mousse—chocolate and cream. Other ingredients, like eggs, add richness and volume, but they can also obscure the flavor of the chocolate. This simple mousse is best made with a relatively dark milk chocolate, so it's not overly sweet. The mousse is poured over a gooey chocolate ganache and topped off with crunchy, salty-sweet toasted almonds.

MAKES 6 SERVINGS

### SOFT GANACHE

3 ounces (85 g) milk chocolate, finely chopped

3 ounces (85 g) bittersweet chocolate (60% to 64%), finely chopped

1 cup (232 g/8.18 oz) heavy cream

### SWEET-AND-SALTY ALMONDS

½ cup (56 g/2 oz) slivered blanched almonds

2 teaspoons (15 g/0.5 oz) light corn syrup

Pinch of coarse salt

### MILK CHOCOLATE MOUSSE

8 ounces (227 g) milk chocolate, chopped

1½ cups (348 g/12.27 oz) heavy cream, divided

### SWEETENED WHIPPED CREAM

½ cup (116 g/4 oz) heavy cream

1 tablespoon (8 g/0.28 oz) confectioners' sugar

½ teaspoon (2 g/0.07 oz) vanilla extract

### *Make the ganache*

1. Place both chocolates in a medium bowl and set aside.

2. Heat the cream in a medium saucepan over medium heat until it just begins to boil. Pour the hot cream over the chocolate and let it stand for 1 minute to melt the chocolate. Whisk until well blended and smooth. Pour the ganache into six 8-ounce glasses, dividing it evenly (just over ¼ cup per glass). Refrigerate the ganache until firm, about 1 hour.

### *Make the almonds*

3. Preheat the oven to 350°F. Line a baking sheet with a silicone baking mat or parchment paper. In a bowl, toss the nuts with the corn syrup and salt until well coated. Spread the nuts on the baking sheet, separating them as much as possible, and bake, stirring once with a spatula during baking, until golden, 6 to 8 minutes. Set aside to cool.

### *Make the mousse*

4. Place the chocolate and ½ cup (116 g/4 oz) of the cream in a large bowl, and set the bowl over a saucepan half full of barely simmering water. Heat, stirring frequently, until the chocolate is

completely melted and the mixture is smooth. Set the bowl aside and let the chocolate cool completely.

5. In the bowl of an electric mixer fitted with the whisk attachment, whip the remaining 1 cup (232 g/8.18 oz) cream at medium speed until it just holds very soft peaks (don't overwhip, or the mousse will be grainy).

6. Scrape about one-third of the whipped cream into the bowl of chocolate and, using a rubber spatula, quickly fold the cream into the chocolate until half blended. Scrape the remaining cream into the bowl and fold it in until the mixture is completely blended and without any streaks.

7. Pour the mousse on top of the ganache in the glasses, dividing it evenly. Refrigerate the mousse for about 1 hour before serving (or up to 8 hours).

## Whip the cream and serve

8. In the bowl of an electric mixer fitted with the whisk attachment, whip the cream, confectioners' sugar, and vanilla at high speed until the cream holds medium peaks.

9. To serve, spoon some whipped cream over each mousse and top with a sprinkling of almonds.

# Individual Warm Chocolate Brioche Bread Puddings

*Bread pudding falls* firmly into the category of comfort food, but it does have its sophisticated side. This pudding combines a rich, dark chocolate custard and cubes of buttery brioche. I've added some rum, which adds a musky sweetness, but if you prefer, you can substitute an equal amount of milk. I make this dessert in individual ramekins, because I think bread pudding looks a little lumpy when it's spooned into a dish. If you can't get your hands on a loaf of brioche, challah is an excellent substitute.

**MAKES 8 SERVINGS**

⅓ cup (37 g/1.3 oz) unsweetened Dutch-processed cocoa powder

1¾ cups (406 g/14.3 oz) heavy cream

½ cup (100 g/3.5 oz) granulated sugar

½ cup firmly packed (108 g/ 3.8 oz) light brown sugar

1½ cups (363 g/12.8 oz) whole milk

¼ cup (60 g/2.1 oz) dark rum

2 teaspoons (8 g/0.28 oz) vanilla extract

¼ teaspoon (1.6 g/0.06 oz) salt

4 large eggs

240 grams/8.4 ounces brioche or challah, cut into 1-inch cubes (5½ cups)

Demerara sugar, for sprinkling

Sweetened whipped cream, for serving

1. Place the cocoa powder in a large bowl and set aside.

2. In a small saucepan, combine the cream and sugars and cook over medium-high heat, stirring occasionally, just until the sugar is dissolved and small bubbles begin to form around the edge of the pan. Remove the pan from the heat and gradually whisk the mixture into the cocoa powder, whisking constantly to make a smooth mixture. Whisk in the milk, rum, vanilla, and salt. In a medium bowl, whisk the eggs until blended, then whisk them into the cream mixture. Stir in the brioche cubes, making sure they are all coated with the chocolate custard mixture. Cover the bowl and refrigerate the mixture for 1 hour (or up to 1 day).

3. Preheat the oven to 325°F. Butter the interiors of eight 6-ounce ramekins or custard cups and place them in a roasting pan. Divide the bread mixture among the ramekins, filling them. Spinkle each pudding with some demerara sugar. Pour hot water into the roasting pan until it comes almost halfway up the sides of the ramekins. Cover the pan with aluminum foil and bake the bread puddings for 20 minutes. Remove the foil and continue to bake the bread puddings until they are just set, 30 to 40 minutes longer. Carefully transfer the ramekins to a wire rack and let cool for 10 minutes before serving warm with sweetened whipped cream.

# Double Chocolate Éclairs

*A rich chocolate pastry cream* takes the place of plain vanilla custard for the filling of these traditional French pastries. The choux pastry shells are fairly easy to make, but try to avoid making them on a humid day, as they can soften up quickly, and they're best when crispy.

MAKES ABOUT EIGHTEEN 4½-INCH ÉCLAIRS

**SPECIAL EQUIPMENT:**
Pastry bags; small, medium, and large plain tips

**CHOCOLATE CUSTARD CREAM FILLING**

6 large egg yolks

½ cup plus 1 tablespoon (112 g/ 3.9 oz) granulated sugar

¼ cup (30 g/1 oz) cornstarch

2½ cups (605 g/21.3 oz) whole milk

2 tablespoons (28 g/1 oz) unsalted butter, cut into ½-inch cubes

5 ounces (142 g) bittersweet chocolate (61%), finely chopped

1½ teaspoons (6 g/0.21 oz) vanilla bean paste or extract

**CHOUX PASTE**

⅓ cup (78 g/2.7 oz) water

⅓ cup (80 g/2.8 oz) whole milk

1 tablespoon (12 g/0.42 oz) granulated sugar

¼ teaspoon (1.6 g/0.06 oz) salt

5⅓ tablespoons (75 g/2.6 oz) unsalted butter, cut into tablespoons

⅔ cup (88 g/3 oz) all-purpose flour, sifted

3 large eggs

(CONTINUED)

### Make the filling

1. In a bowl, whisk together the yolks, sugar, and cornstarch.

2. In a small saucepan, bring the milk to a gentle boil. Remove the pan from the heat and whisk about ½ cup of the hot milk into the yolk mixture to temper it. Return the entire mixture to the sauce-pan containing the remaining milk. Place over medium-high heat and bring to a boil, whisking constantly. Continue to boil, whisking constantly, for 1 minute. Remove the pan from the heat, scrape the bottom of the pan with a spatula, and whisk until smooth. Whisk in the butter and chocolate until melted. Quickly strain the custard through a fine-mesh sieve into a medium bowl. Whisk in the vanilla. Press a piece of plastic wrap directly onto the surface of the custard, let cool to room temperature, and then refrigerate for 2 hours (or up to 3 days), until well chilled.

### Make the choux paste and bake the éclairs

3. Preheat the oven to 400°F.

4. In a medium saucepan, combine the water, milk, sugar, salt, and butter and bring to a full boil over medium-high heat, stirring frequently. Remove the pan from the heat, add the flour all at once, and stir vigorously with a wooden spoon until the flour is com-pletely incorporated and the mixture pulls away from the side of the pan. Return the pan to the heat and continue to cook for another minute, stirring, to dry out the dough a bit. Transfer the paste to the bowl of an electric mixer fitted with the paddle attachment and let it cool for 2 minutes.

on the baking sheet, spacing them 2 inches apart. Bake for 8 to 10 minutes, until the cookies are puffy, appear slightly cracked, and are no longer shiny. Let the cookies cool on the baking sheet (they are very delicate at this point) for 10 minutes. Carefully transfer the cookies to a wire rack and cool completely. Repeat with the remaining dough. Store the cookies in an airtight container at room temperature for up to 1 week.

# Chocolate-Almond-Coconut Bars

*These wickedly indulgent* brownies were inspired by the Almond Joy candy bar, my favorite childhood treat. The fudgy brownie base is topped with a sticky coconut layer into which whole toasted almonds are embedded, arranged so that each portion gets an almond. The filling is then covered with a half-dark, half-milk-chocolate glaze. Pure joy.

MAKES 16 BARS

### CHOCOLATE-ALMOND BROWNIE LAYER

4 ounces (113 g) bittersweet chocolate (62%), chopped

8 tablespoons (113 g/4 oz) unsalted butter, cut into tablespoons

2 large eggs

1 cup (200 g/7 oz) granulated sugar

½ cup (66 g/2.3 oz) all-purpose flour

½ teaspoon (2 g/0.07 oz) vanilla extract

½ cup (60 g/2.1 oz) blanched whole almonds, toasted (see page 13) and coarsely chopped

### COCONUT-ALMOND LAYER

1½ cups (120 g/4.2 oz) unsweetened shredded coconut

⅓ cup (108 g/3.8 oz) light corn syrup

16 whole blanched almonds, toasted (see page 13)

(CONTINUED)

## *Make the brownie layer*

1. Preheat the oven to 325°F. Line a 9-inch square baking pan with aluminum foil, letting the foil overhang two opposite edges by at least 2 inches. Spray the foil with nonstick cooking spray.

2. Place the chocolate and butter in a heatproof bowl set over a pot of barely simmering water and heat, stirring occasionally, until the mixture is completely melted and smooth. Remove the bowl from the heat and allow the mixture to cool for 10 minutes, until just warm.

3. In a medium bowl, whisk together the eggs and sugar until blended. Whisk in the cooled chocolate-butter mixture. Using a rubber spatula, stir in the flour until well blended. Stir in the vanilla and almonds. Scrape the batter into the prepared pan.

4. Bake for 35 to 40 minutes, until the brownies begin to crack on top (a toothpick inserted into the brownies will come out with moist crumbs clinging to it). Set the pan on a wire rack and let cool completely. Once cool, refrigerate the brownies until chilled, at least 2 hours.

## *Make the coconut-almond layer*

5. Place the coconut in the bowl of a food processor and pulse until finely chopped. Add the corn syrup and pulse until the coconut is evenly moistened.

6. Remove the brownies from the refrigerator and, using the foil ends as handles, lift them out of the pan. Invert the brownies onto

CHOCOLATE GLAZE

2 ounces (57 g) high-quality
milk chocolate, finely chopped

2 ounces (57 g) high-quality
semisweet chocolate (61% or
62%), finely chopped

½ cup (116 g/4 oz) heavy cream

2 tablespoons (41 g/1.4 oz)
light corn syrup

a cutting board and peel off the foil. Re-invert the brownies so they
are right side up. Using a long, serrated knife, trim off about ⅛ inch
from each edge of the brownie square. Using a metal spatula, spread
the coconut mixture over the brownies in an even layer. Go over
the coconut again with the spatula to make the layer as flat and even
as possible. Arrange the almonds, evenly spaced in rows of four by
four, on top of the coconut, pressing down to make them stick.

### Make the glaze and glaze brownies

7. Place the milk chocolate and semisweet chocolate in a medium
bowl and set aside.

8. In a small saucepan, bring the cream and corn syrup to a gentle
boil over medium-high heat. Pour the hot cream over the chocolate
and gently whisk until the chocolate is melted and the glaze
is smooth.

9. Place the brownie square on a wire rack set on top of a foil-lined
baking sheet. Slowly pour the glaze over the brownie square, covering the top completely and allowing it to spill over to cover the
sides. Tip the square up on one side to let any excess glaze that is
pooling in the center slide off. The almonds should be covered with
a light coating of glaze, but you should still be able to see them all.
Refrigerate the brownies until the glaze is set, at least 30 minutes.

10. Cut the brownie square into 16 brownies. Serve the brownies at
room temperature or chilled, as you prefer. Store the squares in an
airtight container in the refrigerator for up to 5 days.

*Chocolate*

# Chocolate–Black Currant Tea Tart

*Dark and fruity* black currant tea goes very well with chocolate—the two strong flavors complement each other beautifully without one overwhelming the other, as in this seductive tart. The chocolate and black currant filling—a rich, quivery custard—is set in a deep chocolate crust. If black currant is not your cup of tea, Earl Grey is another good choice. Either way, serve each slice of this rich tart with a generous spoonful of whipped cream.

MAKES ONE 10-INCH TART, SERVING 8 TO 10

### CHOCOLATE CRUST

1⅓ cups (176 g/6.2 oz) all-purpose flour

¼ cup (28 g/1 oz) unsweetened Dutch-processed cocoa powder

⅓ cup firmly packed (71 g/2.5 oz) light brown sugar

⅛ teaspoon (0.8 g/0.03 oz) salt

9 tablespoons (127 g/4.5 oz) unsalted butter, cut into ½-inch chunks and frozen for 15 minutes

2 large egg yolks

1 to 2 tablespoons (14 g/0.5 oz to 29 g/1 oz) heavy cream

### CHOCOLATE–BLACK CURRANT TEA FILLING

1⅓ cups (309 g/10.9 oz) heavy cream

3 black currant tea bags (black tea)

8 ounces (227 g) bittersweet chocolate (60% to 62%), chopped

¾ cup (181 g/6.4 oz) whole milk

2 large eggs

⅓ cup (66 g/2.3 oz) granulated sugar

(CONTINUED)

## Make the crust

**1.** Place the flour, cocoa powder, brown sugar, and salt in the bowl of a food processor and process until blended. Scatter the butter pieces on top and process until the mixture resembles coarse crumbs. Add the yolks and 1 tablespoon (14 g/0.5 oz) of the cream and mix until the mixture just begins to come together as a dough. If it seems a little dry, add the remaining 1 tablespoon (14 g/0.5 oz) cream. Pat the dough into a 4-inch disc, wrap in plastic wrap, and refrigerate for at least 1 hour (or up to 3 days).

**2.** Preheat the oven to 350°F. On a lightly floured work surface, roll out the dough to a 12-inch circle. Roll the dough up onto the rolling pin and drape it over a 10-inch tart pan with a removable bottom. Press the dough snugly into the pan, then roll the pin over the top of the pan to remove the excess dough. Prick the bottom of the crust all over with a fork at 1-inch intervals and place the tart pan on a baking sheet. Line the tart shell with parchment paper and fill with pie weights or dried beans. Bake for 15 minutes. Remove the paper (along with the weights) and bake the crust for another 15 minutes, until it is no longer shiny. Let the tart shell cool on a wire rack while you make the filling. Reduce the oven temperature to 300°F.

## Make the filling and finish the tart

**3.** Place the cream in a small saucepan and bring to a gentle boil over medium-high heat. Remove from the heat. Stir in the tea bags,

½ teaspoon (2 g/0.07 oz)
vanilla extract

Pinch of salt

GARNISH

Unsweetened Dutch-processed
cocoa powder, for dusting

making sure they are immersed, cover the pot, and allow the mixture to infuse for 15 minutes.

**4.** Place the chocolate in a medium bowl. Remove the tea bags from the cream, squeezing them gently to release some of the liquid they have absorbed, and discard them. Add the milk to the cream and heat over medium-high heat until it begins to bubble around the edges. Pour the hot cream mixture over the chocolate and let it stand for 1 minute. Whisk until the chocolate is melted and the mixture is completely smooth.

**5.** In another medium bowl, whisk the eggs, sugar, vanilla, and salt until smooth. Whisk half the chocolate mixture into the egg mixture, then whisk the egg mixture into the remaining chocolate mixture until well blended.

**6.** Place the tart pan on the baking sheet and slowly pour the filling into the crust. Bake the tart for 30 to 35 minutes, until the center is set and only slightly wobbly (but not liquid). Let the tart cool completely on a wire rack.

**7.** Once cool, serve the tart immediately, or refrigerate until ready to serve. The tart can be served at room temperature or chilled, as you prefer. Dust the edge of the tart lightly with sifted cocoa powder before serving.

*Chocolate*

# Better-than-Hostess Cupcakes

*There are lots of recipes* for Hostess cupcake knockoffs out there, and here's mine: Fudgy chocolate cupcakes filled with a creamy vanilla buttercream and topped with a shiny dark chocolate glaze that elevates the cupcakes to the category of adult treats. A squiggle of royal icing gives them that iconic Hostess look. If you want your cupcakes to have that straight-off-the-machine appearance, the key is to get the squiggle just right, so pipe a few practice rounds on a plate before tackling the tops.

MAKES 12 CUPCAKES

SPECIAL EQUIPMENT:
Pastry bag and medium plain or star tip

CHOCOLATE FUDGE CUPCAKES

¾ cup plus 2 tablespoons (112 g/4 oz) all-purpose flour

½ cup (56 g/1.9 oz) unsweetened Dutch-processed cocoa powder

½ teaspoon plus ⅛ teaspoon (3.12 g/0.11 oz) baking soda

⅛ teaspoon (0.8 g/0.03 oz) salt

6 tablespoons (85 g/3 oz) unsalted butter, softened

¾ cup (150 g/5.3 oz) granulated sugar

1 large egg

1 teaspoon (2 g/0.07 oz) vanilla extract

¾ cup (181 g/6.4 oz) sour cream

CREAM FILLING

16 tablespoons (227 g/8 oz) unsalted butter, softened

¾ cup (96 g/3.38 oz) confectioners' sugar

¼ cup (58 g/2 oz) heavy cream

½ teaspoon (2 g/0.07 oz) vanilla extract

(CONTINUED)

## Make the cupcakes

1. Preheat the oven to 350°F. Line a standard 12-cup muffin pan with cupcake liners.

2. In a medium bowl, sift together the flour, cocoa powder, baking soda, and salt and whisk to blend.

3. In the bowl of an electric mixer fitted with the paddle attachment, beat the butter on medium-high speed until creamy, about 30 seconds. Gradually add the sugar and beat at high speed until light, about 3 minutes. Reduce the speed to medium and add the egg, mixing well and scraping down the sides of the bowl as necessary. Mix in the vanilla extract. Reduce the speed to low and add the dry ingredients in three additions, alternating with the sour cream in two additions and mixing just until blended.

4. Divide the batter among the cupcake cups and bake for 20 to 25 minutes, until a toothpick inserted into center of a cupcake comes out clean. Let the cupcakes cool in the pan set on a wire rack for 15 minutes, then turn out the cupcakes onto the rack to cool completely.

## Make the filling and fill the cupcakes

5. In the bowl of an electric mixer fitted with the paddle attachment, beat the butter at medium speed until creamy, about 1 minute. Gradually add the confectioners' sugar and beat at high speed until well blended and light, about 3 minutes. Add the cream and

## CHOCOLATE GLAZE

4 ounces (113 g) semisweet or bittersweet chocolate (60% to 62%), finely chopped

½ cup (116 g/4 oz) heavy cream

2 tablespoons (42 g/1.5 oz) light corn syrup

## ROYAL ICING SQUIGGLE

2½ cups (320 g/11.3 oz) confectioners' sugar

3 tablespoons (45 g/1.6 oz) liquid pasteurized egg whites

1 tablespoon (15 g/0.5 oz) warm water

vanilla and beat for another minute. Scrape the filling into a pastry bag fitted with a ¼-inch plain or star tip, such as Ateco #2.

6. Use a paring knife to cut a small X in the center of the bottom of each cupcake. Hold a cupcake upside down, letting the top rest on your fingers. Poke the pastry tip three-quarters of the way into the X on the bottom of the cupcake and squeeze in some filling, stopping when you feel a slight pressure on the top of the cupcake. Repeat with the remaining cupcakes. Set the filled cupcakes aside while you make the chocolate glaze.

### Make the glaze and glaze the cupcakes

7. Place the chocolate in a medium bowl. Combine the cream and corn syrup in a small saucepan and bring to a boil. Pour over the chocolate and stir until the chocolate is completely melted and the glaze is shiny. Dip the top of each cupcake in the glaze, tapping to remove the excess. Place the cupcakes on a wire rack and let the glaze set for 30 minutes. (You will have some glaze left over since it's easier to dip the cupcakes in a larger amount of glaze. Store the glaze, covered, in the refrigerator for up to 1 week.)

### Make the royal icing and add the squiggles

8. Combine all the icing ingredients in the bowl of an electric mixer fitted with the whisk attachment. Beat on high for 5 minutes, scraping down the bowl occasionally. Scrape some icing into a small parchment cone or a pastry bag fitted with a very fine plain tip, such as Ateco #101. Pipe a row of curlicues horizontally across the center of each cupcake. Serve the cupcakes at room temperature or slightly chilled. They can be stored, covered, in the refrigerator for up to 3 days.

*Chocolate*

# Brooklyn Blackout Cupcakes

*The most popular recipe* in my book *The Cake Book* is undoubtedly the Brooklyn Blackout Cake. For chocolate lovers, it's the Holy Grail of cakes. Here's a junior version in cupcake form. I changed the pudding recipe slightly to make it more chocolaty, but otherwise the recipe is the same, just adjusted to make the correct amount of each component. The result is everything a knock-your-socks-off chocolate cupcake should be.

MAKES 24 CUPCAKES

### CHOCOLATE PUDDING FILLING

¼ cup (50 g/1.76 oz) granulated sugar

2 tablespoons (15 g/0.5 oz) cornstarch

⅛ teaspoon (0.8 g/0.03 oz) salt

2 cups (484 g/17 oz) milk

4 ounces (113 g) bittersweet chocolate (62%), finely chopped

1½ tablespoons (21 g/0.75 oz) unsalted butter

1 teaspoon (4 g/0.14 oz) vanilla extract

### CHOCOLATE BLACKOUT CUPCAKES

1½ cups (198 g/7 oz) all-purpose flour

1 cup (112 g/4 oz) unsweetened non-alkalized (natural) cocoa powder

1½ teaspoons (7.5 g/0.26 oz) baking powder

1½ teaspoons (7.5 g/0.26 oz) baking soda

1 teaspoon (7 g/0.25 oz) salt

2 cups (14 oz/400 g) granulated sugar

2 large eggs plus 1 large egg yolk

(CONTINUED)

## Make the filling

1. In a small, heavy-bottomed saucepan, stir together the sugar, cornstarch, and salt. Gradually whisk in the milk, making sure there are no lumps in the mixture. Cook over medium heat, stirring constantly with a heatproof silicone spatula, until the mixture thickens and just begins to bubble around the edges. Remove the pan from the heat and pass the mixture through a fine-mesh sieve into a bowl. Add the chocolate and stir until it is completely melted. Add the butter and stir until melted. Stir in the vanilla. Press a piece of plastic wrap directly on the surface of the pudding and refrigerate until chilled, at least 4 hours, but preferably overnight.

## Make the cupcakes

2. Preheat the oven to 350°F. Line two 12-cup standard muffin pans with cupcake liners.

3. In the bowl of an electric mixer, sift together the flour, cocoa powder, baking powder, baking soda, and salt. Add the sugar and, using the paddle attachment, mix at low speed until blended.

4. In a medium bowl, whisk together the eggs, egg yolk, buttermilk, melted butter, and vanilla. While mixing the dry ingredients at low speed, add the egg mixture in a steady steam. Scrape down the sides of the bowl with a rubber spatula, then beat at medium speed for 1 minute, until well blended. With the mixer on low speed, add the coffee, mixing just until blended. Remove the bowl from the mixer stand and stir the batter from the bottom of the bowl a

1 cup (242 g/8.5 oz) buttermilk

8 tablespoons (113 g/4 oz) unsalted butter, melted

2 teaspoons (8 g/0.28 oz) vanilla extract

1 cup (240 g/8.5 oz) hot brewed coffee

FUDGY CHOCOLATE FROSTING

4.5 ounces (127 g) unsweetened chocolate (I use Scharffen Berger), chopped

4.5 ounces (127 g) bittersweet chocolate (61%), chopped

24 tablespoons (340 g/12 oz) unsalted butter, softened

3 cups (384 g/13.54 oz) confectioners' sugar

1 tablespoon (12 g/0.4 oz) vanilla extract

few times to thoroughly blend the batter (it will be thin). Pour the batter into the prepared cups, dividing it evenly (each cup should be about two-thirds full).

**5.** Bake the cupcakes (both pans should fit on one oven rack) for 30 to 35 minutes, until a cake tester inserted into the center of a cupcake comes out clean. Let cool in the pans on a wire rack.

### Make the frosting

**6.** Put both chocolates in a medium heatproof bowl and set the bowl over a pot of barely simmering water. Heat, stirring frequently, until the chocolate is completely melted. Remove the bowl from the heat and set the chocolate aside to cool until tepid.

**7.** In the bowl of an electric mixer fitted with the paddle attachment, beat the butter at medium speed until creamy, about 30 seconds. Gradually add the confectioners' sugar and beat at high speed for 2 minutes, until light and creamy. Beat in the vanilla extract. With the mixer on low speed, add the cooled chocolate, mixing until blended and scraping down the sides of the bowl as necessary. Raise the speed to high and beat for 1 minute, until slightly aerated. Use the frosting immediately, or cover well and keep at room temperature for up to 3 hours before using.

### Assemble the cupcakes

**8.** Using a paring knife, cut a 1-inch-diameter cone from the center of the top of each cupcake, reaching almost to the bottom, and remove it. Set the cake scraps aside. Fill a pastry bag fitted with a ⅜-inch plain tip, such as Ateco #4, with the chilled filling. Pipe the filling into the cavity in each cupcake, filling it to the top.

**9.** Process the cake scraps in a food processor to form fine crumbs.

**10.** Spread the top of each cupcake with a generous amount of the frosting (or pipe it on with a medium star tip, such as Ateco #6, if you prefer). Sprinkle a generous amount of the crumbs onto the frosting on each cupcake. Serve at room temperature or slightly chilled. The cupcakes can be stored in the refrigerator for up to 3 days.

# Triple-Chocolate Bundt Cake

*This cake relies* primarily on cocoa powder for its chocolatiness—which, since it has very little cocoa butter in it to temper its flavor, makes a big impact. I've also added some finely chopped bittersweet chocolate to the batter, so you get small pockets of chocolate in every bite, and I glaze the cake with a dark chocolate glaze.

MAKES ONE 10-INCH BUNDT CAKE, SERVING 12 TO 14

## TRIPLE-CHOCOLATE CAKE

2 cups (265 g/9.3 oz) all-purpose flour

½ cup (56 g/2 oz) unsweetened Dutch-processed cocoa powder

2½ teaspoons (12.5 g/0.44 oz) baking powder

½ teaspoon (3.3 g/0.12 oz) salt

18 tablespoons (254 g/9 oz) unsalted butter, softened

1¾ cups (350 g/12.34 oz) granulated sugar

2 teaspoons (8 g/0.28 oz) vanilla extract

4 large eggs, at room temperature

¾ cup (181 g/6.4 oz) whole milk

4 ounces (113 g) bittersweet chocolate (60% to 62%), finely chopped (⅔ cup)

## DARK CHOCOLATE GLAZE

5 ounces (142 g) semisweet or bittersweet chocolate (60%), finely chopped

⅔ cup (154 g/5.4 oz) heavy cream

3 tablespoons (61 g/2.1 oz) light corn syrup

## GARNISH

Chopped walnuts, toasted (see page 13), or cacao nibs

## *Make the cake*

**1.** Preheat the oven to 350°F. Generously coat the interior of a 10-inch (12-cup) Bundt pan with vegetable shortening. Dust the pan with flour.

**2.** In a medium bowl, sift together the flour, cocoa powder, baking powder, and salt.

**3.** In the bowl of an electric mixer fitted with the paddle attachment, beat the butter at medium speed for about 1 minute, until creamy. Gradually beat in the sugar. Raise the mixer speed to medium-high and beat for 2 minutes, until the mixture is well blended and light. Scrape down the sides of the bowl and beat in the vanilla and then the eggs, one at a time, mixing well after each addition and scraping down the sides of the bowl as necessary. With the mixer on low speed, add the flour mixture in three additions, alternating with the milk in two additions and mixing just until blended. Remove the bowl from the mixer stand and stir in the chopped chocolate. Scrape the batter into the prepared pan.

**4.** Bake the cake for 50 to 60 minutes, until a toothpick inserted into the center of one section of the cake comes out clean. Let the cake cool on a wire rack for 10 minutes, then unmold the cake and let cool completely.

## *Make the glaze and glaze the cake*

**5.** Place the chocolate in a medium bowl. Combine the cream and corn syrup in a small saucepan and bring to a boil over medium-high heat. Pour the cream mixture over the chocolate and stir until the chocolate is completely melted and the glaze is shiny.

**6.** Place the cake and the wire rack over a parchment paper– or foil-lined baking sheet. Slowly pour the glaze over the top of the cake, covering most of it. Sprinkle the cake with the walnuts or cacao nibs. Refrigerate the cake for about 30 minutes, until the glaze is set. Store the cake, covered with a cake dome, at room temperature for up to 5 days.

# Zach's Dark Chocolate–Raspberry Pavé

*This recipe comes from* my friend Zach Townsend, owner of Pure Chocolate Desserts by Zach, a website specializing in chocolate cakes and desserts. Zach has a passion for chocolate, and his French-inspired desserts are as indulgent as they are elegant. This pavé (so named because its rectangular shape resembles a paving stone) is one of Zach's signature cakes, and combines thin layers of a rich dark chocolate and raspberry cake with a whipped dark chocolat–raspberry ganache. After you make the cake and ganache, you will have a little leftover raspberry puree. Sweeten it to taste and serve it alongside the cake. Because of this dessert's intensity, a little sweet whipped cream is also a mandatory accompaniment.

MAKES ONE 3½-BY-12-INCH CAKE, SERVING 10

SPECIAL EQUIPMENT: Instant-read thermometer

### DARK CHOCOLATE GLAZE

6 ounces (170 g) semisweet chocolate (55%, preferably Valrhona), finely chopped

¾ cup (174 g/6.13 oz) heavy cream

3 tablespoons (37 g/1.3 oz) granulated sugar

3 tablespoons (45 g/1.5 oz) water

### RASPBERRY PUREE

3 cups (340 g/12 oz) frozen unsweetened raspberries

3 tablespoons (37 g/1.3 oz) granulated sugar

### DARK CHOCOLATE CAKE

4 ounces (227 g) dark chocolate (55%, preferably Valrhona), finely chopped

12 tablespoons (170 g/6 oz) unsalted butter, cut into tablespoons

(CONTINUED)

## Make the glaze

1. Place the chocolate in a medium microwave-safe bowl (you'll be warming it up in the microwave later). Place the cream, sugar, and water in a small saucepan and bring to a boil over medium heat, stirring occasionally to help dissolve the sugar. Pour the hot cream over the chocolate and let it stand for 1 minute, then stir until the chocolate is completely melted and no bits of chocolate cling to the sides of the bowl, at least 2 minutes. Cover the bowl and refrigerate the glaze until ready to use.

## Make the puree

2. Place the raspberries in a microwave-safe bowl and microwave at 50 percent power for 2 to 3 minutes, just until they are thawed (don't allow them to come to a boil, as this will degrade their color and flavor). Press the raspberries and their juice through a fine-mesh sieve into a bowl (discard the seeds). Stir the sugar into the puree. Cover the bowl and refrigerate the puree until ready to use for the cake and ganache.

## Make the cake

3. Spray the bottom and sides of a 9-by-13-inch baking pan with nonstick cooking spray. Line the pan with a piece of parchment

Pinch of salt

¼ cup (66 g/2.3 oz) Raspberry Puree (from page 349)

4 large eggs, separated

5 tablespoons (62 g/2.2 oz) granulated sugar, divided

½ teaspoon (1.5 g/0.05 oz) cream of tartar

½ cup (57 g/2 oz) cake flour, sifted

WHIPPED DARK CHOCOLATE-RASPBERRY GANACHE

5 ounces (142 g) semisweet chocolate (55%, preferably Valrhona), finely chopped

¼ cup plus 2 tablespoons (100 g/3.5 oz) Raspberry Puree (from page 349)

¼ cup plus 2 tablespoons (91 g/3.2 oz) heavy cream

4 tablespoons (56 g/2 oz) unsalted butter, at cool room temperature, cut into tablespoons

GARNISH

Fresh raspberries

Sweetened whipped cream

paper so that it covers the bottom and sides of the pan. Spray the paper with nonstick cooking spray.

4. Place the chocolate and butter in a medium heatproof bowl set over a pot filled one-third full with barely simmering water and heat, stirring frequently, until melted and smooth. Stir in the salt. Place ¼ cup (66 g/2.3 oz) of the raspberry puree in a small microwave-safe cup and heat in the microwave at 50 percent power until just warm, 10 to 15 seconds (do not heat it higher than 110°F). Stir the warm raspberry puree into the chocolate mixture just until blended and the mixture is smooth. Set aside to cool until thickened to the consistency of mayonnaise. (The spatula will begin to leave trail marks. This can take up to 20 minutes, depending on the temperature of your kitchen. You can place the bowl in the refrigerator for 2 minutes, stirring frequently, to speed up the cooling; return to low heat if it begins to thicken too much.)

5. While the chocolate mixture is cooling, preheat the oven to 300°F.

6. In the bowl of an electric mixer fitted with the whisk attachment, whip the egg yolks with 2 tablespoons plus 1½ teaspoons (31 g/1.1 oz) of the sugar at high speed until thickened and light, about 7 minutes. Fold the melted chocolate mixture into the egg-yolk foam until no streaks remain. Transfer the mixture to a medium bowl. Wash and dry the mixer bowl and whisk attachment.

7. Place the egg whites and cream of tartar in the cleaned bowl of the mixer and, using the whisk attachment, beat on medium-high speed until medium peaks begin to form. Continue whipping while slowly adding the remaining 2 tablespoons plus 1½ teaspoons (31 g/1.1 oz) of the sugar until stiff peaks form. Sift the flour over the chocolate mixture and fold it in just until no traces of flour are visible. Quickly stir one-third of the whipped egg whites into the chocolate mixture to lighten it, then gently fold in the remaining whites in two additions, maintaining as much volume as possible and folding just until no streaks of egg whites remain. Scrape the batter into the prepared pan and spread it out evenly, making sure to spread it into the corners.

*Chocolate*

**8.** Bake the cake for 20 to 25 minutes, until it loses its sheen on top and a toothpick inserted into the center comes out clean. Let the cake cool completely in the pan on a wire rack. Once cool, gently press a piece of plastic wrap against the surface of the cake and refrigerate for at least 2 hours.

### *Make the ganache*

**9.** Place chocolate in a medium bowl set over a pot filled one-third full with barely simmering water and heat, stirring frequently, until melted.

**10.** Place ¼ cup plus 2 tablespoons (100 g/3.5 oz) of the raspberry puree in a small microwave-safe cup and heat in the microwave at 50 percent power until just warm, about 15 seconds (do not heat it higher than 110°F).

**11.** In a small microwave-safe cup, microwave the cream on high for 30 seconds, or until just below a boil. Pour about one-quarter of the hot cream over the chocolate while stirring the chocolate vigorously with a silicone spatula. Continue adding the rest of the cream, stirring vigorously and waiting until the previous amount is fully blended before adding more. Gently stir the warm raspberry puree into the chocolate mixture, then stir in the butter until emulsified. The ganache should look smooth and glossy. Let the ganache sit at room temperature undisturbed and uncovered for 30 minutes.

**12.** Cover the bowl of ganache with plastic wrap. Refrigerate for at least 30 minutes, until slightly chilled. The ganache should remain soft but have a slight chill to it. (If you're making the ganache ahead, refrigerate it overnight, but then let it sit out at cool room temperature before using, until it has softened but still has a slight chill.)

### *Trim the cake*

**13.** Use the edges of the parchment to lift the chilled cake from the pan. Set the cake on a cutting board and, using a long, serrated knife, trim off ⅛ inch from each of the four sides. Loosen the cake from the parchment by carefully sliding a long offset metal spatula that has been lightly sprayed with nonstick cooking spray between the bottom of the cake and the parchment paper; use the edge of the parchment to hold the cake in place while performing this step. Slice the cake down the center lengthwise to make two long strips of cake. Cover the strips with plastic wrap and refrigerate. The cakes should remain cold when composing the cake. (The cakes can be wrapped in plastic wrap, then heavy-duty aluminum foil, and frozen for up to 1 month.)

## Whip the ganache

**14.** Right before you're ready to assemble the cake, scoop the ganache into the bowl of an electric mixer fitted with the whisk attachment and whip just until fluffy, about 30 seconds; do not overbeat. *Note:* This ganache can break and become grainy easily, so be sure to carefully control the temperature when making it (do not overheat the puree or the chocolate). Once ready to whip, whip the ganache just briefly (no more than 30 seconds at medium speed), or it could break down and become dry and grainy; you are just looking to lighten it and make it spreadable. The ganache whips best when it's soft and scoopable but maintains a slight chill.

## Assemble the cake

**15.** Place one of the cake rectangles on a work surface (preferably a small cutting board that can easily be moved into and out of the refrigerator). Spread about half the ganache on top of the cake layer, being sure to bring the ganache all the way to the corners. (If the ganache has firmed up too much, you can warm it slightly by dipping the bowl into warm water and stirring it until spreadable.) Place the second cake layer on top and then cover the top and sides of the cake with a thin coating of ganache. Set the cake in the refrigerator and leave uncovered for about 30 minutes for the ganache to set, then cover the cake with plastic wrap pressed against the cake all around. Refrigerate for at least 1 hour.

## Glaze the cake

**16.** Spray a wire rack lightly with nonstick cooking spray and place it over a baking sheet. Remove the cake from the refrigerator and place it on top of the rack.

**17.** Warm the glaze by placing the bowl in the microwave and heating it at 50 percent power in 10-second spurts, stirring after each time, until it registers 90°F on an instant-read thermometer (if the glaze gets too hot, let it cool at room temperature, stirring frequently). Pour the glaze quickly over the chilled cake, starting around the top edges to allow the glaze to evenly cover the sides, then covering the center. You may have to scoop up some of the remaining glaze from the baking sheet to finish covering the corners. Work quickly, before the glaze begins to set. To remove excess glaze from the top of the cake, gently shake the baking sheet to allow the glaze to flow over the edges. Use a toothpick or pin to pop any bubbles that may have formed on the surface. To prevent leaving marks, do not touch the glaze with the spatula once the cake is completely glazed. Pour any leftover glaze through a sieve into a freezer bag and freeze indefinitely to use again at a later time.

*Chocolate*

**18.** Let the cake sit undisturbed for about 5 minutes, until the glaze has stopped dripping, then place it back in the refrigerator to set completely. Once the glaze is no longer dripping, run two offset metal spatulas under the cake to lift it off the glazing rack and place it on a cake board or serving platter.

**19.** Garnish the top of the cake with fresh raspberries. Serve slices of the cake with the leftover raspberry puree and some sweetened whipped cream. Press plastic wrap against the exposed sides of any leftover cake to help it stay moist and store it in the refrigerator for up to 5 days. Bring the cake to room temperature before serving.

# Love-Struck Chocolate Cake with White Chocolate–Coconut Filling

*Nothing says "I love you"* like a heart-shaped cake. Here's the best Valentine's Day dessert I can think of — two layers of moist, fudgy chocolate cake filled with a white chocolate–coconut ganache and covered in a dark chocolate glaze. Make sure to prep the pan as directed, or you may just end up with a broken heart.

MAKES ONE 9-INCH LAYER CAKE, SERVING 8

SPECIAL EQUIPMENT: Two
9-inch heart-shaped (or round)
cake pans

DEVIL'S FOOD CAKE

1½ cups (198 g/7 oz)
all-purpose flour

⅔ cup (74 g/2.6 oz)
unsweetened non-alkalized
(natural) cocoa powder

1¼ teaspoons (6 g/0.22 oz)
baking powder

½ teaspoon (2.5 g/0.09 oz)
baking soda

½ teaspoon (3.3 g/0.02 oz) salt

2 large eggs

1¾ cups (350 g/12.3 oz)
granulated sugar

¼ cup (56 g/2 oz) vegetable oil

4 tablespoons (56 g/2 oz)
unsalted butter, melted and
cooled

1 teaspoon (4 g/0.14 oz) vanilla
extract

1¼ cups (360 g/12.7 oz) brewed
coffee, warm

(CONTINUED)

## Make the cake

1. Preheat the oven to 350°F. Grease the bottom and sides of two 9-inch heart-shaped (or round) cake pans with shortening. Line the bottoms of the pans with parchment paper cut to fit, then grease the paper. Dust the paper and the sides of the pans with flour and tap out the excess.

2. In a medium bowl, sift together the flour, cocoa powder, baking powder, baking soda, and salt. Whisk to combine and set aside.

3. In the bowl of an electric mixer fitted with the whisk attachment, beat the eggs at medium speed. Gradually add the sugar and beat at high speed until pale and fluffy, about 2 minutes. Reduce the speed to medium and beat in the oil, butter, and vanilla. Reduce the speed to low and add the flour mixture in three additions, alternating with the coffee in two additions, beginning and ending with the flour, and stopping to scrape down the sides of the bowl with a rubber spatula as necessary. Mix just until blended. Remove the bowl from the mixer stand and give the batter a few stirs with the spatula to make sure it's completely blended. Divide the batter between the pans.

4. Bake for 20 to 25 minutes, until a toothpick inserted into the center of each cake comes out clean. Let the cakes cool in the pans on wire racks for 15 minutes, then unmold the cakes onto the racks to cool completely.

## WHIPPED WHITE CHOCOLATE-COCONUT GANACHE

1½ cups (348 g/12.3 oz) heavy cream

1 cup (90 g/3.16 oz) unsweetened shredded coconut

6 ounces (170 g) high-quality white chocolate, chopped

## CHOCOLATE GLAZE

6 ounces (170 g) bittersweet chocolate (62%), finely chopped

¾ cup (174 g/6.13 oz) heavy cream

3 tablespoons (60 g/2.1 oz) light corn syrup

## GARNISH

½ cup (45 g/1.6 oz) unsweetened shredded coconut

## *Make the ganache*

**5.** In a small saucepan, combine the heavy cream and coconut and bring to a gentle boil over medium-high heat. Remove the pan from the heat, cover, and allow to infuse for 1 hour.

**6.** Strain the cream (discard the coconut) and measure it; you should have 1 cup. If you have too much or too little, adjust the amount accordingly by adding or removing a little cream. Return the strained cream to the saucepan. Place the white chocolate in the bowl of an electric mixer. Return the cream to a gentle boil over medium-high heat. Pour the hot cream over the chocolate and let it stand for 30 seconds. Gently whisk the mixture until the chocolate is completely melted and the mixture is smooth. Cover the bowl and refrigerate the ganache for at least 4 hours, until thickened.

## *Assemble the cake*

**7.** Place one of the cake layers right side up on a cake plate.

**8.** Place the bowl containing the ganache in the mixer stand and, using the whisk attachment, whip at medium-high speed until soft peaks form (do not overwhip the ganache, or it may become grainy). Spoon 1 cup of the whipped ganache onto the cake layer on the plate and spread it into an even layer, up to the cake edge. Place the second cake layer on top, upside down. Spread half of the remaining ganache around the sides of the cake in a smooth, thin layer to cover the gap between the layers. Cover the remaining ganache and refrigerate it, and the cake, for at least 1 hour.

## *Make the glaze and glaze the cake*

**9.** Place the chocolate in a medium bowl. Combine the cream and corn syrup in a small saucepan and bring to a boil over medium heat, stirring occasionally. Pour the hot cream over the chocolate and let it stand for 1 minute, then stir until the chocolate is completely melted and no bits of chocolate cling to the sides of the bowl, at least 2 minutes. Let the glaze stand for 5 minutes.

**10.** Lightly spray a wire rack with nonstick cooking spray. Remove the chilled cake from the re-frigerator and slide it from the cake plate onto the wire rack. Place the rack on top of a parchment paper– or foil-lined baking sheet. Pour the glaze quickly and evenly over the chilled cake, starting around the top edges to allow the glaze to evenly cover the sides, then covering the center of the cake. Place the cake, still on the wire rack and baking sheet, in the refrigerator to chill for 1 hour.

### Garnish the cake

**11.** Transfer the cake back to the cake plate. Slip three strips of waxed paper under the edge of each section of the cake. Using your hand, pat the coconut all around the side of the cake. Remove the waxed paper. Transfer the reserved chilled ganache to a pastry bag fitted with a plain ³⁄₁₆-inch tip, such as Ateco #801. Pipe small dots of ganache around the edge of the top of the cake. Refrigerate the cake until ready to serve. Serve the cake near, but slightly cooler than, room temperature. Store the cake in the refrigerator for up to 5 days.

*Chocolate*

# Devil's Food Layer Cake with Milk Chocolate–Malt Frosting

*This may just be* my favorite chocolate layer cake of all time. I adapted the devil's food cake recipe from a recipe by New York pastry chef Richard Leach that was featured in *Chocolatier* magazine years ago. It's *very* moist and *very* chocolaty. I frost it with a not-too-sweet milk chocolate frosting subtly flavored with malt. The final garnish is a light dusting of sifted malt powder. This would make the ideal birthday cake for the chocolate lover in your life.

MAKES ONE 8-INCH LAYER CAKE, SERVING 10

### MILK CHOCOLATE-MALT FROSTING

9 ounces (255 g) high-quality milk chocolate (I like Scharffen Berger or Guittard), finely chopped

9 ounces (255 g) high-quality bittersweet chocolate (60% to 62%), finely chopped

1½ cups (363 g/12.8 oz) heavy cream

¼ cup (82 g/2.9 oz) light corn syrup

½ cup (60 g/2.1 oz) malted milk powder

1 teaspoon (4 g/0.14 oz) vanilla extract

16 tablespoons (226 g/8 oz) unsalted butter, softened

### DEVIL'S FOOD CAKE

2¾ cups (364 g/12.8 oz) all-purpose flour

1¾ teaspoons (8.75 g/0.3 oz) baking soda

1 teaspoon (5 g/0.17 oz) baking powder

1½ teaspoons (10 g/0.35 oz) salt

(CONTINUED)

## Make the frosting

**1.** Place both chocolates in the bowl of an electric mixer and set aside.

**2.** In a medium saucepan, heat the cream and corn syrup over high heat until the liquid comes to a gentle boil. Remove the pan from the heat and whisk in the malted milk powder. Pour the hot cream mixture over the chocolate and allow to stand for 2 minutes to melt the chocolate. Gently whisk until the chocolate is melted and the mixture is smooth and glossy. Whisk in the vanilla. Place the bowl in the mixer stand and, using the whisk attachment, begin mixing at medium-low speed. Gradually add the butter, 1 tablespoon at a time, mixing until it is completely blended into the frosting. Refrigerate the frosting, loosely covered, until firm enough to spread, about 1½ hours (if you refrigerate the frosting for longer, you may need to let it soften at room temperature before using).

## Make the cake

**3.** Preheat the oven to 350°F. Grease the bottom and sides of two 8-inch round cake pans. Line the bottom of each pan with a round of parchment paper and grease the paper. Dust each pan with flour.

**4.** In a medium bowl, whisk together the flour, baking soda, baking powder, and salt.

16 tablespoons (226 g/8 oz) unsalted butter, softened

2½ cups (500 g/17.6 oz) granulated sugar

1 cup (82 g/2.9 oz) unsweetened non-alkalized (natural) cocoa powder

3 large eggs, at room temperature

1 teaspoon (4 g/0.14 oz) vanilla extract

1 cup (240 g/8.4 oz) hot freshly brewed coffee

1 cup (236 g/8.3 oz) hot water

GARNISH

1 teaspoon (2.5 g/0.09 oz) malted milk powder

**5.** In the bowl of an electric mixer fitted with the paddle attachment, beat the butter at medium speed until creamy, about 1 minute. Gradually add the sugar and beat at high speed until light, about 4 minutes. Reduce the speed to low and add the cocoa powder, 1 tablespoon at a time, scraping down the sides of the bowl with a rubber spatula as necessary and mixing until blended. Add the flour mixture in three additions, mixing until the mixture is crumbly. Add the eggs, one at a time, and then the vanilla, mixing until the batter is doughy. Gradually add the coffee and water and mix until blended. Remove the bowl from the mixer stand and, using a rubber spatula, blend the batter so that most of the lumps have disappeared (a few remaining lumps are fine). Divide the batter evenly between the prepared pans.

**6.** Bake the cakes for 45 to 50 minutes, until a toothpick inserted into the center of each cake comes out clean. Let the cakes cool in the pans set on wire racks for 20 minutes. Invert the cakes onto the racks and let cool completely.

### Assemble the cake

**7.** Stir the frosting with a rubber spatula until smooth. Using a long, serrated knife, cut off the domed top of each cake layer so that it is level. Set the scraps aside. Using the same knife, cut each cake layer horizontally in half to make a total of 4 layers. Place one of the layers on a cardboard cake round or cake plate and spread ½ cup of the frosting on top, covering it completely. Top with another cake layer and repeat the layering, ending with the last cake layer. Spread the remaining frosting over the top and sides of the cake.

**8.** Place half the cake scraps in the bowl of a food processor and pulse the processor on and off until the cake is broken into crumbs. Pat the crumbs gently around the sides of the cake. (The remaining cake scraps are for snacking.)

**9.** Right before serving, sift the malted milk powder over the top of the cake. Store the cake in the refrigerator up to 5 days; bring to room temperature before serving.

# SOURCES

### AMADEUS VANILLA BEANS
Great prices on bulk vanilla beans and extracts from Madagascar, Tahiti, Indonesia, Uganda, and other exotic locales.
310-670-9731
amadeusvanillabeans.com

### AMAZON
This is a great source for baking equipment as well as hard-to-find ingredients including silicone baking mats, cake pans (round and heart-shaped), disposable pastry bags and pastry tips, digital scales, parchment paper sheets, cardboard cake rounds, almond flour, and natural orange blossom water.
amazon.com

### BEANILLA PREMIUM VANILLA
An excellent source of vanilla beans from around the world as well as natural flavors, extracts, and baking ingredients.
888-261-3384
beanilla.com

### BOB'S RED MILL
A variety of grains and flours, including almond flour, hazelnut flour, and semolina.
800-349-2173
bobsredmill.com

### BRP BOX SHOP
A great selection of reasonably priced brown boxes for all your baked goods, including cake, cookie, and cupcake containers. They also carry tin tie bags for cookies and confections.
BRPboxshop.com

### CHOCOSPHERE

This online source offers a great selection of chocolate products from high-quality
brands, including Valrhona, Scharffen Berger, Guittard, and Felchlin.

877-992-4626

chocosphere.com

### CREATIVE COOKWARE

A great selection of bakeware, including cake pans, cake turntables and stands, cookie
cutters, measuring spoons and cups, madeleine molds, kitchen scales, and cherry
pitters.

creativecookware.com

### GOURMET FOOD STORE

An impressive selection of gourmet food products, including crème fraîche, fleur de
sel, spices, and European chocolates.

877-220-4181

gourmetfoodstore.com

### GUITTARD CHOCOLATE COMPANY

This American-based chocolate maker produces chocolate in blocks, large chips, and
powders for amateurs as well as pastry chefs. The E. Guittard Collection vintage
product line contains blends and single-bean varietal chocolates including white,
milk, and bittersweet.

800-468-2462

guittard.com

### KEREKES

Full line of pastry, baking, and cake decorating supplies, including pastry bags and tips,
cardboard cake rounds, and bakeware.

800-525-5556

BakeDeco.com

### KING ARTHUR FLOUR

This consumer site offers a full line of flours, including pastry, bread, cake, whole
wheat, and organic varieties. They also have nut flours, spices, extracts, chocolate,
cocoa powder, and baking pans and equipment.

800-827-6836

kingarthurflour.com

## L'EPICERIE

Excellent line of high-end pastry ingredients, including nut flours, chocolate, and hard-to-find extracts and flavorings. As a bonus, L'Epicerie allows you to order their products in small quantities.

866-350-7575

lepicerie.com

## MY SPICE SAGE

Great selection of ground and whole spices and dried herbs, including dried food-grade lavender.

877-890-5244

myspicesage.com

## NIELSEN MASSEY

High-quality vanilla beans, vanilla bean paste, powder, and extract in Madagascan, Bourbon, Tahitian, Mexican, and organic varieties.

800-525-7873

nielsenmassey.com

## PAPER MART

Love the selection of decorative packing materials from this site. They have bakery boxes of all kinds, cardboard cake rounds, cello bags, and ribbons for all your baked goods.

800-745-8800

papermart.com

## VALRHONA

This French chocolate maker produces a line of premium chocolate favored by top pastry chefs as well as passionate bakers, including me. Valrhona pioneered the production of high-quality chocolate from carefully controlled sources and started the trend of featuring the percentage of cocoa solids in chocolate. They also have led the way toward chocolate from known origins and quality beans. The product line includes white, milk, and dark chocolate in bars or pellets.

718-522-7001

valrhona.com

# ACKNOWLEDGMENTS

*There are many* I'd like to thank for helping me with this book:

Thanks to my editor, Stephanie Fletcher, for the varied skills she brought to this project, from hands-on editing of the text to gentle suggestions regarding the photography and propping. I consider myself very lucky to have landed in her extremely capable hands. To Shubhani Sarkar, Melissa Lotfy, and Rachel Newborn, who all contributed to the book's art direction and design, and to Jamie Selzer, who seamlessly navigated the production process. To Deri Reed, for her precise copyediting. And to Natalie Chapman, publisher of Houghton Mifflin Harcourt's culinary division, for her continued support.

To photographer Andrew Meade, whose talents with a camera are matched only by his affability, sense of humor, and strong work ethic. And to food stylist Claire Perez, who somehow managed to coordinate all the propping and food styling during the mind-numbing heat of August in South Florida without breaking a sweat. And to Emman Eugenio, Dwayne Sinclair, and Kathy Stauffer, who all contributed their considerable talents and good humor during the photo shoot. I couldn't have done it without you (and it would've been way less fun). Thanks also to Chef David Pantone and Manfred Schmidtke of Lincoln Culinary Institute in West Palm Beach for sending your top grads my way.

To the chefs and cooks who generously gave me ideas or recipes: Robert Ellinger, François Payard, Lace Zhang, Zach Townsend, Jacquy Pfeiffer, Francisco Migoya, Colleen Grapes, Meredith Kurtzman, Marshall Rosenthal, Dennis Teets, Lisa Baron, and Elise Favilla.

To my loyal foodie friends, who helped in countless ways throughout the two years of this project: Judith Sutton, Matt Stevens, Jeff Dryfoos, Jacques Bergier, and Stephanie Banyas. To Lisa Morgan, for tasting all those cakes, pies, and cookies. To my lovely neighbors Mary and Dave Grey, for occasionally taking a surfeit of desserts off my hands. To all my tennis buddies, who surely tired of listening to me talk about this book between sets.

To my wonderful husband, Dick Eggleston, for putting up with it all, and to my incredible ninety-two-year-old mother for her lifetime of love and support.

And most of all, to Mickey Choate, my beloved agent and good friend, who left us suddenly and far too soon. I love you, Mickey—you are irreplaceable.

# INDEX

Whipped Vanilla Bean Cheese-
cake with Blueberry
Sauce, 202–4
Granita, Espresso, with Mascarpone
Cream, 299
Granola Streusel, Frozen Vanilla Yo-
gurt Parfaits with, 31–32
Grapefruit
choosing, 142
Red, –White Tea Sorbet, 152
Green Apple Sorbet, 111

## H

Hand Pies, Blueberry, with Lemon
Glaze, 82–84, *83*
Hazelnut(s)
Ice Cream Sandwiches, 224–26
Meringue Cookies, 224–26
toasting, 13
Holiday Bark, White Chocolate,
219–20
Homemade Crème Fraîche, 20
Homemade Vanilla Extract, *26, 27*
Honey
about, 4
Apple Cake, 136
Frozen Café con Miel Parfaits
with Caramel-Walnut
Espresso Topping, 293–95,
*294*
-Vanilla-Chamomile Ice Cream,
29
Honeycomb, Peanut, 223

## I

Ice Cream
Honey-Vanilla-Chamomile, 29
Lemon Buttermilk, 150
Lemon Cheesecake, 183
Orange Blossom–Cinnamon,
with Blood Orange Sorbet,
153–54
Sandwiches, Hazelnut, 224–26
Strawberry–Pink Peppercorn, 75
Ultra-Dark-Chocolate, 321
Ingredient notes
chocolate, 9–10
dairy products, 5–6
eggs, 6–7
fats, 7
flavor accents, 8–9
flours, 3
gelling agents and thickeners,
4–5
leaveners, 7

nuts, raisins, and coconut, 8
sugars and sweeteners, 3–4

## J

Japanese-Style Cheesecake with
Fresh Raspberries,
200–201

## K

Key Lime Pie, My Favorite, 165–66

## L

Lavender and Strawberries, Vanilla
Bean Panna Cotta with,
35–37, *36*
Leaveners, types of, 7
Lemon(s)
-Blueberry Parfaits, *144*, 145–47
Buttermilk Cupcakes with White
Chocolate–Lemon Frost-
ing, 167–68
Buttermilk Ice Cream, 150
Cheesecake–Ginger Tart,
193–94
Cheesecake Ice Cream, 183
choosing, 142
Citrus–Olive Oil Cake, 172
–Cream Cheese Pound Cake,
173
Glaze, Blueberry Hand Pies with,
82–84, *83*
Layer Cake, Light, *174*, 175–76
-Raspberry Buttermilk Tart,
148–49
Lime(s)
choosing, 142
-Coconut Mousse Cake, 177–80,
*178*
Cream Tart with Ginger–Cream
Cheese Crust, 160–61
Key, Pie, My Favorite, 165–66
Meringue Bars, 157–58
Meringue Cheesecake Pie,
Frozen, 162–64, *163*
Linzer Hearts, Pistachio, with Sour
Cherry Filling, 232–33

## M

Macarons
Caramel Almond, 268–71, *269*
Espresso, 307–8
Macaroons, Pistachio and Coconut,
231
Madeleines, Orange-Scented, 155–56

Malted Vanilla Buttercream Filling,
Vanilla Whoopie Pies with,
46–47
Malt–Milk Chocolate Frosting, Devil's
Food Layer Cake with,
358–60, *359*
Maple (syrup)
–Cream Cheese Frosting and
Candied Walnuts, Apple-
sauce Cake with, 128–29
for recipes, 4
-Walnut Caramel Apples, *112*, 113
Marshmallows, Vanilla-Flecked,
38–39
Mascarpone
buying, 6, 182
Cream, Berry-Topped Phyllo
Cups with, 70–71
Cream, Espresso Granita with,
299
Custard Tart, 191–92
Frosting, Orange Cupcakes
with, 169–70, *171*
Tiramisu Parfaits, 186–88, *187*
Topping, Espresso Layer Cake
with, 313–15
Mendiants, White Chocolate, 219–20
Meringue. *See also* Macarons
Bars, Lime, 157–58
Big Vanilla Pavlova with Fresh
Berries, 50–51
Cookies, Hazelnut, 224–26
Lime Cheesecake Pie, Frozen,
162–64, *163*
Milk, for recipes, 5
Mint
Cream, Fresh, Strawberry Short-
cakes with, 79–81, *80*
Raspberry Pâtes de Fruits,
67–69, *68*
Mousse, Two-Tone Milk Chocolate,
with Sweet-and-Salty Al-
monds, 326–28, *327*
Muffins, Blueberry, Extra-Crumbly,
96–97

## N

Nut butters, 212. *See also* Peanut
Butter
Nuts. *See also* Almond(s);
Hazelnut(s); Peanut(s);
Pecan(s); Pistachio(s);
Walnut(s)
storing, 212
testing for freshness, 8, 212
Toasted, 13